SHARP NOTIONS

SHARP NOTIONS

ESSAYS FROM THE STITCHING LIFE

EDITED BY MARITA DACHSEL & NANCY LEE

ARSENAL PULP PRESS
VANCOUVER

ARSENAL PULP PRESS
Suite 202 – 211 East Georgia St.
Vancouver, BC V6A 1Z6
Canada
arsenalpulp.com

The publisher gratefully acknowledges the support of the Canada Council for the Arts and the British Columbia Arts Council for its publishing program and the Government of Canada and the Government of British Columbia (through the Book Publishing Tax Credit Program) for its publishing activities.

Arsenal Pulp Press acknowledges the xʷməθkʷəy̓əm (Musqueam), Sḵwx̱wú7mesh (Squamish), and səlilwətaɬ (Tsleil-Waututh) Nations, custodians of the traditional, ancestral, and unceded territories where our office is located. We pay respect to their histories, traditions, and continuous living cultures and commit to accountability, respectful relations, and friendship.

A portion of Carrianne Leung's essay, "What Story?" was previously published in *Send My Love to Anyone* issue 4, April 2021.

Excerpts and images from *Jan Wade: Soul Power* (Vancouver Art Gallery and Information Office, 2022) are reprinted with permission of the artist and the Vancouver Art Gallery.

Cover image by Lia Pas, *she breathed*
Cover and text design by Jazmin Welch
Edited by Marita Dachsel and Nancy Lee
Copy edited by Catharine Chen
Proofread by Jesmine Cham

Printed and bound in Canada

Library and Archives Canada Cataloguing in Publication:
Title: Sharp notions : essays from the stitching life / edited by Marita Dachsel & Nancy Lee.
Names: Dachsel, Marita, editor. | Lee, Nancy, 1970– editor.
Identifiers: Canadiana (print) 20230225764 | Canadiana (ebook) 20230225896 | ISBN 9781551529257 (softcover) | ISBN 9781551529264 (EPUB)
Subjects: LCSH: Sewing—Psychological aspects. | LCSH: Fiberwork—Psychological aspects. | LCSH: Textile crafts—Psychological aspects. | LCSH: Canadian essays—21st century
Classification: LCC PS8367.S49 S53 2023 | DDC C814/.60803564—dc23

For our moms, who taught us everything.

CONTENTS

TWO STICKS AND A STRING:
An Introduction from the Editors

It's just two sticks and a string. That's my glib answer when someone compliments my hand-knits, declaring that they could never do something like that. It's just two sticks and a string—if I can do it, anyone can. Of course, this isn't completely true. I didn't begin by knitting lace, cables, or colourwork. It took years to build those skills, and I'm still learning. I'm far from a master knitter, but it brings me joy, a sense of accomplishment that I can literally wear on my sleeves.

I do marvel at the technology of knitting, at what two sticks and a string can create. Knitting is a relatively new technology, particularly in comparison to its sister techniques, and is believed to be about a thousand years old, though its presumed precursor, nålbinding, has been practised for at least 8,500 years. Weaving is even older, with evidence that it was practised since at least 7,000 BCE. And string, or thread, which is needed for knitting or weaving, is much older. The earliest preserved string is dated about 15,000 BCE, but we know, based on sculptures, that the technology to produce string is at least forty thousand years old.

I'm using the term *technology* deliberately. Cloth and fibre are ubiquitous, and the basic technologies so old that we generally take them for granted. These technologies, excluding knitting, are older than the wheel. In ancient times cloth was a major industry, fuelling expansion and connection between peoples and cultures, even beyond the storied Silk Road. I often wonder if we overlook the importance of fibre technologies because of their strong association with women.

I don't knit only because I admire the technology or the history, but recently I have been thinking of my familial history in relation to the craft. My mother taught me the basics, enough to earn the knitting badge in Brownies, then I promptly stopped knitting until days before learning I was pregnant with my third child. It was January, a minus-forty-degree cold spell in Edmonton. My husband was out of town for a few weeks, and my mother was visiting, helping me manage two young sons. I wanted to relearn how to knit, and she retaught me the basics. Since those cozy days in Edmonton, I've turned to the internet and to my friend Nancy for tutorials and support. I've been knitting on and off for over a decade now.

I don't know why I had a sudden impulse to pick up two sticks and some string. Now, twelve years later, I could expertly bullshit my way to an explanation—I wanted to create something tangible, somehow my body already knew it was pregnant and was urging me to nest, I wanted to create a matrilineal connection—but at the time, it was none of these. I can't tell you why I returned to two sticks and string that night in Edmonton, but I can tell you one reason I keep at it.

As a child of immigrants who came to Canada as adults from different parts of the world and for different reasons, leaving their families of origin behind, I had a longing for connection that I now recognize as a longing for culture. My nana had been a knitter; my mother has memories of curling up in the chair behind her as Nana tucked one long needle under her right arm and knit quickly in a style I have since learned is called "lever knitting." (She also tatted, sewed, embroidered, and crocheted.) My mother learned to knit at age five, but not lever style. I wonder, if I had grown up near my nana, would she have taught me? Was this how her own mother had knit?

On my mother's side, almost every matrilineal generation since the 1850s moved away from their family of origin, from Scotland to various locations in Australia and then to New Zealand, then finally, to Canada with my mother. My mother assumes her grandma Hardy used to knit (she had six children and one couldn't pop into a store to buy sweaters back then) but remembers only her fine embroidery (she monogrammed everything with a cursive *H*). Did my great-great-great grandmother Amelia learn from her own grandmother while a servant at Glamis Castle back in Scotland, before she turned fifteen and her family settled in Australia? Or, perhaps, did my nana learn to lever knit from a friend, one of her fellow farmer's wives? With every move, connections to the older generations have been severed and knowledge, stories, and relationships lost.

As I knit, I think of the hands of my matrilineal line doing similar work, making similar motions, creating a body memory, connecting me to the women before me (though they weren't simultaneously streaming videos or watching their kid's taekwondo practice). I wonder what they knit and for whom. I want to learn about the patterns and practices of my ancestors, and I've begun to learn about the histories of knitting and other fibre arts.

Archeologists and fabric historians can learn much from a scrap of fabric. Styles, techniques, and fibres reveal when, where, by whom, and sometimes why a piece was created. A tunic found in Tutankhamen's tomb revealed a tapestry weave made specifically for Tutankhamen in the Egyptian style, yet the bottom embroidered panels were done in the Syrian style; true embroidery was unknown at this time in Egypt. While experts cannot say specifically where the panels were created, the fact that they do know they were made by Syrian artisans over three thousand years ago will not cease to impress me.

In our technology-laden world, it's almost impossible to imagine that we have lost some fabric technologies. Dhaka muslin was a gauzy fabric that was transparent and so light one could pull a full ninety-one-metre bolt through a ring. It was popular across continents for at least two thousand years, a favourite of the ancient Greeks and Romans, Mughal emperors and their wives, and eventually Empress Josephine and Jane Austen. It was made with a rare cotton grown solely along the banks of the Meghna River and involved a sixteen-step process to create. Colonialism and imperialism destroyed the craft, and by the twentieth century, the technology and knowledge to make Dhaka muslin was lost.

Closer to home, I find myself deeply moved by the traditions of the people on whose land I live. The Coast Salish peoples have a rich tradition of weaving, spinning, and knitting that includes the Cowichan sweater. For thousands of years, they spun mountain-goat fur, dog hair, and plant fibres together to weave textiles. The Salish Woolly Dogs were kept separate from the other village dogs to ensure there was no crossbreeding, and they were fed a diet of fish to keep their fur luxurious. There is evidence that dog domestication in this area is at least six thousand years old and that the woolly dogs was a distinct breed for at least three thousand years. The few known photos of this breed show them to have been ridiculously cute spitz-like pups who were clearly adored. Amid the violence of colonization, the dogs were unable to be kept separated, and settler dogs spoiled the breed lines; the Salish Woolly Dog died out in the early twentieth century. If only there were a way to revitalize the breed. When I brush my own floofy dog or see one of her hairs entwined in stitches of my work-in-progress, I think of those woolly dogs and wonder if I should learn to spin.

I'm not concerned that the world will lose the knowledge of spinning just because at some point, the women in my family stopped learning how to spin. But I do wonder what regional techniques and threads of culture have been or are becoming lost. Thanks to the internet, I have learned many knitting techniques I could not have learned from my mother, such as my preference for the cable cast on to start projects. I no longer remember the cast on she taught me and have not been able to find an online tutorial that resembles what I recall. Her own mother taught her how to cast on. Are there repercussions to these seemingly inconsequential choices?

Culture, whether we are aware of it or not, is as woven into the fibre arts we create as the threads themselves. I wonder, as I knit, what my knits will one day reveal about me.

—MARITA DACHSEL

In the twenty-first century, we don't need to knit, embroider, weave, bead, make lace, or spin, but many of us do. Why? In our expedited consumerist culture, where everything is discounted and a mere click away, why weave a cloth for drying your dishes? Why knit a pair of socks? Why hand piece a queen-size quilt? Nonpractitioners may view these "hobbies" as illogical—the time they take, the cost and storage of materials, the learning curve, the patience required—but as you'll see from the essays in this collection, these minor annoyances rarely register with those who love fibre arts. For us, there are profound, beautiful, and sometimes heartbreaking answers to the question, "Why?"

If you're lonely, stitching is company; if you're stressed, it's a reprieve. Stitching can be a time machine, making dull stretches pass faster, or slowing the frantic pace of modern life to the awareness of a single tiny gesture. While I tend to be a bit stitch promiscuous (I knit, crochet, embroider, quilt, sew), like Marita, I was taught to knit by my mom, who is now, in her retirement, a prolific source of hand-knit socks for friends and family. I have memories of my auntie Margaret knitting for her children, of my grandmother knitting a large brown cabled cape, and each week on Instagram, I admire my auntie Monica's latest knitted creations.

When my grandfather was first hospitalized near the end of his life, my mom went to sit with him every day, from morning until evening. She fed him breakfast and lunch, made sure he was comfortable, then sat in a chair by his bed and quietly knit cotton dishcloths. When I asked if she needed more yarn from home—these were long days, and even a giant ball of craft cotton would soon be depleted—she said there was no need. She was knitting, then unravelling the same dishcloth over and over. The knitting's purpose was meditative, not productive. The cloth grew stitch by stitch, arrived at its finished form, then diminished stitch by stitch as she wound it back into a ball. My grandfather, eyes closed and silent in his hospital bed, was also unwinding, returning to some original state of being.

This story reminds me of two things. First, for most of us who practise fibre arts, the finished object is rarely the point. It's a vehicle, a catalyst for what we want: to engage in peaceful practice; to challenge ourselves with new learning; to create something where once there was nothing; to hold a loved one in our thoughts for hours as we make; to not only express but also experience the tactile, the textural, the slow and incremental growth of a project as we create. Like so many practices, the fibre arts process is its own reward.

Second, those of us who love fibre arts tend to reach for them at life's most challenging times. They are a life preserver, a way to keep our heads above water in rough seas. Sometimes, the reliability of a knit stitch, the steady rocking of a quilting needle, the solid structure of a loom is all we have. In many ways, that's how this anthology came about. Two exhausted, overworked middle-aged women who had said to one another many times, "This knitting project is the only thing keeping me going," started to wonder if anyone else felt the same. If knitting, crochet, embroidery, and quilting were our lifelines, were others having the same experience?

In January 2022, we put out a call for personal essays on the fibre arts, uncertain if anyone would be interested in writing such a thing. Submissions began appearing in our inbox almost immediately, and we were overwhelmed by the response, not only by the number of essays we received but by the depth of emotion and vulnerability in each piece. We read every submission with care, knowing these writers had taken the risk of revealing themselves, of sharing the intimate intersections of life experience and fibre arts practice. Perhaps the pandemic had made people more introspective, more attuned to what mattered, or perhaps it was the fibre arts themselves opening people up, connecting them to their most challenging truths. Every essay read like an urgent communication.

The selection process took time, and to be honest, we could have edited several anthologies from the work we received. It was difficult to let many of them go—essays that moved us, left us smiling or wiping away tears. In the end, our curatorial priority was to include as broad a range of experiences and processes as possible, from new practitioners to experienced artists to nonpractitioners, from birth to death with every challenge of life along the way, from dismantling the traditional to reclaiming cultural knowledge and identity, from spiritual reckoning to the complexity of illness and disability, from the beauty of nature to the threat of environmental collapse, from the discovery of self to the power of community, from the art studio to the kitchen table.

You'll discover in these pieces how individual a writer's relationship to fibre arts can be, a distinct braiding of perspective, life experience, and practice. At the same time, some constants emerge: practice as a lifeline, practice as contemplation, practice as a space to step into in order to make sense of life's most difficult challenges or greatest joys. We hope that after reading these essays you'll be inspired by the many possible answers to the question, "Why fibre arts?" and, if you find yourself passing a yarn shop or fabric store or craft aisle, that you'll listen to that little voice inside you that says, "Why not?"

—NANCY LEE

THE BOYFRIEND-SWEATER CURSE

JUSTINA CHONG

A year after we start dating, my boyfriend asks me to make him a green grandpa cardigan with enormous pockets and brown elbow patches. He wants the pockets so his hands won't feel restless without a cigarette.

I have never been so excited to knit anything. How better to say *I love you* than to wrap the person you love in something you've made?

When my sisters and I were small, my mother made us sweaters with lambswool imported from the Patricia Roberts Knitting shop in London. She taught my twin and me to knit when we were twelve, after we moved to Markham without my father, who stayed in Hong Kong to work. After she relinquished her life as a tai tai, a lady who lunches; after she learned to drive at thirty-seven because we would not have a chauffeur in Canada; after she took on the burden of taking care of three daughters in a creepy six-bedroom house in the suburbs all by herself.

The first things my twin and I knit were red headbands for our dog, but our interest in knitting disappeared when we got a home internet connection, around the time my mom switched to white wine after spilling red on her bedroom carpet. Why waste time knitting when we could chat on ICQ with friends on the other side of the planet, whose lives, no matter how fast we typed, were running ahead without us? It was hard not to feel left behind. *I chose baby-blue elastics for my braces yesterday. The boys had a "babe talk" at camp and named all the girls they liked. I'll mail you some Oxy face wash in a Ziploc bag.*

I didn't pick up a pair of knitting needles again until my final year of undergrad, when a Christmastime bout of shingles left me holed up in my aunt's spare room in Mississauga. My mother had moved back to Hong Kong by then, so my aunt would take me in over the holidays. My shingles coincided with two critical events. First, the Boxing Day sale at Michaels, where Lion Brand Thick & Quick yarn could be had at half price. Second, my twin emailed me an invitation to Ravelry, the online community for knitters and crocheters. That winter, I knit more chunky hats and wrist warmers than my friends could wear.

A Ravelry search turns up the perfect grandpa-sweater pattern. My Toronto Public Library branch has a copy of the pattern book. I get a library card for the occasion. My boyfriend comes with me to the yarn store and picks out some green Cascade Yarns Eco+ wool. Then it's time to cast on.

For weeks I take my boyfriend-sweater project everywhere I go. Knit knit knit, purl purl purl, row upon row of stockinette stitch at the park, on the porch, on the 501 Queen streetcar, on the subway.

But just as I'm binding off, my boyfriend breaks up with me. He thinks we don't really understand each other, like something is missing. He might be right. His emotions are hard to read. Blank, even, like he would prefer to be alone inside his head. He's four years older and does things real adults do, like smoking, drinking black coffee, using an electric toothbrush, reading Thomas Pynchon, and watching arty movies that don't make sense. Sometimes his cynicism frightens me; no doubt my optimism disgusts him. Our arguments, though rare, usually conclude with him declaring, "When you're in your late twenties, you'll be jaded too." I don't want him to be right. He tends to avoid eye contact, but when he breaks up with me, he stares straight into my eyes, and it looks like somebody has drawn tiny petals around his pupils with a Micron pen.

My sisters console me over GChat. "It's for the best," says the younger one. "Why would you want to be with someone who doesn't want to be with you?" I don't tell my mother about the breakup, because I know she wouldn't be able to disguise her glee over the telephone. She thinks I deserve "more" than dating someone from a small town who went to art school.

When later I return to get my things, his apartment smells the way it did the first time he invited me over, like the upholstery of a car baking in the sun. There are dishes in the sink, strands of noodles caked to the bottom of a saucepan. I fight my instinct to wash them. The sweater, still damp, lies on the bedroom carpet where I spread it out to dry after blocking. I haven't yet sewn on the buttons, pockets, and elbow patches. It occurs to me that he will never sew them himself, so the cardigan goes into the box along with my toothbrush, books, and underwear—onto the subway, all the way home.

Time to ask Ravelry for advice. What to do about the sweater? All seventy-five thousand stitches were knit and purled with him in mind. But if I were to give it to him now, would that make me a chump?

Several Ravelers say my predicament makes them laugh out loud. Others are not so amused. *Do not, I repeat, DO NOT under ANY circumstances give this piece of your soul to someone who doesn't deserve it. You have a dad around? Brother? Yourself? Infinitely better choices*, writes one. *Will you enter the world of dumped chumps? I THINK NOT.* Another writes: *Strangely, I had a similar experience knitting this very same sweater. Even the request for "an old man sweater." Only I never sewed buttons on it when we broke up—just left it at the house. Maybe he wears it, maybe the dog sleeps on it. Who can say?* Yet another writes: *Regarding one of the other replies: you live in a world where men sew on buttons and pockets?*

To prove to myself that I'm a generous person with a capacious heart, that I will never become jaded as he predicted, I resolve to give him the sweater. I'm okay with entering the world of dumped chumps.

I sew on the buttons, pockets, and elbow patches and weave in all the ends.

We meet at a restaurant in Chinatown for the sweater handover. The cuffs of his hoodie are pulled over his hands, like he's trying to expose as little of himself to me as possible. When we sit down, he scoots his chair farther away. It feels like meeting a strange animal for the first time. Be careful or you might startle him. Does he feel the same? I force my breathing to be imperceptible, lift single pieces of chicken and celery from the dishes on the table without disturbing the surrounding food, and leave the silences between us alone instead of filling them with banter. Measuring my movements like this is unbearable. When we leave the restaurant, I hand him the sweater. As soon as he pulls it on, his face contorts into that of a person I don't recognize. He's grinning, teeth showing, eyes curved into half moons. It's almost cartoonish. "I love it. I'm going to keep it forever!" he says.

His reaction fills me with delight and sustains me for days. In my mind, he wears the cardigan all the time, while sketching in his notebook, pumping air into his bicycle tires. Even the thought of bike grease on the ribbed cuffs is endearing. He stashes pens, tire levers, and a lighter in the pockets, leans on the elbow patches as he scans his RSS feed on the computer. He even wears it to sleep. He loves the sweater so much.

A week later, we walk the perimeter of a park nearby. Some girls are chasing each other on bikes, singing "Baby" by Justin Bieber. I match my strides to his, silent and deliberate, my arms across my chest so I won't unconsciously reach for his hand. He's wearing the grandpa sweater, his hands burrowed deep inside the pockets. A week's worth of feelings for us to pick apart, poke holes in, turn upside down and inside out. We're still curious about each other. We swallow the inkling that something is missing and get back together. We survive the Boyfriend-Sweater Curse.

This is how we met: I was sitting on a bench at dusk waiting for a migraine to pass so I could bike home. He sat down next to me. We talked until two in the morning, avoiding eye contact the way quiet people do when they think they might like each other. Instead, we stared at the bare branches above us as the sky became dark and my nose turned cold.

A year after surviving the sweater curse, we move in together. Though our jobs aren't great—he's an underpaid office assistant with the workload of a project manager, and I type closed captions for *Animal Miracles* and *Winx Club*—we eke out a modest living by combining our wages. Uninspiring jobs mean we have more free time than most. We fill it with creative projects, read in parks, go for bike rides, talk for hours, and take turns making food and unloading the dishwasher. After dinner, we walk along the beach and laugh at Labrador retrievers wrestling in the sand. We watch movies on the couch and eat ice cream in our underwear. Our favourites are Raspberry Lemon-Lime Sherbet and Moose Tracks from Kawartha Dairy. One summer, on our way back from a camping trip, we stop by a Kawartha Dairy outpost in Bobcaygeon. Our ice cream melts before the cashier can count out our change.

I knit us hats, scarves, mittens, sweaters, and things for his family too. Extra-warm Newfoundland-style mittens for his brother living in Nunavut, a lilac shawl for his mother to wear to church, toques for his father and sister to wear on hunting trips, and a yellow cape for his niece.

My mother is frustrated that my life is stuck in Nowheresville, Ontario, with a go-nowhere relationship and go-nowhere career. She doesn't need to articulate her disappointment when she calls on the phone; it's the sound of the ice cubes clinking in her vodka. "I think you should move back to Hong Kong and find a job here," she says, over and over, like if she says it enough times, it will come true. My sisters have jobs she can brag about: my twin works for a Hong Kong publishing company and gets cast in insurance commercials, while my younger sister lives out of a suitcase in Dubai or Minneapolis or Moscow as a management consultant. I'm living hand to mouth, but it's not all bad. A former teacher gives me a couple of gigs writing scripts for a children's television show, an agent adds me to his roster, and a production company invests money to develop my ideas into a cartoon. Even though all of this sounds promising, my mother isn't impressed. I tell myself it takes time to cultivate a creative career. Someday things will pan out, and my mother won't be so ashamed of me. I send her photos of things I knit, hoping to bond over the hobby we share, but she only sends one-word responses like *nice* or *good*. Or she doesn't reply at all.

In my aunt's basement one Easter, I find a plastic tub my mother left behind when she moved away. In it is a half-finished knitted baby sweater in a luxurious pastel angora yarn dotted with popcorn bobbles. Attached is a row counter indicating her progress: 137 rows. She would have counted out the stitches in Cantonese. She must have felt overwhelmed by the task of knitting not one but two sweaters for her baby twins, the way knitting socks feels daunting because you can't stop at the one. My mom had dreams for us, of Ivy League schools; walk-in closets full of cream-coloured clothes and lush fur coats; faithful, well-pedigreed Chinese husbands from old-money families; hired help at home. In her dreams, there is no room for me to do the dishes, ride a bicycle, or make things with my hands.

The plastic tub also contains the front, back, and half-finished sleeves of a camel-coloured cable sweater, sized for an adult. Who was my mother knitting this for? She never made anything for herself. I take the pieces home, finish each sleeve, and sew it all together. My mom has always hated seaming sweaters, but it's my favourite thing about knitting.

I send my mom a photo of the finished pullover, a special mother-daughter project. But she doesn't remember knitting it. If my mother won't acknowledge me for finishing the work she abandoned twenty years earlier, maybe the universe will. Every time I pull the sweater over my head, I pray she will love me even though I might never fulfill her dreams.

My mother visits Toronto once a year to dote on her parents and gossip with her sisters in person. Between barbecues and mah-jong at my aunt's house and birthdays at the Mandarin buffet, it's difficult to catch a moment with just her. Whenever we do spend time alone, it's usually at a restaurant. Each of these meals ends with us not speaking for months. One June afternoon over lunch at a cafe near Toogood Pond Park in Unionville, I give her a summer shawl I've made for her in a turquoise cotton yarn. The colour reminds me of a Tiffany's box. Expensive, like her. She tucks the shawl into her handbag without looking at it. A goose honks. She tells me I should leave my go-nowhere life and move to Hong Kong to make something of myself. I tell her no. Lunch ends.

The shawl goes missing within a week. I feel silly. How could I have thought she might be happy to receive something so rustic? I decide to never knit for her again. She doesn't speak to me for half a year. She's punishing me for being okay with my mediocrity. When she finally calls me again, her speech is slurred. I put my phone down on the table and let her talk to herself, on and on with her opinions about how I should live my life.

But I love my life. For my twenty-seventh birthday, the boy I love bakes me a chocolate cake from scratch, takes me ice skating by the harbour, and gives me a hand-drawn coupon for a Goldie Hawn–a-thon with complimentary popcorn. For months the coupon remains tucked inside my journal, unredeemed. I still don't have a full-time job and haven't had scriptwriting work in years. My TV show ideas at the production studio are going nowhere. Life stagnates. My agent phones every six months to give me a pep talk. Each time, he asks me to write scripts for my portfolio so he can pitch me to producers. Each time, I say I'll do it, but I never do. Instead, I scan the classifieds on Craigslist and take whatever crappy hourly job I can get.

One morning, my boyfriend plunks a mug of cold coffee into the dishwasher full of clean dishes. We bicker. I run the dishwasher again. Later, as I scour the supermarket flyers for the best deals on President's Choice detergent, I wonder: Is this how I want to spend my life? Watching my friends and sisters shoot ahead in their professional lives? Dreading phone calls from both my agent and my mother? Washing my boyfriend's boxers because he won't do laundry unless I remind him to? I love him, but I can't see a way out for myself in Toronto. I give in to my mother's nagging and buy myself a one-way ticket home.

My boyfriend seems open to the idea of coming with me, but we discover Hong Kong will be too expensive. We set our sights on

Chengdu in mainland China. Rent is cheaper and jobs easier to come by. I find him a job posting at a Dutch Chinese gaming company and convince him to apply.

My plan is foolproof. I will be nearer to my mother, study Chinese at the university, and take up part-time work at the same start-up as my boyfriend. My job will be marketing educational apps for children. My boss will notice my wit, creativity, and potential and ask me to invent cute animal characters to spice up their fictional app universe. They'll invite me to write scripts and stories. Meanwhile, my boyfriend will work as a game designer and beef up his portfolio. After we've tempered ourselves into respectable, employable people, we will move to Hong Kong. My mother will be pleased.

For his Skype interview, my boyfriend trims his beard and puts on the pants and button-up shirt I persuaded him to buy at a Loblaws Supermarket the year before. "You can wear these for weddings and job interviews!" I said. The company offers him the job.

When we visit his parents in their hometown to celebrate his mother's birthday, we tell them about our plan to move. His father dusts off the atlas, lays it on the coffee table, and searches for China as though it's the back of an earring on the pavement. I point out Hong Kong and Chengdu.

"You can't take my baby to China. It's so far away!" his mother says, like I'm an alien snatching him from her arms. Her eyes are red and wet. It's the first time she's referred to my boyfriend as her baby. It dawns on me that I'm my own mother's baby too, that we haven't lived on the same continent since I was fifteen. The hours we've spent together in the last ten years wouldn't fill a single week. To my mother, I am frozen in time as a teenager in boarding school; to me, she is a voice who drunk-dials me every now and then. As adults, we are strangers.

On the GO bus home, I weep thinking about how my boyfriend's parents have woven me into their family. At Thanksgiving we ate the wild turkey his father shot. His mother made me a Christmas stocking, wrote my name on the cuff with a Sharpie. They brought me along to summer family reunions in Huron County. The night his niece was born, we stayed up solving MindTrap puzzles until his brother-in-law called, then we rushed to the hospital to welcome the baby. Taped to his parents' fridge is a picture of my boyfriend and me, sitting back-to-back and smiling at the camera while we wait for his brother to go skydiving.

In the weeks before my flight, I knit my boyfriend a light-grey pullover in Rowan Pure Wool, an upgrade from the more economical Cascade 220 I usually knit with. The sweater is made up of a tedious knit-knit purl-purl checkerboard stitch. Completing the sweater feels more urgent than all the other things that must be taken care of—closing my bank account, cancelling my phone contract, saying goodbye to my friends. I add dark-grey elbow patches and sew a handmade label bearing his name to the inside of the neckband.

I give him the sweater the morning he drives me to the airport. We eat cold slices of pepperoni pizza in the departure hall. Then I fly to Hong Kong and wait for his decision about the job in Chengdu.

My parents are thrilled about my return. They kiss me on the head whenever they walk by—my mom because she's happy I've left my go-nowhere life, my dad because I've finally lifted my mother out of her misery. I stay in a spare room in their apartment, the one my father naps in and uses as a study. I empty my suitcases over the college hoodies and workout clothes my sisters have left behind in the drawers. My existence here seems to be superimposed on everyone else's, but it doesn't matter. This is temporary. We're moving to China soon.

I barely talk to my mother because I'm busy hunting for apartments in Chengdu, looking up local yarn stores, befriending an Asian American Raveler who lives there. I can see it all so clearly:

she and I will spend Tuesday evenings knitting in our favourite cafe. My boyfriend and I will join her bike gang. We'll zip around the city at midnight, squat on the curb eating jianbing and spicy skewers, guzzle cans of lukewarm Wanglaoji tea as the sun comes up. It's so easy to imagine that I can feel it in my fingertips. When I tell my mother about my excitement, she speaks in a very measured way, as if she's pulling each word out of her mouth on a long string: "If he moves with you to China, it will be the hardest thing you face together. If he doesn't, then you have your answer."

One month later, my boyfriend calls me. "I'm not moving to Asia," he says. I have my answer. The Boyfriend-Sweater Curse is real. Our time together is complete.

For weeks I wake up in tears. Somehow, I figure out that I can survive by imagining a parallel life inside my head, one in which our time together keeps unfolding, and we're flipping pancakes, riding bikes, eating ice cream, lying in the grass holding hands and looking at the clouds through the leaves.

Sometimes if I imagine something, it's as good as done.

Over the next six years in Hong Kong, my life blossoms. I get a job I love at a software company. I make friends, move into my own apartment, have romantic relationships, go on adventures. I see my parents every Sunday. I learn to sew my own wardrobe. I wander Hong Kong's hiking trails and travel to Australia, Vietnam, Korea. Even though I walk the same streets and say hello to the same people every day, the city still feels exciting years later. The ornery cat in the Chinese medicine shop. The curve in the track where the tram enters Central and the view opens up like a postcard. A fruit seller prying open a durian with a meat cleaver. The pink sky and blue-grey sea, the sound of waves hitting the concrete pier as the sun sets over Lantau Island.

My mother is proud to see me grow. She drinks less. I move to Shanghai to learn Chinese, just as I had hoped to years before. For the first time in my life, I have my own dreams. I want to become fluent in Chinese, travel around China, and write stories about the people I meet. Now that we don't live in the same city, my mother and I don't talk as often. Instead, she sends me WhatsApp stickers, a cartoon rabbit blowing violent kisses over and over. She doesn't knit anymore because it irritates the skin on her hands.

I don't knit much either because it's hard to find yarn on Taobao. Not my favourite yarn anyway, that scratchy, durable, 100-percent wool that makes you smell like a wet sheep when you get caught in the rain. The kind that people in Canada like. This type of yarn doesn't seem to appeal to mainland Chinese tastes. In any case, my mother is glad I'm diving into my Chineseness. She hopes I'll meet a nice Shanghainese man to marry. They're known for being good at cooking and housework.

But can Shanghainese men sew buttons and pockets onto hand-knitted sweaters?

I saw my ex-boyfriend two years after our breakup, when I visited Toronto one July for my cousin's wedding. We agreed to meet near my Airbnb, at the corner of Queen and Spadina.

His hair was white at the temples. We hugged. I expected one whiff of his musk to intoxicate me with familiarity, but he looked like a dad and smelled like a stranger.

We walked west. I had to shield my eyes from the evening sun. The waiter at the Vietnamese restaurant seated us on the patio. My neck was roasting in the sunshine. We had sat at the same table years before, after a trip to Romni Wools nearby. I had bought some Noro yarn to make him a colourful stripy scarf.

Over bowls of cold vermicelli, he told me about his life. He lived with his girlfriend. His niece was big now, and his brother had moved back to Ontario from up north. He told me tales of Tinder from right after our breakup and that he earned income as a writer and still worked on his art. Time had marched on. The food at the restaurant wasn't as good as I remembered. My cup of water smelled like a dirty dishrag.

Now it was my turn to tell him about my life. As I spoke, I searched his face for some sign that he cared, but there was none. He had always been hard to read.

Once, years before, he had watched a mosquito feed off my cheek for five minutes without saying anything. When I realized what was happening, I slapped the mosquito and felt the bite grow hot and puffy. Maybe I had mistaken his passiveness for gentleness.

I struggled through dinner, lost in my thoughts. Did he still wear anything I had knit for him? Had he donated all of it to Value Village? A stranger was probably sitting in a coffee shop wearing that green grandpa cardigan, sipping an Americano, looking at memes on his phone while crumbs of biscotti clung to the stitches of the sweater I had knit for someone I loved in another life.

Next door, people clamoured in a queue for Hong Kong–style egg waffles and matcha ice cream. "Do you want to get ice cream?" I asked.

"I don't think my girlfriend would like it if I got ice cream with you."

I said nothing. I would have felt the same way in her shoes.

We walked back in the direction of my Airbnb and said goodbye. I remembered my friend was having an art show down the street. We had met through our exes and called each other the happy remnants of past relationships.

In the basement gallery, I was absorbed into a sea of strangers. I tried to focus on a lithograph. It depicted a classic Toronto summer sidewalk scene: people drinking on a stoop and a Cavalier King Charles Spaniel peeing on a sandwich board. With warm beer and bodies pressed up against each other, the room was stifling. All evening I had felt out of place, like a character who had wandered into the wrong book. For so long I had seen myself in terms of the roles I played in other people's stories. My identities as a girlfriend and daughter had given me a sense of belonging. Without those, who was I? As I thought about the life I was building in Hong Kong, my joyful existence, I understood: I belonged to me. How lucky I was to know this. How lucky I was to choose the life I wanted to live. Outside, a streetcar rolled by. I pushed my way through the crowd and walked up to the street, swinging my arms in the cool night air.

THE CAROLE QUILT

ELIANE LESLAU SILVERMAN

We swim in the Salish Sea year-round. In wetsuits, face down with masks and snorkels, we swim every season, each Sunday at least and usually once more during the week. We are never fewer than two and sometimes as many as twelve women. Yes, the water is cold, but it is clear, and in our gear, hearing our own breath, we become part of the ocean, joining the busy crabs, the quiet purple or aqua sea stars, the eel grass, the undulating iridescent kelp. We leave behind the complicated realities of our lives. Anxieties about demanding work, personal relationships, the planet, and our beloved children or grandchildren diminish as we swim through icy salt water. Often, we reach an almost meditative place, lost within and supported by the ocean. She is not exactly our mother, as she is indifferent to us, and yet she nourishes us with profound challenges of strong current or wild chop and the deep peace of repetition, our arms and legs steadily working. She holds us up while we do our part, squeezed into wetsuit gear from head to toe, tight and restrictive yet also freeing, since without it we could not survive the low water temperatures. We see life under the surface and become part of it.

We have swum together for nearly twenty years. A few members of the group have moved away; new people join us. We live on Salt Spring Island, off the coast of British Columbia, between Vancouver Island and the mainland. How could we not swim, we whose element is the salt water, when we live on a small island? We call ourselves the Salt Spring Seals, a name we came upon early, laughing at ourselves and yet loving our capacity to brave the ocean. We are clumsier and noisier than the actual seals, who sometimes observe us, even dance underneath and around us, and our gestures are heavier—the crawl or the breaststroke—but we are amazed as we call each other over to see an opalescent nudibranch or the return of a chunky purple starfish. Black and sleek as the seals in our gear, our bright-blue or yellow fins, our pink or green plastic snorkels add a note of the earth world we inhabit, remind us that we cannot live in this element forever but must clamber back to dry land, return to the tug of gravity.

Back on land, we struggle out of our wetsuits, boots, gloves, hoods. Snorkels and fins shed. We sometimes need each other's help with zippers, or with pulling at the ankles of our suits. The neoprene sticks to our skin as if we were vacuum sealed. Even the sleeves sometimes need help coming off, especially since we suffer more shoulder injuries or experience stiffness as we age. Twenty years is a long time. We share tips about gear, about the tides, about the weather that may be changing. Maybe more rain; snow, even. There is a photo of the two oldest of us, me and Ellen Mae, in our midsixties fifteen years ago, standing at Vesuvius Beach in our wetsuits, in the snow. We talk about past swims. "Diana, do you remember the time we sat on this bench watching the snow front from Vancouver Island coming toward us like a solid white curtain?" We always discuss the swim we have just experienced, forty-five minutes long in dead winter, over an hour in high summer. Anne says it isn't even worth getting into the gear for less than an hour. The suits are tight, the winter suits heavy. We joke that putting on the gear is half the exercise; even worse is getting out of it.

Finally, wearing clothes that we can slip into modestly, we have our tea, always Bengal Spice, and crystallized ginger, because it takes the salt taste out of our mouths and warms our insides. Newer members bring baked treats and occasionally Lay's potato chips. That's a great occasion. We sit on logs, huge rocks, or benches, depending on where we have swum, and discuss the day's swim—what we saw if it was clear, or how murky it was. The ocean never disappoints us. We have sea stars and anemones, rushing schools of small fish and beautiful grasses that let us know by their bend how fast the current is flowing. Seals sometimes make eye contact; we are in love with them. On a few occasions, we have seen sea lions, way too close. They are probably benign, but even a little curiosity from an eight-hundred-pound creature is daunting. No two swims are ever the same; the light shifts, the tides change, the temperatures always surprise. The wind, the chop ... so much to talk about. We have become friends, even Seal sisters. We know a lot about each other: birthdays and favourite cakes, diseases and surgeries. After I recently had an operation, the others brought me dinners, calling themselves Seals on Wheels. We pass books around. We pride ourselves on the good food we serve at potlucks. Twenty years, for some of us, of being with each other and the Salish Sea.

Late last summer, one of us, Carole, suffered a terrible event. Her son Tony, not much older than forty, died in a car accident. He was her beloved redhead. Married to Caitlin, he had two small children. The enormous loss of an adored man was evidenced by the outpourings of feelings and generosity to his family. His death left a great big hole in many hearts. Carole spent some months afterward in Vancouver with his young family, consoling and grieving at the same time.

The magnitude of the event left us all shattered, deeply saddened, and vulnerable. We knew that loss lurked everywhere. But we swam.

And we pondered. What could we do for Carole? Not much—that kind of grief is so personal, the loss incomprehensible. Six months after the death, Pat proposed that we make a quilt, a recognition of Tony's death, a signal of Carole's loss, and a representation of our love for her. We'd had occasion in the past to utilize my experience as a quilter: in support of a Seal with breast cancer, one with a hip replacement, another breast cancer, and for celebrations too, like the Sea Capers Parade. A lot happens in twenty years.

The process began in my studio. Knowing twelve Seals would be participating in the project, I picked out five background fabrics so the quilt would have coherence and continuity. I cut them into twelve-inch squares, laid them on my work table, and added many different fabrics to the selection so that each person could pick her own combination of textiles. There was netting and veiling; there were hand-painted and commercial fabrics, in all their beauty and promise. I loved the moments when each Seal came to my studio, sometimes alone and sometimes with a friend, and pondered the textiles for her contribution. It was a moment of beginnings and, for some of us, of trepidation. Seals may be great swimmers, but they are not necessarily needlewomen.

While not every Seal felt she could contribute to the project, the process and the finished piece held a cherished place in all our hearts. Those who contributed their creativity and their labour put their best selves into it. One by one, two by two, they came over and asked questions as they thought about what they wanted to express in their squares. Some of them returned for more fabric or more embellishments. Many of us talked on the phone, working through ideas. Some of the sewers and makers found it an awkward and difficult process; others felt at home and familiar with creating with textiles. But deep thoughts about loss, empathy for Carole's grief, and excitement at creating beauty—everybody had those.

Little by little, the finished twelve-inch squares came back to my studio. And, interestingly, not a single piece referenced Tony's death or a theme of loss. Instead, they spoke of vibrancy, beauty, and our love for the ocean. Of the water and the ocean floor, our familiar home. Octopuses adorned with sequins, grasses couched with wool and silk and moving with the current, a Dungeness crab carefully pieced. One heavily embroidered maroon kelp bed, and another swaying, outlined in careful stitches of brown wool thread. Sea stars, purple and red, nestled in a happy clump deep within the crevice of a rock. Two red octopuses adjoined each other, one an abstract representation of the creature in tropical waters, its neighbour decorated with tiny coral beads. A ubiquitous moon jelly, translucent and deceptively sweet, and an adorable French angelfish flirting with the coral, a memory of our several visits to Bonaire in the Caribbean, far from our own very cold water. More jellyfish, their tentacles animated by the current, reproductive organs carefully created by shiny thread embellishing their shimmering domes. Sand dollars, beautified with buttons, positioned next to sea stars, a delicate red heart peeking through the waves. On Anne's squares of fabric, she'd printed two photographs of anemones and snails taken with her GoPro, which accompanies her frequently, providing a strong contrast to the fine stitchery outlining details of the images. And finally, an opalescent giant Pacific nudibranch, the elegant dancing invertebrate we all love so much, made of transparent folded fabric, raised up and announcing itself.

We all fell in love with our squares. They were expressions of our very hearts and our whole beings. Each piece was brought to me, held out and handed over by its designer as if it were her first-born. I laid out the pieces on a white sheet, arranging and rearranging them until I had a good balance of texture, colour, and weight. Navy-blue sashing allowed each piece to stand on its own and yet live in unity with the others. I admit to a feeling of reverence when quilting the piece. A quilt made by a community to whom I owe my ocean self demanded fidelity to the group, unlike even the pieces I make for friends and family; each woman had made a square I had to honour. The binding was bright orange, which I chose to remind us of so

Salt Spring Seals, *The Carole Quilt*, 2021. | Photo: Janet Dwyer Photography.

many losses: our beautiful brilliant orange sun stars, many legged, slowly pulsating on the ocean floor, killed by the growing heat of the water and by a virus. They wasted, their legs turning white before our eyes, before finally disappearing entirely five years ago. Perhaps they will return. Or perhaps not.

Upon the quilt's completion, a Seal who is a professional photographer took it home and photographed it under studio lights. I missed the quilt's powerful presence—profound, important, like the ocean itself or like my Seal sisters—when it left my studio. Our first Seal, Diana (I like to call her the mother of us all), reproduced a quotation from each of us on paper to scale with the quilt, representing through language yet another expression of our caring about each other. Each of us signed with a gold pen.

We arranged a date with Carole when everybody could be there to present her the quilt, without telling her why we would be gathering in her driveway during this difficult time of COVID. We carpooled, as we usually do, thinking to spare the environment, down to the south end of the island, carrying not only the quilt but, of course, snacks and tea—where there are Seals, there is food! The big moment ... Carole would be surprised, we knew.

When we had all arrived in her driveway, we called Carole to come out of the house. In winter clothing like all of the rest of us on that chilly afternoon, she looked a bit bewildered, but smiled in her usual welcoming way at all of us standing in a circle. Two of us lifted the folded quilt from the trunk of my car and slowly opened it, raised it up high. Silence first, then tears all around. We explained the process, with its sewing challenges and its joyful creativity, so that she could be part of it. She accepted the gift graciously and later created a space for it in her small house, offering it an iconic place akin to altar, in fact. She joined in a bit tentatively and then wholeheartedly as we talked about the ocean, reminisced about our many years together, ate, laughed, cried, froze in the cold, and felt renewed. The joyous moment was punctuated and intensified by grief; it always accompanies us humans on land, though it's sometimes ameliorated in the water. The water supports us. The ocean nurtures us.

Sadly, the story doesn't end there. A few months later, Catherine's daughter Michelle, also only in her early forties, died unexpectedly in her apartment in Vancouver. The loss begins again, or continues, as grief must. We have already wondered what we might do for Catherine. It is too soon to know. Plant a tree, maybe, or bring weekly desserts? We must live with the knowledge of tenuousness and fragility for a while still. We will see what we choose to make for her. Meanwhile, we swim on, and as the water warms up, our hearts may begin to thaw.

PROTECTION

ANNE FLEMING

On Halloween in 1981, after the Princess Leias and Morks had stopped knocking at the door, my mother and I repaired to the plaid couches in the basement to watch *Friday the 13th* on TV. My idea. I was seventeen and woefully out of step with acceptable teen knowledge of horror movies. I had not seen *Halloween*. I had not seen *The Amityville Horror*. I had not seen *The Texas Chainsaw Massacre* or *Black Christmas*. None of them.

Not that I was a fan of horror movies. I was (am) too susceptible to them for that, even the black-and-white ones that littered late-night TV, the ones I *knew* were bad. There was one about a baseball player who has a hand transplant. From a murderer. The hand *has* to kill.

I had read what I needed to in order to be au courant in the late 1970s: *Ghost Story* and *Flowers in the Attic*, a couple of Stephen Kings, *The Exorcist* (do not ask me to touch a Ouija board). But movies I had not seen. Luckily: Citytv.

Not long before, my mother had taken my sister and I each aside at different times with a catalogue of knitting patterns to ask me what sweater I thought my sister would like and my sister what sweater she thought I would like. I said Sheila would like an argyle pattern; Sheila said I would like a Cowichan-style sweater-jacket. So while we watched *Friday the 13th*, Mom was knitting the argyle. I was eating leftover Halloween candy and learning what a jump scare was.

In the movie, teens, warned en route by a sketchy local not to go there, start showing up at a newly restarted summer camp. They run into the woods and get killed, they open doors and find people there who shouldn't be there. There's something looking through the window. There's a dead body in the top bunk and there's somebody under the bed. The killer's moving through the woods, and there's this light churring sound in the background (*ch*-ch-ch-ch) that's his motif, which, despite my own fear, I would later use to freak out my friends.

I'm scrunching up into a ball, watching through my fingers.

Mom's knitting.

"Oh!" she says, not just unfazed but impatient, the knitting needles going snickslip snickslip against the *ch*-ch-ch-ch. "This is ridiculous!"

And it seems to me like knitting itself is her protection.

Against fear. Against susceptibility to manipulation, to pop culture, to soundtrack, to what needs to be known, against being duped as I am being duped by this ludicrous low-budget thing.

If the first image I give you of my mother is the time she knit through *Friday the 13th*, saying, "Oh, this is ridiculous!" what do you think about who she is? Who do you see when you hear my mother knits and finds horror movies ridiculous?

She would have been fifty-one at the time. At fifty-seven, she was diagnosed with Parkinson's disease. She was director of senior support services at a social service agency in Toronto. People with Parkinson's and their families comprised a significant portion of their caseload. She knew the disease's inexorable decline, whether slow or fast. She knew the loss of mobility, of muscle control, of facial expression, of independence, of ability to swallow, to speak, to think. She knew if she told people at work, they'd feel sorry for her and treat her differently. She'd shift categories, she'd be demoted in other people's minds. She knew this was wrong but true. She knew people wouldn't intend to treat her differently, but they would.

For the next eight years at work, she kept her diagnosis secret. After retiring, she became a vocal advocate and volunteer for people with PD. She stayed physically active. She hiked and canoed and bicycled. She discovered her dyskinesia changed relative to her surroundings. Outdoors, it was largely absent. Indoors, it was worse, and in narrow spaces, corridors, and hallways, worst of all. She spent a lot of time outdoors.

Indoors, she kept her hands active. She knit. She wanted to knit sweaters for all her grandchildren, nine of them at the time, before she wasn't able to anymore. Out came the pattern books for each grandchild to choose their sweater. She completed those nine sweaters and then a tenth for my kid, a baby sweater, which didn't count in her reckoning as a grandchild sweater. She had one more sweater to make. It was still on the needles when she died at eighty-one. She hadn't been able to knit for at least five years. The last year or so, she'd found it hard to communicate. She'd get halfway through a sentence, a phrase, and lose her thread. For a while, her eyes still spoke. And then, even they said less and less.

When I brought all her knitting stuff home to Vancouver, I left that sweater on the needles. It was only about twelve rows of knitting, bunchy and full of dropped stitches, not at all like her usual even rows. She'd never outright abandoned the project, never pulled out all the stitches, never given up.

There it remained, a testimony of intention.

A few years after watching *Friday the 13th*, I was a counsellor at a summer camp where we stayed up later and later each night in the staff lounge, talking and smoking, in love with each other's company. Sometimes I'd make the Jason sound: *ch*-ch-ch-ch. Our hearts in our throats. Five or six of the staff were knitting Icelandic sweaters in rose or grey or blue. It was a bit of a fad in 1983. You'd get a kit: a pattern, ten balls of Elenka yarn, a set of five- or six-millimetre circular needles, double-pointed for the sleeves. I had the notion at the time that circular needles were a new invention, suddenly making knitting easy. There was no blanket-stitching the seams of front and back together, no purling, even—just going round and round and round, fat yarn, fat needles, knitting up fast. Regularly that summer, though, one of the knitters would swear, "Fuck," having made a mistake or noticed a mistake, and "Fuckity fuck," then pull out rows and rows of stitches, pick them back up again, "Damn," and start over.

I loved sweaters.

I loved those sweaters.

When I put on a sweater (by *sweater*, I mean wool sweater—there is not really another kind), well, it sounds too obvious, but it almost disappears, and it is warm. Down is like this too, and even lighter. It's like wearing warm air. Humans are so inadequate.

I had been told all my life: wool keeps you warm even when it is wet. Subtext: wool protects.

I decided if and when I ever made a sweater, it'd be one of those Icelandic ones. And if I made a mistake, and I surely would, I would not pull it out. I would just keep going. Who cared if there was a flaw in the pattern? The aesthetics didn't matter. The warmth. The warmth mattered.

This was true, but there was something else going on.

A few years later again, I was about to start work at a winter outdoor ed centre in Ontario. School groups would come up for three or five days at a time, and we'd take them out on snowshoe hikes, teach them to ski and build winter shelters and be comfortable in the snow. Seemed like a good time to knit myself a sweater.

I'd got a haircut early that fall, short enough to prompt my mother to ask if I was a lesbian. "Yes," I allowed. She had feared this for some time. She and I had been at loggerheads over what I wore since I was three and out of the cute smocked dresses she had made me. She found my bent for the masculine incomprehensible—deliberate and perverse, a repudiation of a self she imagined for me. On my end, it was a simple truism: this is who I am.

Relations with my parents that fall sucked.

But my Christmas present was a trip to the yarn store with Mom to pick out the wool and the needles and then a knitting lesson: cast on, knit, purl, increase, decrease, and Fair Isle knitting, how to carry the strands when it came to the yoke.

When we were children, my sister and I had a little hand-knitting toy, a tube with four hooks on top. I can't remember now how it worked, but it was weirdly satisfying to do. Pull yarn, wrap around peg, wrap around next peg, pull a strand, I don't know, and out came a tube of knitted yarn. I think you were meant to then sew it into a coil to make a mat or a pot holder or something. I don't remember ever doing that. Just making the tubes themselves. Odd, useless crafts. The point of crafts is utility.

Unless you think the point is the making, not what is made.

YouTube tells me it is called French knitting (an insult to the French, no? Like they're not manually dexterous enough to manage real knitting?).

Corking. That's what we called it. Corking. My sister called this up from the well of her memory.

The point I am trying to get to is the simultaneous simplicity and complexity of the loop. In knitting, you can take a line and make it a plane. That alone is geometrically interesting. A kind of magic.

In corking, you take a line and make it a bigger line, a tube.

You go from one dimension to two, or you go from one to three.

But first you have to go from three to one.

A friend of my mother's had a spinning wheel. Our childhood dog, a collie, shed her magnificent undercoat each year, garbage bags full of it. Under the guidance of our mother's friend, my sister carded and spun our dog's fur into a fine, soft yarn. Took volume and turned it into line.

Knitting is a series of loops inside loops next to loops. When we tied up the boat at the dock, we did a slip knot and then slipped another loop through the first loop, another loop through that loop, another loop through that until we had about eight, and the end got tucked through the last one. When we came to leave again, we untucked that end and pulled. Out all the knots came, sloop, sloop, sloop, sloop, hop in the boat, and we're off.

We knit our boat to our dock. We pulled the stitches out to cast off.

After my mother died, my father went through a period of regretting he had not valued her more—her abilities, her acuity, her intellect. She was smarter than he was, he said regularly, and it went without saying that he was very smart, because he had one of those jobs that people use as a touchstone for intelligence. But he felt it in a new way after she was gone. I think for the first time, he saw her as a person and not just a gendered person, a woman. It came to him in a new way, *whom* he had lost.

One evening, as an adult, I was doing the dishes after some family event, a task I quite liked because it was quiet in the kitchen, tucked away from the loud debate that characterized so many family dos.

My father came into the kitchen and said, "You shouldn't have to be doing this."

That made no sense to me. "Who should?" I asked.

I mean, yeah, my brothers, but that wasn't what he meant.

Later it came to me that in the house my father grew up in, there were servants. I don't think he was conscious of it, but what he'd meant was, "There should be servants to do this."

The notion that anyone is above housework is disturbing.

I am not above housework. My father is not above it. Nobody is. Some people do it for a living, and we should value them.

My mother did it throughout her life, and we should value her.

My father did learn to value it, a little, later on, when he was meal planning and grocery shopping and cooking because Mom could not.

My brother said something once about my father being *reduced* to wiping his wife's bum. Dad himself did not feel that way. He might even have said he was honoured to do it.

And still, he didn't value her fully until her whole life was a whole life, with an end to it.

Children's household chores were not gendered in our house. We all washed the dishes. We all cleaned the bathrooms and vacuumed and took out the garbage. We all did yardwork. We all washed the windows. We scraped and sanded and varnished and painted. When my mother went back to school, we each took turns cooking dinner one night a week.

But there were some things my brothers never did, and sewing and knitting were two of them. They were across the line.

I have thought about gender all my life.

The way that certain women look at me (how to describe them fairly?), outraged, aghast, or baffled and irked; the dismissiveness, lifelong, of some men. The double takes, the duration of the gaze that wonders. Not malicious, mostly,

but curious, the *It's Pat* phenomenon. (It's
funny how you can tell the difference between
a malicious gaze and a curious one.) I got used
to this.

I do not think I have thought expansively enough.

I have thought in reaction to.

The unfairness of boundaries. The arbitrariness of skirt and pant.

I have been made comfortable through female
exceptionalism: You don't play trombone like a
girl at all!
[Oh, I am a better girl because I am more like a
boy.] [Wait.]

I have succumbed to twoism. Two

ways of thinking—that there are two
categories within which there is broad
conformity, naturally occurring. These
categories are fixed. If someone comes along
who does not conform, it's not that they do
not fit the category but that the category must
be expanded to include them. Then, make
another category within the category. Mannish.
Effeminate. // And the other way:

if someone comes along who does not conform,
who feels they do not fit the category, they place
themselves in the category that does fit. // But
this is the same, or almost the same. // Because
there are not only the two categories, and there need not be. //

"You knit?" with that little emphasis on "you" that means, "No, not you, that is so unlikely." It gives me a spark of pleasure as much as anything that might be construed to be the reverse, like, "You play hockey?"

On a superficial level, I just like the idea of refusal, of not *not* choosing things for their failure to be masculine. If I let my masculinity be as assailable as men do by refusing to associate with the feminine, am I not just as wrong, just as limited, just as blinkered as they?

When I asked you to picture my mother, a fifty-one-year-old woman knitting while pooh-poohing horror movies on television, I imagine you thought of someone matronly, maybe someone a bit dumpy, someone, above all, domestic. Because I would. How is it that I have learned to imagine knitters this way? If I catalogue the individual knitters of my acquaintance in my head, they are varied—an outdoorsy gay man who for a time knit professionally for fashion designers, a Utilikilt-wearing straight man who works in IT, two teenage sons of friends of my parents', my stylish and kind step-grandmother.

And then there's the question of what *domestic* means. (For that matter, what does *dumpy* mean? How do I use that word? I think I must retract it.) What does a woman who is domestic look like? What does she think about? Is she important or trivial? If my mother had no concerns except that her house be well run—clean, in good repair, etc.—she would be no lesser than if she wrote seven books and successfully lobbied government to end clear-cutting. Most of her middle-class friends did some kind of volunteer work; many of them did as she did and returned to work after the youngest was old enough to be left alone. Some of them did not; some of them were alcoholics. They suffered, those women, I think.

Why am I even putting knitting in the category of the domestic? How do I define the domestic? I haven't thought it through. Domestic. Of the domicile. The home. Cooking and cleaning and caring for children clearly fall into this category, along with their attendant offshoots of meal planning, grocery shopping, activity planning, and so on, but so too do household maintenance, yardwork, etc.

Now, knitting isn't really *for* the family or the household. If you want to efficiently clothe yourself, your spouse, and your children, you sure as heck don't knit.

So I've been on a false chase all this time.

But I remain interested in the domestic. I have plans for another essay on the role it plays in children's books.

When my mother was a child, most of her clothes were homemade, first by her mother and then by herself. And what she had was so much less than what we have now. What she considered important to have in one's wardrobe was:

1 very nice dress (a party dress, a dress to wear to special events)
1–2 regular dresses for everyday wear
2–3 skirts
4–5 blouses to mix and match with the skirts
2 pairs of slacks to mix and match with the blouses
2 cardigans
1 sweater
1 pair of jeans for camping or yardwork
1 set of ski clothes (ski pants, turtleneck, ski sweater, ski jacket)
2 shorts-and-top sets
2 nighties (one summer, one winter)
1 dressing gown
1 winter coat

Within the scope of this wardrobe, almost everything could be made by hand, except perhaps the winter coat. Oh, or anything that needed to be serged, like the turtleneck.

By the time she had children, most of these items would be store bought and not handmade. Mass production meant it was cheaper to buy them than make them. Still, each year, she made certain things. For herself. For my sister and me. Pedal-pushers. Culottes.

One item my mother made for herself in her early twenties was a wool dressing gown, which she used from the time she made it to the time she died at eighty-one. There she is wearing it in photos, just after marriage. There she is wearing it, hand on her hip, age fifty or so, squinting into the morning sun at the cottage, where it hung between daily use on cold mornings on a peg on the back of the door. After she died, it was still in perfect shape. It is made of a tartan of deep red with yellow, green, and black accents, narrow at the waist and slightly flared in the skirt. It fits neither my sister nor me. I did not want to give it away, this exquisitely made garment, but I thought maybe I could make something of it. I had been making slippers out of old sweaters for some time now. My sister had care of the summer cottage. I could make a tea cozy for the cottage. Which I did. It was hard to cut into the dressing gown. But I thought of all the old clothes my mother had cut up and turned into quilts. I can look at the orange quilt she made for me and recognize an apron, the pedal-pushers, a floral dress of my sister's. So I took a deep breath, placed my fingers through the handle of the scissors, and opened the blades. And stopped. Admired the finely made loop for the waist-belt. The neat seams. The perfect line. I put down the scissors and tried the dressing gown on once more. It lay on me light and heavy the way wool can. It was tight in the shoulders and snug at the waist. Even if it had fit, I could not have worn it. The same fabric in a men's cut, absolutely. I sighed. I refocused.

This is what we do. We take the old and make new with it.

It turns out that knitting *is* a form of protection. "Knitting is the saving of life," wrote Virginia Stephen to Leonard Woolf sometime before she married him. (Ultimately, of course, we know knitting did not save her.) Esther Rutter uses this quote in her history of knitting in the British Isles, *This Golden Fleece*, to introduce a section cataloguing studies showing that knitting reduces heart rates and lowers blood pressure and reduces PTSD-induced flashbacks and so on.

Knitting is the saving of life.

The domestic with nothing else can be the death of it. The same Virginia Woolf, saved for a while by knitting, in 1927 turned her wit and intellect to the question of women and fiction in the form of two lectures intended for women's colleges. The resulting book, too long for even two lectures, is one of those resonant and pivotal volumes whose main point is easy to encapsulate: to write, you need money and space. You need a room of one's own.

Coincident with my writing this essay, my pre-ordered copy arrived of poet Sina Queyras's book *Rooms*, about their relationship with *A Room of One's Own*. The pleasure of cracking this new book open sent me back to *AROOO*, as Queyras calls it. One thread of it sees Woolf looking for and failing to find women writers before Aphra Behn, sees her imagining Shakespeare has a sister with the same spirit, the same mind as he. What happens to her? Her parents tell her to make stew and mend stockings. And marry. And when she refuses to marry and is beaten by her father and runs away to London like her brother, does she end up on the stage, writing plays? No. She ends up pregnant by the actor-manager of the company and kills herself at the age of seventeen.

But Woolf too considers the value of the domestic in *AROOO*.

> In my little street ... domesticity prevailed. The house painter was descending his ladder; the nursemaid was wheeling the perambulator carefully in and out back to nursery tea; the coal-heaver was folding his empty sacks on top of each other; the woman who keeps the green-grocer's shop was adding up the day's takings with her hands in red mittens ... I thought how much harder it

> is now than it must have been even a century ago to say which of these employments is the higher, the more necessary. Is it better to be a coal-heaver or a nursemaid; is the charwoman who has brought up eight children of less value to the world than the barrister who has made a hundred thousand pounds? It is useless to ask such questions; for nobody can answer them.

There is a great deal more to exclaim over in rereading *A Room of One's Own*, but I'll limit myself to a quick mention of these lines, which struck me: "Two sexes are quite inadequate, considering the vastness and variety of the world" and "If an explorer should come back and bring back word of other sexes looking through the branches of other trees at other skies, nothing would be of greater service to humanity."

In 1928, Virginia Woolf was saying that only two sexes were inadequate, that somewhere in the realm of possibility existed a world with many sexes. The mention of "other trees" and "other skies" suggests to me that the very multiplying of gendered possibilities brings us new trees and new skies. We see everything anew.

She is not quite the visionary wonder I am making her out to be. In their context, these quotes are more conventional than they seem here—the first quote in its entirety is, "It would be a thousand pities if women wrote like men, or lived like men, or looked like men, for if two sexes are quite inadequate, considering the vastness and variety of the world, how should we manage with one only?"—and yet there is something about the base assumption "two sexes are quite inadequate" that is very close to contemporary queer ideas.

The Christmas after that horror-movie Halloween, under the tree were the sweaters. For me, a cream, beige, and grey argyle that I'd thought was for Sheila. For Sheila, a zippered Cowichan she'd thought was for me. I had to work to hide my disappointment. Argyle? Sorry, no. And then too my mother's version of a good fit on me has never been my version of a good fit. So the argyle sweater was always too small. I wore it only a few times, to family events, where Mom would see me wearing it, where it might lodge in photos. But I never gave it away. On each go-through of the closet, it sparks not joy but something as important: honouring. Memory. And now I am on the lookout for a yarn that will complement it when I deconstruct and reconstruct it.

After the awkward and painful Christmas that followed my coming out, as I was saying goodbye to my parents in the front hall of their house before heading up to the outdoor ed centre, my father said, "I'll always love you, Anne, but I'm ashamed. I am deeply ashamed." He pulled me toward him to give me a hug. I stood stiffly. I don't know what I said.

Almost everyone at the outdoor ed centre knit. John and Ray knit. Joanne and Geri knit. We knit together, companionably, around the fire, which was in a small dining room in the same building where the children washed their faces and brushed their teeth. There too we were in love with each other's company. One time we were knitting like this when a group of twelve-year-old girls burst in in their pajamas. They advanced on me in a clump, with nervous laughter. "When we first got here, we thought you were a boy," one of them said. "We thought you were cute," said another, while her friends whacked her arm and told her shut up, they did not. "We're tomboys too," the first one said. "But we were wondering. Don't most people grow out of it?"

I shrugged. "You don't have to."

At night, in my little room in the building that housed the bathrooms and the winter kitchen, I listened to Joan Armatrading on the tape deck and knit. Knit a round, another round, another, wondering when to stop, when to call it a night, adding dimension, turning a line into a tube, a little addicted to this transformation. I heard my own voice in my head. "You don't have to."

I made mistakes. I kept going. I started the sleeves. I made mistakes. I kept going. I joined the sleeves to the body. Time for the yoke, the really time-consuming bit. I applied my mother's teaching, carrying the red, the white, and the grey strands of yarn across the shifting pattern. I made mistakes. I kept going. Two months in, I almost had a sweater. Just the collar left to do. With the needle still in the stitches around the neck, I tried it on, gently put my arms in the body of the sweater, probed for one armhole. Yup. Okay, other hand poised at the other armhole. Here we go. Next gesture would be stretching the arms into the sleeves, pulling the head hole over my head, pulling the body down. But no. My arms were not going anywhere. There was no room for my arms. I had attached the sleeves to the body wrong. I had made a mistake. Not the kind you can keep going from. The kind that made the sweater literally unwearable. I had to pull it out. The whole yoke.

At first, I was anguished. How could I save this? What could I do?

Then I thought it was funny. I had been so adamant, refusing to go back over mistakes. I was getting my comeuppance.

Now I think it wasn't only that. My *I'm not going to pull it out* attitude was an assertion of masculinity or a repudiation of femininity or some combination of the two, as if caring about how the sweater looked was feminine and petty, whereas caring only about its warmth was masculine and wise.

We are wrong about things so frequently. We fail to imagine beyond what we have known. My parents thought queers were ostracized, pathetic, and sad. That was what they'd learned and also what time—and all of us letting ourselves remain knit together—let them unlearn. My father thought women were less than men until that thought too unravelled. I can't even catalogue all the times I've seen beyond what I know just enough to know I've been wrong.

Those flashes, though, of what might be. We have those too.

What if we took gender's sweaters and turned them into slippers?

What if we took gender's dressing gown and turned it into tea cozies?

What if we took gender's three dimensions and carded it? Tore it up and broke it down and turned it into one dimension and spun it anew, then knit it up into two dimensions and then pieced those two-dimensional things together the way we wanted and put them on our three-dimensional bodies however we wanted?

SPIRIT MATERIALS

SADIQA DE MEIJER

I've not embroidered for long—three years or so, since the summer that Amy and I began our project. We are having a conversation of questions and answers exploring faith. Her Jewish origins, my Muslim and Christian ones, our present spiritual compasses. We'd been preoccupied with the subject, she as a visual artist and I as a writer, so we merged what we knew and wanted to find out into a mutual undertaking. She started with one embroidered question for me: *when someone asks your religion, what happens internally?* I stitched an answer and another question and sent them back to her. And so it goes on. We work on strips of near-white cloth, approximately as tall as a pen, often wider than the span of our arms—mine are torn from an old bedsheet, boiled in tea to take out the harsh glare—and then we mail them between Nova Scotia and Ontario by affordable, unregistered mail, a small gesture of faith within the process. Someday, we'll sew all the fragments together, and the conversation will be longer than a skein of geese.

A line of geese in flight resembles a row of running stitches. If it were one, there would also be a goose in every gap, but on the reverse side of the sky's fabric. The bird thread moves; its lagging end isn't knotted, and the leading goose follows a needle darting in and out of the cloth. Skilled stitches are evenly spaced and of the same tension as the backing material. Is that how a flying goose feels—at one with the currents of air?

Resting lines also hold an elapsed movement; a line has time in it, as painter David Hockney has said. A start, an end—though that sort of temporality is difficult to locate in life. When did I begin this embroidery? In answering Amy's stitched question, or twenty-five years earlier, at our first hello? In florals across the knees of my grade ten jeans, or on a stiff plastic grid, with clumsy and deliberate kindergarten hands? Perhaps the beginning was longer ago, with a gesture that could germinate again in my body because my grandmother had made it, as had hers, and hers, by the light of a flame, chewing a scrap of tobacco.

Other starts and stops are ingrained in my materials. The cotton grew in Egyptian fields that boys sprayed with toxins carried on their backs. My sewing bag is printed with a guide to a shorthand invented in 1888; *start* looks almost like a downward crawling snail, and *stop* like a cursive *r*. The phrases that Amy and I lay down in thread could outlast our fingers.

What I've learned so far is to start, as with prayer, by washing my hands. To lay the blank cloth on the table, not the floor, with its nails and seams. To write out my answer and question with a fabric marker whose ink will later vanish in seconds under the tap. To buy the good eighteenth-century brand of embroidery floss, because others don't have the same lustre, and they break off. To split its six strands and use two at a time. To know that a small deviation from the intended line will soon alter its entire course. To resist the lure of progress and stop to free the needle from the thread, undo errant stitches with its metal tip, and start again. To locate dormant pockets in the schedule of my hands—the intervals of phone conversations, or online meetings, or sitting out on the wooden porch steps—when they can be writing with thread. I tried to work out there in the rain once, under what seemed like a sheltered edge, but some drops still struck the fabric and caused such quick erasures that I lost the line.

Rain looks like running stitches when we watch it falling close to us—a fastening of cloud and ground with water thread. I've found that my eyesight is not as sharp as it was when Amy and I first became friends, and we seemed for months to be immersed in one long sunlit conversation. The needle's eye, the stitch's exit, softened. From far away, a raining cloud appears to wear a gauzy skirt of downward lines. I have a dimmer, wider vision now; every weather lives in it.

For the words, we use the backstitch, a strong stitch of two lengths forward, one length back. This choreography requires more hours and thread than the running one, but it makes an unbroken line, thin and smooth on the front of the fabric, more ragged on the back, where each stitch is a double. A backstitched, cursive script, both the thread and letters forming lines that return in small looped increments to where they've been and then continue forward. When I write, my mind moves like that—rereading the last sentence, pulling ahead into a new one—but there isn't the pale markered outline to follow.

Is that what makes me feel so held and settled when I stitch? Or maybe it's the slowing down, the words that materialize outside the

NEXT PAGE: Sadiqa de Meijer and Amy Rubin, a selection of questions and answers from *The Woolgatherers*, 2020–present. Embroidery floss on linen. | Photo: Asad Chishti.

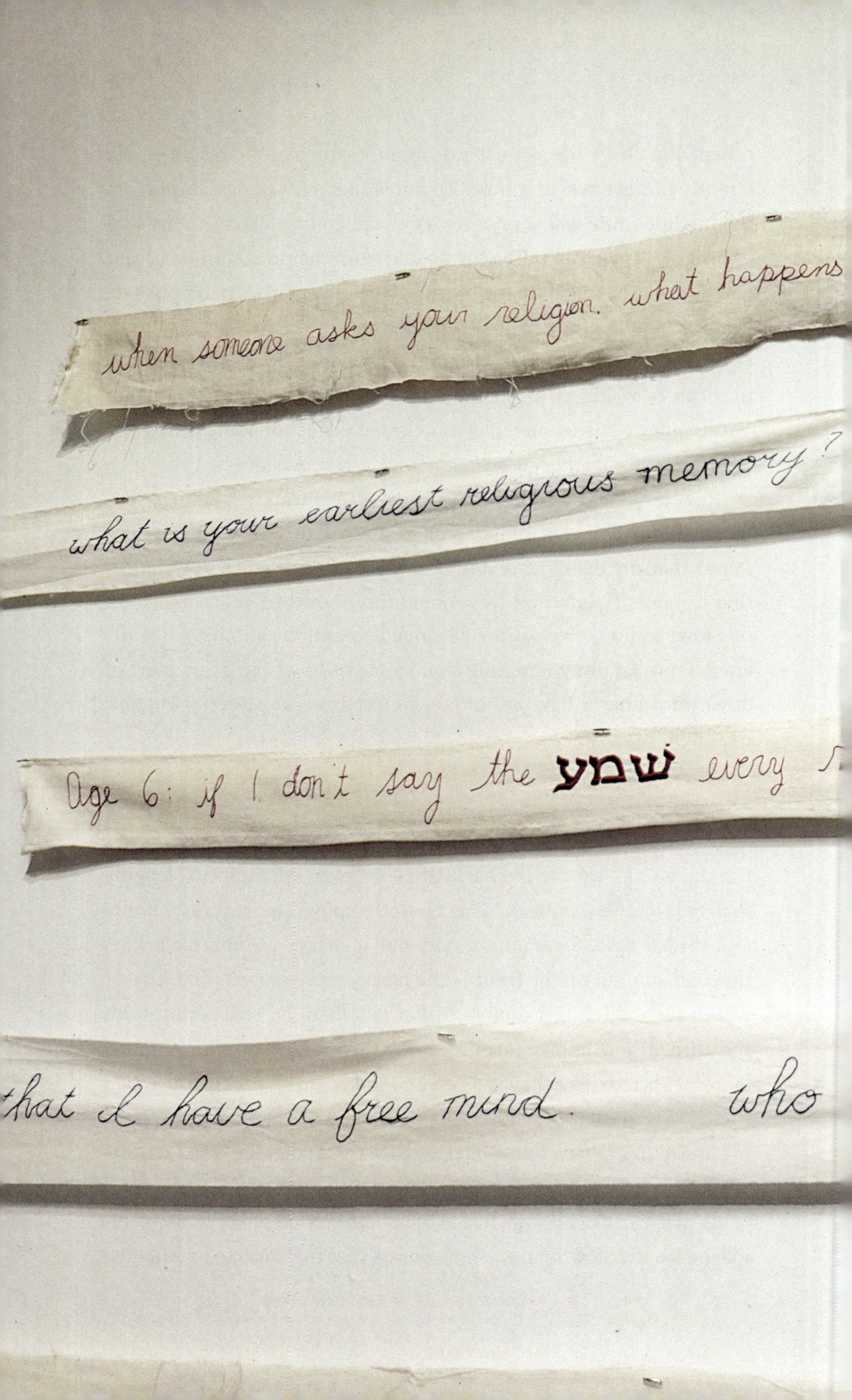
when someone asks your religion, what happens
what is your earliest religious memory?
Age 6: if I don't say the שמע every
hat I have a free mind. who

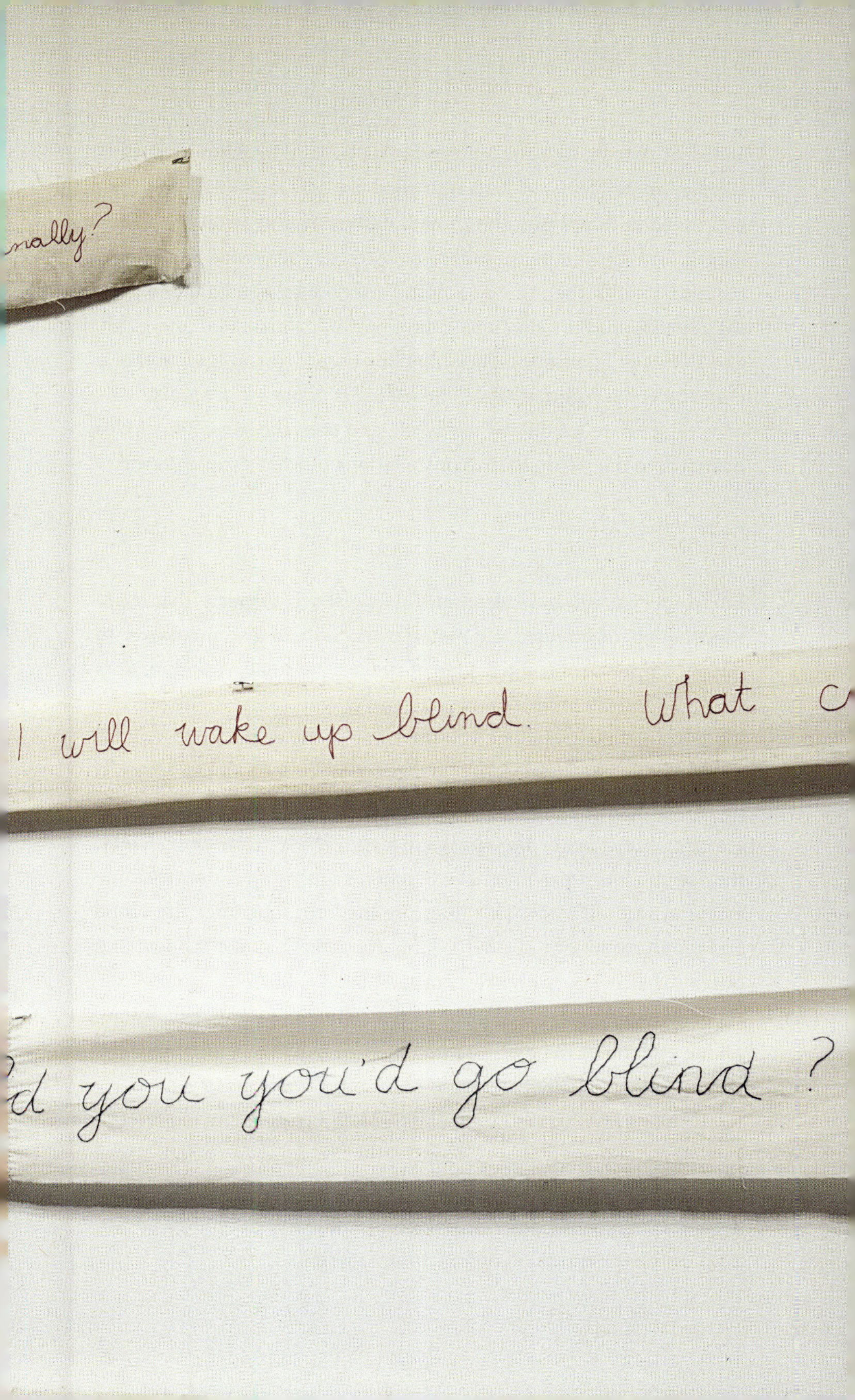
nally?
I will wake up blind. What c
d you you'd go blind ?

speed of speech, or texts, or typing, or writing by hand. It doesn't happen immediately; at first, my mood prevails, and I'm sure it gets expressed in how I pull the thread, its resulting tension and stitch length, and the number of times I have to start again and leave a tiny telltale hole. But then there's a shift. I am doing this with my fingers, the repetition of a rising and falling motion, with metal and cloth, and I start to admire the dark-blue line that forms in their wake. It is steady, it has a good shape. The feeling is praise—I am praising its unfolding existence quietly to myself, and then the sensation circles outward, to the room, to the constellations of what surrounds me.

Embroidery is an embellishment; its presence suggests that there was enough, of minutes and material and skill, to give them over to beauty. Evidence of some degree of peace. The small, round mirrors that one grandmother sewed onto my salwar kameez, the smocking that the other stitched into the front of my summer dress. Our project is and isn't like that—we too are lucky to have the room to do this slow work, but our purpose is not to decorate the fabric. In a sense, questions of the spirit arise conversely from embroidery; they seem almost ornamental when life is untroubled, then become essential when it's not. This crawling medium magnifies the visual and temporal weight of their asking. Its demands take the hedging out of my answers. If I make a rushed mistake, I bleed.

Embroidery also takes place in the telling of stories, but we are asking each other to be plain: *what is your earliest religious memory? when do you feel belonging? what in this world belongs to you?*

Time is a line, and in our ancestries it is a tree, and in experience it is elastic. One day, I was standing in farmland in spring, and a gunshot sent up a flock of resting geese. They scattered outward in pulsing circles from one centre like a puddle's surface after a raindrop, another expression of how time functions.

The women who made me were centres from whom children and bread and clothing and prayers and curses and skills moved outward. Not all of them were literate; a few generations ago, perhaps none of them were. They possessed great knowledge, obviously; I feel it lurking tidally inside the quiet sewing hours. Some of them practised the Punjabi art of phulkari, using the darning stitch and untwisted silk to pattern shawls for their daughters' dowries. Others on the North Sea coast cross-stitched finely detailed initials into their sons' woollen vests for identification if they were lost at sea. I sense the devotion imbued in those needlework gestures, whose makers might find me a lapsed student, shockingly unskilled at anything past basic stitches. But the conversation, the inquiry into what matters in this life between Amy and me, between those relatives in their sewing circles, between all of us and our own minds—I'd like to imagine that as an intricate, knotted, frayed, astounding, and still somehow seamless whole.

NEXT PAGE: Sadiqa de Meijer and Amy Rubin, part of an answer from *The Woolgatherers*, 2020–present. Embroidery floss on linen. | Photo: Asad Chishti.

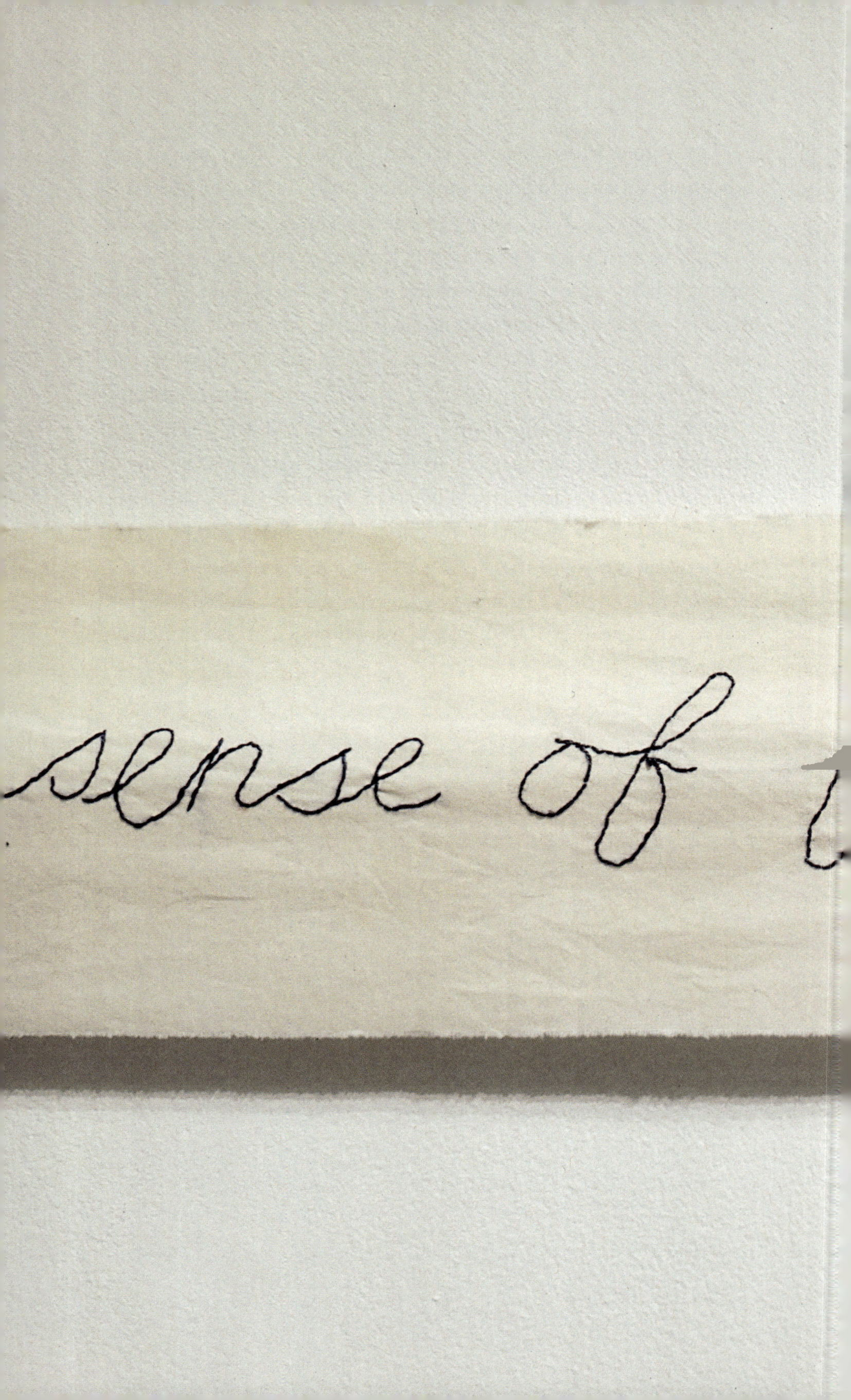
sense of

with

PERFECT IMPERFECTIONS

KELLY S. THOMPSON

A glossy book, *Knit Your Own Dog*, is splayed in my lap alongside a lined notebook, where I track completed rows. The black-and-white yarn I've chosen for my project is soft but durable—perfect for my soon-to-be nephew—and designed for easy washing, which is important because my sister, Meghan, throws everything in her machine on hot and prays to the laundry gods to spit out something that resembles what she put in.

A stitch slips as I try my hand at the formidable challenge of turning a heel, part of the pattern for the anvil shape of a bull terrier snout. "Fuck." For some reason, I'd thought myself talented enough to modify a pattern for a white bully into a replica of my own Pot Roast, his black-and-white splotches, the black heart marking his stomach, as if drawn with a Sharpie. I am not, it turns out, talented enough, as evidenced by the seven open tabs in my internet browser. *How to increase in purl. What is YO in knitting pattern? Perfectly turn a heel.*

Disembodied hands on YouTube demonstrate at incomprehensible speeds, then I try to mimic what I see. I have cried three times, and it's only been an hour.

"How goes the progress, Martha?" Meghan asks, her voice blaring through the speakerphone. She's been calling me this for years now, short for Martha Stewart, because I like hosting dinner parties and making my own bone broth and recently needle-felted a field mouse who had fishing-line whiskers and wore a cap fashioned from an acorn. Despite having a perfectionist personality exacerbated by high anxiety, I am a dabbler in countless art forms, a master of none, somehow content in art's absence of exactitude. There's the writing, of course, but also watercolours, bookbinding, violin, cake decorating, and knitting. Other kids, Meghan included, used to call me a dork, but now in my thirties, I'm on the right side of cool, or so the hipster lifestyle tells me.

"I don't know. I'm worried it looks like an anteater." I inspect the misshapen, unstuffed mass of white and black, finding it hard to imagine it taking dog form. "I just wanted to, I don't know, make something. For the baby." What I want is to give to my nephew a representation of the thing I love most in the world, or an iota of the calm I feel with my dog snoring on my lap. I want him to know me even in the absence of me. Unable to have my own children, the closest I will come is my sister's boy, but in some ways, it feels like enough. We've always filled the gaps for one another.

She snorts. "Thank God he'll have an aunt like you. I can barely make an edible cookie." Meghan is a shitty cook, a shamelessly bad housekeeper. She admits she's professionally lazy, with skeptical ethics and zero stick-to-it-iveness. When Grandma Helen gave us knitting lessons as kids, Meghan often disappeared to climb trees with the neighbour's kids while I tried producing pointless squares filled with holes that unravelled by the time we got home. But I liked the idea of a handmade signifier, some physical representation of an experience—a souvenir, but infinitely more special. At the end of those muggy summer days, my sister always returned to me, and we'd collect clay at the creek, which we shaped into figures and let dry in the sun the following morning. Or roll down the steep hill at the end of the lane and cover ourselves in grass stains.

I huff air through pursed lips so that my bangs puff up in a cloud. "This is turning out like garbage. It's going to be garbage." I throw the needles and yarn to the floor, startling Pot Roast. He nudges one of the balls with his nose, considers giving chase, then settles back into a patch of sun to nap.

"Stop pulling a Helen, Kell."

Grandma Helen had such a negative self-view that "pulling a Helen" became a family euphemism for putting yourself down. "I shouldn't be giving lessons," she once said to me in the middle of casting on. "I'm not a very good knitter. I can never get the tension quite right." Or that tasty pie she'd made? Well, she had overworked the pastry, so it lacked a flaky crumb. Her weight? Always too much (but then who was she to resist a Cheez Whiz sandwich on Wonder Bread?). Mom says I take after Grandma—a worrier, a perfectionist. Stuck with a permanent feeling of never having done something well enough, a sense of not quite stacking up.

I sigh and pick up the needles. "Grandma said you can't wreck a piece of knitting. That it's just a matter of figuring out where you went wrong and learning how to fix it."

"See? Now that's the right attitude." I hear Meghan slurp from a mug. "You've got this."

When I finish mini stuffed Pot Roast for my nephew, I'm impressed with the likeness. I snap a photo of the live version staring at his woolly doppelgänger and send it with a whooshing text to my sister.

It's perfect ♥, she types back. *He'll love it.*

I kiss Pot Roast on his real-life snoot and give him a liver cookie. Homemade by me.

Four years later, Meghan punches at the controls of the rented hospital bed that occupies her entire living room. My husband is outside playing with her two young children, entertaining them so she can rest.

"Cup of tea?" I call from the kitchen. The tiny space is a pit, even though it feels like I'm always here cleaning, wiping, scrubbing. But lately, as Meghan's cancer advances, it feels like there are more important things to do than tidy up.

She shrugs, attention focused on the crocheted blankets she hasn't yet finished.

"Your hands look cramped." I set the tea down, chamomile dripping down the mug to leave a puddle of moisture on the laminate floors.

"I'm kind of on a deadline," she says wryly, weaving the crochet needle rapidly. "Get it? *Dead*-line?"

We snort at this, revelling in the death jokes others find off-putting. Meghan was never into crafting, but since she found out her cancer was terminal, she's been a woman obsessed, making fat acrylic throw blankets—one for each family member in a colour of their choosing. "Meghan hugs," she calls them, to wrap ourselves in when she's gone. She's working on mine now: lime green, white, and grey. I hope the yarn will pick up her scent and keep her alongside me as she slips toward death.

Meghan presses the bolus on her morphine pump and leans back, clutching at her stomach until her pupils dilate and her body slackens. Then she takes my hand in hers, her bones radiating heat. "You'll keep the leftover yarn, right? So that if the kids ever need them repaired, you can fix them? No one else will know how, Kell. No one will know."

"I will be the resident tailor of all Meghan hugs." I offer a mock salute and kiss her palm and hope this gives her the peace she needs.

Her eyelids sag closed, and soon she is snoring, hands raised over her head on the pillow like a newborn.

Pot Roast and I receive our diagnoses just a month apart. Rheumatoid arthritis for me and sarcoma cancer for him, which is ironic, considering sarcoma killed Meghan two years earlier. She and Roast were such a bonded pair, him lying at her side in my guest bedroom for the entire duration of her surgical recovery. I don't know if my nephew still has knitted Pot Roast or if, in the madness after such a monumental death, the stuffed dog was donated along with Meghan's shabby clothes.

My hands have been knotting into burly roots for a few years, but there was always a reason to ignore the pain—caring for Meghan in her illness, helping our parents cope with her death, or prioritizing my waning mental health over the physical because the former felt infinitely more life-threatening. But when my wedding ring no longer fits over my knuckles, I finally went to the doctor for tests, and the disease was confirmed.

The medications make me ill, flares leave me writhing with flu-like symptoms, and even after the swelling abates, bony nodules are left like booby prizes. I can barely manage work, much less do the crafts I love, but I'd take all the pills in the world if it meant Pot Roast would live. He has a few months at best, and whenever I look into his beady black eyes, a tide of panic swells and leaves me breathless.

The vet says that sarcoma progresses differently in individual dogs, so there's that hope to cling to. Losing Pot Roast should be easier than the slow, painful death of my sister, who lost more than half her body weight, heaved and heaved litres of vomit, became skeletal in her seven weeks in hospice. The last few years have been a perpetual state of bereavement, anticipatory and prolonged, what comes and what remains. Everything tastes of sawdust. Warm sun does nothing but sting my skin.

It takes a considerable number of anti-inflammatory tablets to help me with my latest project. I've spent hours clacking away with bamboo needles, pausing every so often to sob into Roast's velvety ears. Knitting demands attention, which harnesses my anxiety into an act that produces something worthwhile and, in turn, makes me feel worthwhile. When I'm looping stitch over stitch, I can focus on the product, the creation, instead of the fear of what comes next or pain related to events long past.

The result is chunky scarves for both human and canine companion. But Pot Roast will barely tolerate wearing his, despite the charming horn toggle button that complements the mint wool. When I stand back to admire my handiwork, he looks at me with a sense of indignance. He shimmies and shakes, then drops to the floor in hopes of ridding himself of this personifying shame.

"Fine, fine. Come here."

Before I remove it, I snap a selfie of our matching ensemble, wishing I knew how to use Instagram filters or those apps that slim and blur. When I look at the picture, all I see is my red, swollen eyes, thick with impending loss.

From behind a pandemic Plexiglas barrier, the cashier rings up more than eighty dollars of chunky alpaca yarn as my eyelids brim. It's ridiculous, this price, but I finger the softness and think of Pot Roast in my lap last week as the veterinarian put him to sleep, his eighty pounds weighty in my arms, and the musk of his ears, into which I whispered calming sounds.

"Are you sure you have enough for your whole project?" the woman asks. "We aren't getting any more of this in, so I don't want you running out."

I panic and zoom in on my phone to scrutinize the pattern. I walked into this place with a plan, as if I knew how the fuck to translate a pattern that produces a ten-inch figure into a more huggable size, but so much has changed since my last kick at the *Knit Your Own Dog* can. My rheumatoid arthritis is progressing rapidly. I can hardly hold needles, and again, I have to google every pattern instruction that extends beyond the simplicity of stockinette; my brain can't remember what my hands have already forgotten.

"I, I'm trying to knit my dog." I hold up my phone like this will explain everything, total up my grief on the counter alongside the stitch markers and buttons I thought would make acceptable eyes. But how did I think I could replicate such a curious, impish nature with lifeless pieces of plastic? And how much more info to give? The first knitted Roast, and now the second knitted Roast, and the real living Roast, and the Meghan hug I wrap around my shoulders when it all gets too much. "He died. This book, it has patterns, and I made one before but—" That does it. I cry, big, heaving jags that send a rivulet of snot down the inside of my surgical mask. I swipe at my eyes with the back of my hand and shake my head over and over.

"Oh, love." The cashier tilts her head sideways. "I understand. Lots of folks want to make something to commemorate someone. Or something. Here, let me see." She reaches for my phone and squints at the screen.

I want to tell her it is so much more than that. I am losing myself—big, heaving parts of myself—and if I can't do this one thing perfectly, then nothing will ever be quite right. My second knitted Pot Roast cannot "pull a Helen" in an epic swan dive of my sanity, because I am already holding tight to that tender nature of well-being like an egg in my hand. It is too fragile, and while I can make an allowance for slight imperfections, I need some part of this project to succeed in order to make each day worth living, just as Meghan's stitches gave her reason for being.

"What size needle are you planning on using?"

I sniffle, clear my throat. "Maybe a US 10?"

She nods, considering, and makes some shapes with her hands for scale. "Yes, I think that'll do it. You should be set with these five balls. If you run out, call the store right away, and I'll set aside any leftovers we have and get them sent to you. Okay?"

In less pandemicky times, she might have patted my hand or given me a hug. But Plexiglass separates us, and so she gives an oversized smile.

I stuff the haul into my tote and burst into the fall air, whip off my mask, and blow my nose in the street, my fingers aching from the cold.

Large-size knitted Pot Roast does, in fact, look a bit like an anteater. A misshapen, lumpy anteater. He takes more than three weeks to make, whereas the one I made for my nephew seven years ago was whipped up in two days. As illness grips my joints, I can only work in short sections. A tail here. A front leg there. Then it takes eons to sew up, often because I'm crying so hard I'm unable to see the pattern—from grief or pain, I can't quite say.

The knitted dog uses an entire bag of stuffing, and the alpaca wool is so dense the effigy takes on a hefty quality that would win any pillow fight.

"He sits just like Roastie." My husband, Joe, balances Knitted Roast 2.0 on the kitchen counter. Indeed, he sits right on his arse, just like a terrier, back legs kicked out in an adorable V.

"He's a little, I dunno, weird looking. The head isn't quite right. I messed up the body."

"It's perfect, Kell. Look, he's so snuggly!"

"I think my hands need a month to recover." I hold up my braced arms as evidence. Upon completion, I'd tried to cuddle my new project, but the yarn kept snaring in the three-inch-wide Velcro straps of my RA braces.

"Well, labour of love, right? And hell, it's not like Pot Roast was perfect. Didn't you cry almost every day when he was a puppy? He was so horrible back then, remember?" He pats the fake dog's head and grins at me, even as his own eyes mist.

Whereas Pot Roast was handsome and confident, our new bull terrier, Hamlet, is nervous and lithe. At two years old, Hamlet's red-and-white colouring is pocked with dark freckles, and his black-spotted lips look like he's sloppily applied goth lipstick. He's adorable, but different.

I've never rescued a dog before, and welcoming him into our home sets my nerves on edge and pushes me into a stress-induced RA tailspin. It's so bad that Joe has to cut my meat at dinner and open my pill bottles to shake the medications into my mouth, my maw gaping like a baby bird. In the days leading up to bringing Hamlet home, where I imagined I'd be nesting like a new mom, I'd done nothing but sob, unsure if it was RA-related depression or uncertainty about this new animal in my life. I wanted my old life and all the beings who'd been in it.

When we arrive home, we leash Hamlet and walk him through the house, room by room, to let him sniff and explore. I limp behind Joe and the dog into the bedroom. Hamlet's ears perk high on his forehead, his body tensing into a tight ball of muscle. His nose wiggles in the air. Blood lust.

"Whoa, hold on, buddy." Joe tugs on the lead and tries to settle him, but Hamlet is wild, back legs kicking like a bronco, the whites of his eyes zoning in. His target: Knitted Pot Roast 2.0, perched on the dresser and lording over the bedroom.

"No! Don't let him!" I wail, aware of the melodrama in my voice but unable to stop it. Hamlet leaps and spins like the Tasmanian

Devil, reaching heights we didn't think possible. He snatches the knitted dog in his teeth and proceeds to shake him like a maraca, snapping the neck of the doll in wild figure eights. The scene moves in slow motion. The slap, slap, slap of Hamlet's ears against his head. Joe, reaching for the leash that tethers them, wrestling to pry open our dog's mouth to retrieve our pretend dog, our stand-in, my sepulchre to suffering. Me like an opera performer, dropping to my knees, keening. The effort, the cost, this illness progressing so fast, the disability so stark that I don't know if I'll ever be able to make another, and what then? My boy now gone, my sister. What of all this loss?

"Ham! Drop it, Ham!" Joe booms as he jimmies his collar. Hamlet spits out the knitted dog as if it's gone bitter, then cowers, tail curled under, ears pinned to his curved dome, as if waiting to be hit. My insides quiver. What was Hamlet's life like in the three other homes he had before ours? Was he ever loved enough that his people would knit a mini version of him and cherish that version when he was gone? Was he so imperfect that no one saw the tenderness in him?

Joe takes a moment to wipe the slobber from the stuffed animal and inspect it for holes before righting it on the dresser. "It's fine. Seems fine."

Hamlet remains hunched, shaking. I half crawl, half limp toward him. I take his bristly cheeks in my hands and hold his nose so it meets mine. "Don't worry, sweet Ham. It's okay. You're safe. You're home." He leans into me like he understands every word I say.

A gust of cold air rushes through the front door, and Hamlet looks up at me with disdain, his shaded eyebrows raised as if to say, *Go out? In that?* Our first nor'easter of the season has hit with a wallop, and while the winds have finally died down, the snow left behind has billowed into a pile outside the front door.

I wear so many layers of Gore-Tex that I waddle like the Michelin Man, Hamlet's leash clipped to a carabiner around my waist so as not to tug at my tender hands. My mittens—knitted back when I could make a pair a week to gift them for Christmas—are layered inside with roving wool that has felted into the shape of my hands. Impenetrable and cozy. I had made Meghan a pair, but she never wore them, as though they were to be worshipped, not used.

Hamlet approaches the wall of snow with trepidation and then backs up. *Nope. No way, lady.* He was born in Mexico, so can't say I blame him.

"Do you think he'll be warm enough?" I double-check the Velcro of his winter coat and ensure his winter booties are done up tight.

"Stop fussing," Joe responds. "He'll be fine. We'll warm up once we get moving."

The moment we step outside, icy wind whips my cheeks. And what of Ham's exposed face? "Hold on." I run back indoors, dig through bins of hats and gloves missing their partners, gaiters to keep snow out of boots, until I find the mint-green scarf and its match. Slivers of Pot Roast's black-and-white hair are still embedded in the weave, and I give it a sniff. It smells like home.

I wrap the twin around my neck in three loops and carry the mini scarf out to Hamlet, buckle the toggle around his burly neck. "An extra layer for my sweet baby Ham." Sometimes we call him Spicy Ham, depending on his mood, but today, he is sweet. I kiss his soft ears, and he wags his tail in something I interpret as enthusiasm.

"Hey, I think it matches him." Joe says, patting the dog's side. "Think he's ever seen snow?"

There's a lot we don't know about Hamlet in his life before us, which reveals itself in myriad ways—the way he hides when characters on TV get in an argument, the way he cuddles me when I cry, the way he zeroes in on toys like he has never had a chance to play. Meghan insisted she was going to reincarnate as my next dog, and sometimes, I look at him and wonder.

Hamlet leaps into the air to snap at clumps of snow that land nearby. Joe takes my mittened hand, and together we start our slow amble around the neighbourhood, impervious to the cold.

Kelly S. Thompson, knitted bull terrier next to real-life model, 2021. | Photo: Kelly S. Thompson.

HEIRLOOM

DANIELLE GELLER

> I don't know how the first spider in the early days of the world happened to think up this fancy idea of spinning a web ... but she did, and it was clever of her, too.
>
> —E.B. WHITE, *CHARLOTTE'S WEB*

In 2002, a nineteenth-century Navajo chief's blanket was brought to the stage of *Antiques Roadshow.* The blanket's design was simple, with thick bands of black, white, and blue, but chief's blankets were important trade items for the tribes of the plains, and then for white settlers. The yarn was hand spun from the coarse, curly wool of Navajo-Churro sheep—a Spanish import, bred native—and the textiles were so tightly woven that they were nearly waterproof. Back then, a blanket woven by a Diné (Navajo) weaver could cost a year's wages, or half the cost of a house.

The clip from the episode is still hosted on YouTube, and the blanket is called one of the show's "GREATEST FINDS!"

Ted, the elderly man with the blanket, holds his hands firmly behind his back throughout the appraisal. When the appraiser asks what he knows about the rug, he rolls his shoulders in a small shrug. "It's probably a Navajo," he says, "but that's about all I know."

"Ted, did you notice when you showed this to me that I kind of stopped breathing a little bit?" The appraiser is anxious, giddy. The blanket, he tells Ted, is a first-phase blanket, one woven for Ute chiefs. Though the blanket was likely woven between 1840 and 1860, there is little apparent damage, and though the blanket is wool, it feels like silk. The white and black stripes reflect the natural colour of the wool—if you ever find yourself close to a chief's blanket, you can see that the black bands waver between shades of deep, dark brown—and the blue was dyed with indigo. "This is Navajo weaving in its purest form," the appraiser claims, and then he delivers Ted the good news: on a bad day, the blanket would be worth $350,000; on a good day, it could sell for half a million or more.

"Gee," Ted squeaks, pressing his hand to his chest. "I can't believe this!"

The blanket had been hanging on the back of a chair in his house.

In 2016, *Antiques Roadshow* updated the video's description with a new appraisal, increasing its maximum value to a full million.

My mother was Diné. She was raised in Window Rock, the nation's capital, on the reservation. After she graduated high school, she moved with my white father to South Florida, where I was born, to escape a life of poverty, alcoholism, and abuse—though the life she lived with my father was also one of poverty, alcoholism, and abuse. When I was still little, my mother transferred her parental rights to my dad's mom, with whom my sister and I moved north.

Held apart, the thread between my mother's life and mine wore thin.

But for my college graduation, she gifted me her mother's blanket, striped white and orange and forest green. It was the closest she ever came to sharing something from her family and her home, a people and a place she didn't want us to know.

After she left, as I spread the blanket across my bed, I noticed a blue-and-gold label in one corner that read *Pendleton Woolen Mills*. The discovery was a downward spiral into the commercial history of textile production and one of the great innovations of the Industrial Revolution: the power loom.

When the first-phase chief's blanket was woven, weavers had already begun to automate textile production. The jacquard loom, developed in the wee hours of the nineteenth century, was a machine that produced intricately designed textiles through a system of punch cards, which many historians cite as an early inspiration for modern computing. The meaning of *weaver* as a professional designation shifted from "person who weaves" to "person who operates machine."

In the early history of Pendleton Mills, the company's jacquard operator, Joe Rawnsley, consulted with nations throughout the Pacific Northwest and then the Southwest to design textiles incorporating their preferred colours and motifs. One might look at this history and call it appropriation, exploitation, but Pendleton Mills attained a status of cultural significance. Because handwoven Navajo blankets and rugs are so costly in time and skill, because Navajo textiles hold significant commercial value, most Diné families can't afford them, and Pendleton blankets are gifted at graduations and weddings instead.

I wasn't familiar with this history until I began digging around the internet that night. And even though I discovered the Pendleton blanket had *become* a traditional gift, that *tradition* had shifted shape, I found it hard not to feel disappointed. It was as if my relationship with my mother could be defined only by loss—of family, of tradition, of knowing, of memory.

There's a group of middle-aged guys I like to watch play video games on YouTube. Collectively, they call themselves Neebs Gaming. They play survival games like *ARK: Survival Evolved* (a survival game with dinosaurs); *7 Days to Die* (a survival game with zombies); and *Minecraft* (a survival game built out of colourful blocks). They're professional gamers, by which I mean they do this for a living, though skill-wise, they're only *okay* gamers. The comments sections of their videos are full of their fans explaining basic game mechanics, and some of the most enjoyable moments arrive through their spectacular failures. A fan named Failz Z summarizes it best in a comment on their most recent *Minecraft* series: "This series: genius. The editing: genius. The cinematic feel: genius. These guys trying to survive: fucking idiots."

I sometimes worry that I too will be a fucking idiot if it ever comes to surviving apocalypse.

But what the guys lack in skill, they make up for in storytelling. Their twentyish-minute videos are unscripted and carefully edited down from hours of gameplay, and even voices are edited to reflect their virtual environments (echoing through caverns, gurgling underwater). Leitmotifs persist across the series to signal recurring situations, like turning something simple into something very hard.

In one episode from their latest *Minecraft* series, Neebs, a sweet guy from the south, tries to figure out how to use a loom, which is represented in the game by a single brown block with grey lines running across the top and halfway down one side. The production interface is a confusing grey box with other boxes inside it, and as Neebs's frustration grows, the video switches from his point of view to that of the spectator cam positioned in the corner of the room. "*Nope!*" he yells finally. "Don't understand it. I have a loom, and I have some wool. I should be able to figure this out, right?"

He wiggles the wool block around the interface, but there's no indication he's figuring it out. "Oh, crap," he sighs, then mutters, "Simon's the only person here."

Simon is loveable but inept. He's so bad at video games that it's hard to believe he's been playing them professionally for years. He's often the butt of the joke, the group's punching bag, and the persona he adopts is equal parts confusion and belligerence.

Neebs walks out of his virtual house and scans their virtual neighbourhood and yells, "Simon, are you the only person here?"

Simon isn't home. He's standing under some trees a short distance away, and when he hears Neebs call his name, he turns around to face Neebs's house and the meadow between them blooming with flowers. "I don't know," Simon yells, sounding both confused and amused. "Why?"

Neebs calls to the other buildings in their neighbourhood. "Anybody else who knows how to use a loom?"

"Oh! I know how to use a loom!" Simon, excited and eager to help, bounces toward home.

But Neebs isn't really listening for an answer. Anticipating Simon's incompetence, he just groans. "Of *course* you don't know how to use a loom."

"I know," Simon says, resigned. He always sounds resigned to the things he doesn't know, to the joke that never lands. He's a man who stands crosswise to the world, to which I can relate.

After my mother died, there were many things I resigned myself to never knowing. I would never know the Navajo language, which she hardly knew. I would never know her parents, my grandparents, who had already died. I would never know her favourite colour, her favourite song, her first kiss. I would never know how to see her home through her eyes. So I looked around for something I *could* know and decided I would learn how to weave.

I learned to weave from Jenny Slick, whose mother was a friend of my great-grandmother, herself a woman who weaved.

I learned from Lori Begay, who taught me that weaving is a kind of inheritance. "It was given to you," she told me, as if weaving were embodied knowledge, as if my hands and my heart were born for weaving, just as a spider is born with the art of the web.

I learned to weave in an old trading post. In the conference room of a Quality Inn. In a room at the Heard Museum, an institution dedicated to the preservation of American Indian art, which was full of Diné women, young and old.

I learned to weave in silence and in laughter and in the beauty betwixt and between.

Most recently, I learned to weave from Barbara Teller Ornelas and Lynda Teller Pete, two master weavers of Two Grey Hills. In K'é, the Diné kinship system, I am one of their granddaughters by clan. Their mother and my grandmother were born to Tábąąhá, the Water's Edge Clan. In their class, they gave equal weight to story and craft, and as we wove, they shared family stories and origin stories, some of which they published in their book, *Spider Woman's Children*. "At its core," Barbara writes, "K'é is knowing where you come from, learning language, culture, prayer, songs, and your origin stories."

In one of our origin stories, the Holy People came to Spider Woman's home, a skinny sandstone spire we call Spider Rock. At their behest, Spider Woman travelled to our four sacred mountains to gather materials: from Sisnaajiní in the east, she harvested wood; from Tsoodził in the south, she harvested plants to dye her wool; from Dook'o'oosłííd in the west, she learned weaving patterns from the thunder gods; and from Dibé Nitsaa in the north, she learned ceremonial prayers and songs to bless her weaving. And then the Holy People instructed Spider Woman to share this knowledge with the people, the Diné.

In this way, weaving was given to me.

The introduction to *Spider Woman's Children* was written by Barbara's daughter, Sierra. In that introduction, she describes a quiet, formative moment with her mother in the car. As they drove home from an exhibition of Navajo chief's blankets, her mother made the uncomfortable point that the textiles in the exhibit were woven during the same period of history when Van Gogh was painting wheat fields and sunflowers. "Everyone knows who he is," she recalled her mother saying, "but no one will ever know the names of those weavers."

Ted, the man who brought the blanket onto *Antiques Roadshow*, knew admittedly little about its history. The blanket had come to his family through the foster father of his grandmother. "It was given by Kit Carson," Ted says with a flicker of a smile, "who, uh, I'm sure everybody knows his history ..."

To see him smile, even if the smile is given in discomfort. To see Kit Carson flicker out of the showroom as quickly as he arrived. Kit Carson, the Indian agent who led a scorched-earth campaign against the Diné. Who burned villages and farms and slaughtered entire flocks of Navajo-Churro sheep. Who led a cavalry raid into Canyon de Chelly, a sacred place, where Spider Rock towers above the canyon floor. Kit Carson, who forcibly relocated those he did not kill to an internment camp in Bosque Redondo, where weavers spun yarn not from the wool of their sheep but from upcycled materials like bayeta, a red flannel cloth salvaged from the discarded uniforms of Spanish soldiers.

Textile scholars who write about this period of Navajo weaving describe it as a time of inspiration and innovation: new designs, new colours, new techniques. Some write of the freedom of commercial yarns and the relief that weavers must have felt, unshackled from the labour of shearing, carding, and spinning wool. But when one of my weaving teachers, Lynda Teller Pete, talks about this period in Navajo weaving, it is easier for me to understand.

The land in Bosque Redondo was not fit for farming or for raising sheep.

A quarter of the people interred there died of exposure, starvation, and disease.

Diné women pleaded with commissioners to return the people to Dinéteh, but they were forced to remain until four years later, in 1868, when they were finally given permission to begin the Long Walk home.

Pulling these threads together now, reality emerges: the weavers were doing their best to spin shit into gold.

The *Antiques Roadshow* appraiser did not take into account the blanket's loose association with Kit Carson; if he had, the blanket's value would have inflated by 20 percent. His rationale: the link between the blanket and Kit Carson would be difficult to prove. But on one edge of the chief's blanket, there is an important piece of evidence for its age and provenance: a small hole repaired by a weaver with thread spun from bayeta red.

After Spider Woman returned from her journey to the four sacred mountains, the Holy People visited again, and they gifted her husband, Spider Man, the knowledge to craft her loom and weaving tools from the wood she had gathered. A Navajo loom could be considered simple—traditionally, four logs bound together; today, four straight and symmetrically cut boards nailed tight. A simple design for a transient life. The weaving can be untied from the loom and carried, driven, flown, displaced.

When I began learning how to weave, I bought my first Navajo loom from the husband of one of my weaving teachers. On the last day of class, he set up a folding table and laid out the wooden battens, combs, and spindles he made. I held each comb in my hand—felt its weight and the curve of the wood, which conjured images of juniper roots carved through sandstone—before buying two, one large and one small. The loom I picked was stained a burnt orange and branded with his initials, as one might brand a sheep.

The second, I bought from Lynda's husband, Belvin Pete, a mechanical engineer. His materials—plastic clamps, metal turnbuckles, zip ties—were sourced from a hardware store, not the mesa, but the looms he designed were thoughtfully built to accommodate his mother's and his wife's weaving. He made adjustable looms that could be raised or lowered to ease the tension in one's neck and shoulders and collapsible looms that could fit inside one's luggage and be flown from one city to the next. He had no spare looms to sell me at the workshop, but he shipped one to me later. Disassembled, the pieces were wrapped tightly in clingy green plastic and cushioned with loose grocery bags.

A loom is a tool, a machine. An instrument of labour and productivity. It's an object in which form meets function. At its simplest, a loom is an anchor; at its most complex, it is a network of wires, beams, and circuit boards.

Once, *loom* referred more generally to any object valued for its frequent utility; English refined that meaning to a synonym for *tool*. "An outligger carryeth but onely one loome to the fielde and that is a rake," a seventeenth-century farming book cited by the OED reads. Poking around the internet, I discover that an *outligger* was a girl who followed a scytheman through the fields to gather what he cut. I like to imagine each girl had her own favourite trusty rake, and when she aged out of outliggery, she passed that rake on to a cherished sister or friend.

An *heirloom*, then, is just this: an object whose form and function you hope holds value for the ones whose lives follow yours.

When my mother gifted me her mother's blanket, my younger sister was jealous. She had only received a baby-blue polyester shawl, which my mother said she'd worn while dancing in ceremony. I might have preferred the shawl, but the blanket became a minor resentment that burbled under the surface of my relationship with my sister. I sent her the blanket a decade later, after our mother died. I wanted the gift to be seen as a gesture of pure generosity, but in my mind, the blanket had been tinged somehow by the complicated nature of its value, which I found difficult to ascertain.

When I married my Canadian husband and left my desert home, I knew I wasn't going to find the kind of weaving I had begun to learn in Arizona. Kitchener-Waterloo, sister cities bound by a hyphen, reminded me of central Pennsylvania, a place I thought I had left behind. To combat my depression during that first long winter, I enrolled in an introductory class offered by a weaving guild that rented floor space in a local synagogue.

My husband was skeptical. He has no inherent appreciation for handmade things, and I imagine that he imagined our apartment cluttered with janky scarves that neither of us would wear. But the first hand towel I brought home—even with its uneven edges, clashing colours, and skipped warp threads—began to sell him on the possibility of wife as weaver. One quiet morning, he even joined me at the synagogue to tie dozens of threads to another weaver's old warp.

Tedium aside, the first thing that struck me was how fast this kind of weaving could be.

In Diné weaving, a loom is dressed for one project at a time. The weft is not one thread carried back and forth by a shuttle but many threads passed through the warp by hand. My weaving teachers' hands reminded me of my mother's: small as the bird they might hold, but strong. Diné weavers create tight, dense textiles by beating the weft threads with broad wooden combs, which creates a breathy sound of wood on wool that, my weaving teachers tell me, makes grandmas happy to hear.

A weft count of forty to fifty threads per inch is considered high quality; a fine Two Grey Hills tapestry nears eighty. Daisy Taugelchee, one of the world's famous Diné weavers, could achieve weft counts that exceeded one hundred wefts per inch or more. The hand towels I learned to make, by contrast, rarely exceeded twenty wefts per inch, and the loom itself made this work easy. In the time it took to complete a Diné rug the size of a sheet of paper, you could finish enough hand towels to gift your mother-in-law, the mentors who wrote you letters of recommendation for a tenure-track professorship, and the friends you sorely miss.

Shortly after the class ended, I joined the guild, which I found a little funny. *Guild* wasn't a word I heard used outside of video games, and I wasn't sure what membership entailed. The guild collectively owned and maintained a collection of both table and floor looms, including one so large it was best operated by two weavers seated side by side, but the guild was much more than its machinery. Any day I went, I could find women working. Sometimes they were quiet and focused on their individual projects, but other days they worked together, helping each other dress their looms or troubleshoot a problem. I was much younger than the other women, much less experienced, an apprentice to masters of their craft.

Less than a year later, I accepted a job at a university on Vancouver Island, and shortly after arriving, I looked up the local weaving guild. Their equipment was easy and cheap to rent on their website—twenty-five dollars bought you three months on a floor loom you could take home—but unlike the guild in Kitchener-Waterloo, there was no communal space to work in. Instead of joining, I decided to buy my own loom.

As soon as my quest began, I received more offers than I could accommodate. It seemed like every family had a deceased mother's or grandmother's loom in storage, an heirloom gathering dust. After a university function, a colleague told me about a floor loom that had once belonged to her mother-in-law, a master weaver from the Outer Hebrides. Her husband held on to the loom, hoping to finish her last piece, but thirty years passed, and he never found the time to learn how to weave.

I didn't know anything about Scottish weaving or the Outer Hebrides, an island chain off the west coast of Scotland, before I started digging around online. "From the land, comes the cloth," reads the landing page of the Harris Tweed Authority's website. In their photographs, the Outer Hebrides look almost tropical—white sand, turquoise water—but like most land that borders sea, they're subject to both wind and rain. The cloth born there is dense and rugged to the touch, the colours deep, dark, rich. Each thread of yarn is spun from multicoloured wool in which black meets brown meets blue meets mustard meets yellow-orange-brown, once traditionally derived from a lichen called crotal.

In a follow-up email, my colleague told me her mother-in-law's loom was big and old (all caps, followed by *vintage?* inside parentheses). In the images I found online, Scottish looms were built of lacquered metal stained with grease, the frame weighed down by gear-like wheels, pulleys, and chains. They weren't just big and old—they were unfamiliar, intimidating.

This is the tension: a loom is simultaneously tool and inheritance, but it is often more one than the other.

A few weeks later, I came across a local listing by a seller called whiskeysour: *45" floor loom, bench, warping mill, accessories.* The loom was described as both beautiful and custom built by the weaver's husband, a cabinetmaker, in consultation with weavers. The seller said it was custom designed to reduce fatigue and maximize both tension and speed.

When I told my husband about the listing, he agreed to come see it with me.

The loom was dressed when we arrived. The weaver, a woman named Pat, invited me to test it out, and her husband, Mike, offered my husband a seat. I was nervous to weave in front of someone I didn't know, but she didn't hover too close. I tapped the treadles with my feet and slid the shuttle back and forth while she told me about herself and the loom, whose name was Charlotte. She picked the name from her memory of a grade-school teacher who'd read a chapter from *Charlotte's Web* every Friday afternoon as a way of tricking her students into coming to school.

Pat asked me about my weaving, and I told her about the Diné weaving classes I'd taken, the time I spent in the weaving guild, then she took me upstairs and showed me a Diné Wide Ruins rug she'd bought from a roadside stall on a trip to the Southwest. She didn't have enough cash on hand, so she and Mike had to race between cash machines, skirting withdrawal limits, to pay for the rug on time. She told me the weaver's name, Chimbah Nez, though I had to ask her to remind me of this name when we met again.

Pat told me the only reason she was parting with the loom was because of her hip; she was no longer able to work the floor pedals. At the end of an hour, longer than I had ever spent with a seller, I asked if I could take Charlotte. Pat agreed to let me have her.

A week later, my husband and I rented a U-Haul and drove Charlotte to my office on campus.

A month later, the pandemic. Like everyone else, I transitioned to working from home. And though campus was only a fifteen-minute walk from my apartment, I rarely made it to my office; when I did, I wove only a few inches at a time. I couldn't commit to one material or design, so I wove mismatched bands of wool, cotton, linen. I told myself I just wanted to experiment, to see what kinds of things I could produce. But the longer the pandemic dragged on, the less often I went to campus, the less time I gave myself to weave.

Those long months, I spent more time playing video games than anything else. Every evening after work, I played round after round of *Wingspan*. The birds on each card chirped prettily through my headphones as laundry went undone and dishes piled in my sink. According to my profile, I was playing more than forty hours a week, which filled me with guilt.

Because I have been conditioned to value commercial productivity over beauty or art or enjoyment, *weaver* and *writer* and *gamer* are identities I wear uneasily. I weave, and I write, and I game, and I pray I use my time well.

When I began writing this essay, I knew I wanted to talk to Pat again. I wanted to make sure that I remembered the stories she told me about herself and Charlotte, that I could record their history for when memory fails. The first time we met for tea and crackers, we got caught up talking about things like my writing, provincial politics, and Indigenous rights. I left with book recommendations, a fresh stack of *Handwoven* magazines, and a set of white Rosenthal plates, but no history of Charlotte.

The second time we met, we sat outside with tart strawberries and slices of Mike's fresh-baked banana bread. We talked about art and provenance; labour and production.

Pat first became interested in weaving in the early 1960s, when the clothes being mass-produced were both garish and uncomfortable. I worked in a vintage clothing store throughout high school and college, and it was textiles made during this period that I hated most. The synthetic fabrics were fragile and collected static, which crackled in my hair as I moved between racks. But there was a woman in Pat's church choir whose clothes she loved, and when she discovered the woman wove her own fabric, Pat knew she wanted to learn how. She didn't begin until much later, when she was in her early thirties, the same age as me, when she and Mike moved house and their next-door neighbours, Gladys and Jack, just happened to be weavers. Jack offered to teach her, and Mike asked her if she would like him to build her a loom.

Charlotte was built from pale blond oak reclaimed from a World War II–era air force base. When the building was demolished, rather than burn the materials, the maintenance workers took the wood home. Mike arrived well after the demolition, but when he asked around about wood for a loom, one of the workers mentioned that he had some stored in his barn. He offered a trade: Mike could have the wood for a case of beer and an old power saw.

The oak had likely been harvested in the early 1930s or '40s, and the planks were well seasoned, straight. The wood had been painted with air force blue, which Mike carefully shaved away with a hand plane, though some blue freckles remained. He ordered a few premade components, like the reeds, but he hand-milled most of the metal bits himself. "Betwixt and between, it became a single entity," he told me. "The loom was old before it was ever made."

When Neebs wanders back inside his block house, muttering about string, wool, loom, Simon yells from across the field, "Do you know how a loom works in real life?"

"No, not really!"

"Well, *I* do!" Simon, triumphant. "So there!"

"Okay, well, you know what. Let's go for it." It's easy to imagine Neebs throwing his hands in the air before he walks outside. To imagine the frustration in the act of clicking the door open and closed. "How do I use *this* loom?"

Simon groans. He doesn't know. "I was just trying to make a point!"

Neebs closes the door with a dismissive "yep" muffled by the glass between his avatar and the spectator cam now positioned outside the window.

"About the fact that I'm knowledgeable—"

"Not in this situation!" Neebs walks toward us, the window, and the brown-and-grey block representing the loom. His right arm twitches as if turning a page. He's lost in the crafting interface again, and for the rest of the scene, we watch him through the glass. We're on Simon's side, whether we know it or not.

"Well, in *life*!" Simon yells.

"I look forward to talking to you about real looms in the future," Neebs replies.

The scene closes, absurdly, with Simon yelling about a loom book club, and then it ends, inconsequentially, with the sound of a bleating sheep. Neebs figures out how to use the loom off-camera, and we don't even come to learn what he has made. Digging through the game's wiki, it seems like looms are primarily used to make banners, a decorative item. Functionally useless.

Most games' crafting mechanics are just as simple. Gathered materials like wool and string are fed into boxes that churn out perfect, identical cloth. I sometimes wonder what enters the imaginations of players when they interact with in-game crafting mechanics. I wonder if they ever look at a woven shirt or a cape and think about the chain of production. I often find myself wishing for more Simons, for more people with strong opinions about sandwiches and a genuine appreciation for things like virtual crown moulding and herringbone floors.

After Pat and Mike moved to Victoria, she hardly used the loom he had built for her. She carried the guilt even after Charlotte left her possession. When I asked her why, she seemed startled.

"Well, I haven't thought about it," she said, but her mind started turning. She'd found the beginning, the learning, more exciting than the doing. "I didn't love it enough," she said, then laughed. "No one's ever questioned my dilettantism before!"

I admitted that I hadn't woven as much as I meant to, that I carried some of the same guilt. And the longer I didn't weave, the more guilty I felt.

"Some of us aren't able to focus on just one thing," she told me. "I've judged myself harshly for that." But for her, weaving was a portal, an entry point that deepened her appreciation for the way things used to be done: how weavers imbued culture and tradition into their work and art, and how both work and art reflected life and land.

Sitting there in Pat's garden, sharing the shade of the umbrella Mike had raised for us, I felt at home. Weaving, writing, birding, gaming—all had done the same for me. "Maybe Charlotte understands," I said. Hesitant, because it was a vulnerable thing for me to say. But Charlotte, I hoped, might be a tool shaped perfectly for a dilettante and so, might be happy with me.

In the final pages of *Charlotte's Web*, Charlotte, the spider, tells Wilbur, the pig, that her time is ending. Her last project is a delicately woven sac to hold her eggs. Surprised and amazed, Wilbur reveals he didn't know Charlotte *could* lay eggs, but she remains cool, casual.

> "Oh, sure," said the spider. "I'm versatile."
> "What does 'versatile' mean—full of eggs?" asked Wilbur.
> "Certainly not," said Charlotte. "'Versatile' means I can turn with ease from one thing to another. It means I don't have to limit my activities to spinning and trapping and stunts like that."

Heartbroken but dutiful, Wilbur cares tenderly for Charlotte's eggs after she dies. Come spring, they hatch by the hundreds—514, to be exact. The spiderlings climb to the top of the barn, spin a single strand of web, and let the wind carry them off. Wilbur, in a panic, begs them to stay, but their small voices only cry *goodbye, goodbye, goodbye* as they sail away. Despondent, he collapses and cries himself to sleep, but when he wakes the next morning, he's greeted by three tiny voices, three tiny spiders weaving their webs in the doorway of the barn.

Charlotte's daughters. The next year, Charlotte's granddaughters. And every year, daughters, daughters, daughters weaving their webs.

Everything, Pat told me, comes round again.

A year ago, my husband, my mother-in-law, and I bought an old house together. She planned to live in the downstairs suite once she retired, and my husband and I above. He claimed one of the bedrooms on the main floor for his office, and I claimed the attic, whose slanted ceilings were too low for him. The north-facing skylight filled the room with a gentle light, and I painted the walls yellow, terracotta, and Navajo white. It was easy to see myself weaving in this room come winter, and I was eager to bring Charlotte home.

Shortly before the fall semester began, my husband helped me dismantle the loom in my office. We carried her, piece by piece, to my small Yaris hatchback, and then he helped me carry her up the spiral stairs and reassemble her in the middle of the attic-turned-office.

I have big plans. Huck-lace curtains for the bedroom. A rag-rug runner for the kitchen. New hand towels. Since my ADHD diagnosis, I have kept intense colour-coded daily schedules, and I am better at budgeting time than I used to be. I have made an effort to structure time for not-work things—birding, gaming, writing, weaving—and I have accounted for them all in shining yellow.

SELF MADE

TIKENYA FOSTER-SINGLETARY

My maternal great-grandmother was a maker. I mean that in multiple senses of the word. First, as the story was told to me, she decided in her early adulthood to rename herself. She became Birdie—the only name I ever knew her by. It was fitting, as she was a slight woman, slender and small in stature. She had a soft voice. Of course, I may be remembering her through the gentle lens of memories held by a little girl looking up at her elder's fancy jewellery and carefully curled hair. Now, through the lens of a literary scholar, wife, and mother, I think of her renaming alongside the narratives of enslaved people whose works I teach in my college classes. Frederick Douglass, author of the most well known of these narratives, also chose his own name. After orchestrating an escape from enslavement, he changed his surname to signal his freedom: "I subscribe myself," he writes at the end of his first autobiography, *Narrative of the Life of Frederick Douglass,*

An American Slave.[1] Whenever I teach that text, I think my grandma Birdie also "subscribed herself"; she wrote herself into existence, making herself into the woman she wanted to be.

While her renaming seems somewhat daring and, well, cool to me, Grandma Birdie was also a maker in a more twenty-first-century sense, though she did not live to cross the threshold of the new millennium (she missed it by three months). I remember her strawberry layer cakes and the dolls she made. They sat among the knick-knacks that magically populate the homes of elderly people, everything seeming a million years old. These dolls were delicate brown-plastic ladies with tiny glasses, dainty shoes, and fancy party dresses who posed on the living-room shelves. These dolls were not the kind that little girls played with.

As I was completing the graduate work for my doctorate degree, a wind blew through my life and wiped away nearly every plan I'd made. I had finished the last revisions for my dissertation. Unfortunately, though, not in time for spring graduation. I would have to wait until fall. I had been teaching a couple of classes each term. Suddenly, those classes were cancelled; I had neither work nor school to busy myself with. My husband and I were expecting our first child. But those plans too would have to wait. The pregnancy came to an early and unexpected end without giving us the baby we were hoping for, and we had to wait to try again. I had no business to take care of and very little to do. So, what I did was sit home alone, watching copious amounts of television.

One of the reality shows that caught my attention featured a woman battling a serious illness, trying to heal contentious relationships, and facing a crossroads in her life. She appeared on screen

1 Frederick Douglass, *Narrative of the Life of Frederick Douglass, an American Slave* (Boston: Anti-Slavery Office, 1845), 124, https://docsouth.unc.edu/neh/douglass/douglass.html.

with crochet hooks and yarn. As she sat around the reality show house, making hats, she began to teach some of the other women to crochet. She was both building community and doling out domestic instruction to these women, living out a version of femininity through the work of her hands. I was intrigued. Maybe I could use this medium to help myself too. I popped over to the public library to retrieve books and videos (VHS tapes!) on crochet. Then I stopped at a big-box store to get supplies. As I stood in the crafting aisle, dumbfounded about what I needed, an older woman offered assistance. "No, baby," she said, "you don't want that one." She told me to start with a thicker yarn, better for a beginner, and pointed me toward easy-grip crochet hooks. That would not be the last time a woman I didn't know extended herself in community.

I sat alone at home, making myself into a fibre artist: domestic, cozy, like I was entering a space long ago carved out—or boxed in—for women. I felt heavy from the disappointments I'd experienced, but this new skill took time and stillness to learn, and now I had both. I was a youngish academic, a Black woman, desiring motherhood. On the one hand, didn't I fit snugly into an activity framed around women? On the other hand, was this space, steeped in traditional femininity, for Black women?

The idea of crochet and knitting as tools to make a home was complicated. I knew, both as a Black woman and as a literary scholar, that home was not always fertile and nurturing ground. The time, space, and expense of crafting has often been shouldered by women whose race and class status made them assistants to white women's homemaking rather than agents of their own domestic spaces. The fibre arts are most available to people who have time and resources; the popularity of expensive hand-dyed yarns makes this even more true now. So, when I thought about becoming a crocheter—and a knitter, since people of colour are even more invisible in knitting—I felt a tension in adopting an identity as a maker in the fibre arts. Many women in my family and community could sew, a common skill set for women in previous generations. Segregation would have made sewing and fibre work either necessary or preferable given the expense and indignities of shopping. Purchasing clothes in public, with the likelihood of being followed in stores and prohibited from trying things on, must have been difficult; I'd heard stories of Black people who had to draw an outline of their feet on a sheet of paper in order to find their shoe size in a store. Faced with the risk of embarrassment and the dangers of the law, knitting your own baby layette may have seemed like the better option. Moreover, the domestic work of laundry, mending clothes, or taking in ironing existed alongside the cooking and cleaning work definitive for many of those Black women. While that work provided avenues for Black women to bring income into their own homes, it opened them to the risks of white domestic spaces where their labour was desirable, but their bodies were threatened.

After desegregation, the public and private lives of Black women were much more open. The associations with social risk remained, though. The birthright of younger women like me, raised after segregation, was to breach the public/private divide that kept women in the confines of the home—both white homes and their own homes. Shopping in stores was much easier, so making clothes and home goods was no longer necessary. The desire to gain access to mass-produced products was high. Conversely, the idea of making goods at home must have seemed like a relic of a past better left behind. Sewing your own dress or crocheting a blanket was the stuff of another time—not something you were forced to do. In a way, eschewing the responsibilities of making seemed akin to the way my paternal grandmother talked about childbirth. Doctors, she said, would withhold pain medication from Black women. They would relieve the birth pain of white women, who were presumably fragile and deserving; Black women were made to suffer through labour without relief. Long before I was even thinking about giving birth to my own children, my grandmother told me that I had a right to pain medication. Relief was no longer something that could be withheld from Black women. In a similar way, women who had few choices about their purchases now had many more options. They did not have to accept scraps and could go into the same market spaces as respectable white women.

Emily Matchar's *Homeward Bound: Why Women Are Embracing the New Domesticity*[2] posits that twenty-first-century domestic instruction comes in the form of blogging, social media posting, and the like; these displays of homemaking, she argues, are choices to resist elements of contemporary technology-filled life in favour of older methods of producing the material and abstract comforts of home. These media representations serve as teaching tools for embroidery, jam-making, knitting, etc., intimating that other women should be doing the same. The message, then, is that homemaking is the purview of women, and they need directions to do it properly. Despite the availability of mass-produced food and fibre products, the suggestion that twentieth-century women can and should be making their own items provides a path to mark them as suitable women. Matchar's ideas begin to answer some of the questions I was asking as a Black woman in maker circles. Yes, these activities are tied to our collective ideas about femininity; yes, being Black makes my claim to them tenuous. I did not want to be subject to domesticity that excludes as easily as it includes. But I believed that what drew me to the fibre arts was community and solace and creativity. These features could overcome the damaging messages.

Lorna Hamilton-Brown's study of the racial history of knitting, "Myth—Black People Don't Knit," helps dispel the idea that the fibre arts are defined by whiteness. She notes that the Egyptian beginnings of knitting are often ignored: "Its Western roots seem to be more

2 Emily Matchar, *Homeward Bound: Why Women Are Embracing the New Domesticity* (New York: Simon & Schuster, 2005).

valued."[3] Oral histories have been erased and downplayed to deny the expertise of Black yarn and string makers, succumbing to the white gaze.[4] Hamilton-Brown's dissertation examines the work of painter Harry Roseland, whose depictions of Black women document their expertise. These paintings, like *The Knitting Lesson*, in which a Black woman seems to teach a white woman to knit, are rare media representations of Blackness in knitting, but still, they advance the idea that domestic leisure is intended for the affluent, well-dressed white woman.[5] Hamilton-Brown dismantles the idea that Black people aren't aware of or capable of knitting; additionally, her own work as an artist proves that the fibre arts can be used for social commentary. The points she makes gesture thoughtfully toward the tangle of womanhood and race embodied in Sojourner Truth's "Ain't I a Woman?" speech from the 1851 Akron Women's Rights Convention: "I can carry as much as any man, and can eat as much too, if I can get it. I am as strong as any man that is now."[6]

I've taught this speech several times, usually as an early example of intersectional feminism, with Truth positioning herself at the juncture of race and gender. It highlights the ways in which Black women have been separated from the ideals of frail femininity—the ways I was separated from those ideals. Consequently, her titular question became my question. As I watched my goals dissipate, I asked, "Ain't I a woman?" Where did I belong? Where could I belong? Truth's emphasis on her labour in fields both confirms her physical strength and challenges the marginalization of non-white women, who are generally cut out of feminine domesticity. Hamilton-Brown's work adds that the unfounded association of Black people globally

3 Lorna Hamilton-Brown, "Myth—Black People Don't Knit: The Importance of Art and Oral Histories for Documenting the Experiences of Black Knitters" (master's thesis, Royal College of Art, 2017), 17.

4 Hamilton-Brown, "Myth," 59.

5 Hamilton-Brown, "Myth," 40.

6 Sojourner Truth, "Ain't I a Woman?" (speech, Woman's Rights Convention, Akron, OH, June 21, 1851, transcript by Marius Robinson), TheSojournerTruthProject.com.

with poverty, need, and lack of intellect—perhaps along with other racialized stereotypes like laziness or theft—bolsters the idea that yarn and needlework are reserved for white women.[7]

As a result, Black women, who are thought only to exist outside the fibre-arts world, are seen with suspicion or made invisible in crafting spaces. Vox reports that "hundreds of people of colour have shared stories of being ignored in knitting stores, having white knitters assume they were poor or complete amateurs, or flat-out saying they didn't think Black or Asian people knit."[8] Adella Colvin, owner of LolaBean Yarn Co., recalls the unpleasant shopping experience that pushed her to dye and sell her own yarn: "I was told that their bathroom was for customers only. And I immediately knew what that was about—my appearance, Black woman, Afro ... I couldn't possibly be there to buy yarn."[9] These gatekeeping behaviours ideologically and literally keep out those who do not easily fit acceptable demographic categories. Koritha Mitchell's "Keep Claiming Space!" terms this as "know-your-place aggression." It is a way, she writes, "of reminding targets of their 'proper place,' a way of insisting that certain people should not feel secure in claiming space."[10] Ignoring women of colour or presuming them to be incompetent is a way of narrowing the definition of womanhood to exclude them.

I was not immune to these perceptions; my ignorance had even erased my own family members. After I learned to crochet, I began to bring my yarn and hooks everywhere. That included my grandparents' house during the holidays. I sat in their kitchen, working on a new piece and trying to learn new stitches. My grandfather walked

7 Hamilton-Brown, "Myth," 22.

8 Jaya Saxena, "The Knitting Community Is Reckoning with Racism," *Vox*, February 25, 2019, https://www.vox.com/the-goods/2019/2/25/18234950/knitting-racism-instagram-stories.

9 Anais Amin, "For One Self-Starter, a Bad Experience Spun a New Business Venture," *Marketplace*, November 11, 2021, https://www.marketplace.org/2021/11/11/spinning-a-yarn-business-out-of-adversity.

10 Koritha Mitchell, "Keep Claiming Space!" *CLA Journal* 58, no. 3/4 (2015): 229–44. https://www-jstor-org.ezproxy.auctr.edu/stable/i40181049.

in and said, "Oh, my mama used to do that." I was a bit surprised, as I'd never seen Grandma Birdie with yarn, hooks, or knitting needles. My grandfather left the room and returned a moment later with an entire sweater-vest. It was cream coloured with neat, even stitches. I was stunned. When my grandpa said his mother crocheted, I'd assumed she made simple beginner projects like granny squares. Instead, this vest used an array of stitches and showed careful shaping when Grandpa slipped it on to model. I'd been crocheting for years and was still too intimidated to try a sweater. How had I come to this skill unaware of an existing thread tying me to it? Not only did this discovery defy the messages I had received about who engaged in crafting and who didn't, but it changed the way I saw my own participation. There was no need to question my place in these communities. Without even knowing it, I was directly part of this legacy of Black women's making.

My grandfather pointed to the living room and the metal swords mounted above the fireplace. Unlike my great-grandmother's sweater, these black swords had been on display all my life. My grandfather told me he had made them; he used to weld. Further, my grandfather himself had done embroidery when he was younger and sold his services door-to-door as a means of making a little money. Add to this revelation the fascination I had as a child with my grandmother's sewing machine and my quick childhood stint in learning cross-stitching from my mother, and it turns out I was always a crafter. I began to realize the degree to which this association between crafting and whiteness was misguided. We were an entire family of makers. My entrance into the crafting community was not an anomaly. I could see these activities as part of a broader "making a way out of no way" that was so definitive of Black life and tradition. Necessity may have driven these skills as much as leisure, but the impulse to create is absolutely aligned with what Black folk do and who they are.

Another important element of the fibre-arts world is the community it invites. Knitting and crocheting in public settings clarified that the crafting community is wide and diverse. It wasn't just my own Black family who resisted the little-old-white-lady face of yarn crafts. Over and over, women walked up to me to talk about stitches. One of the first times this happened was on a trip with my Korean-born mother-in-law and her sisters. I was fresh off my string of losses, and crochet was a soothing vessel that soaked up many of my tears. The women in my husband's family saw my yarn and hooks and shared their own stories of crocheting when they were young. During that trip, I completed my first successful piece, a blanket that included a few rows stitched by each of the women in my husband's family. Years later, after my daughter was born and was old enough to learn the single crochet stitch, she tagged along as we ran weekend errands, which included a stop at a brow-threading lounge. As she waited while I received my service, a woman with long black hair and a hint of a South Asian accent showed my daughter a different way to hold the hook. They sat together, making loops from yarn in this space where women gathered to beautify each other. More recently, a Latina grandmother approached me to ask what I was knitting. I was sitting on a bench at an indoor trampoline park, and we were both waiting for our children to finish playing. I was having trouble getting the colour changes right for a striped scarf. "Oh, it's easy. I can show you," she said. She sat beside me, giving me instruction, and then took the needles to demonstrate.

All of these women, with different backgrounds and ethnicities, readily identified me as a member of a community to which we each belonged. As Lorna Hamilton-Brown declared, "Black people don't knit" is a myth pretty easily dispelled. Likewise, these other women of colour were not outside the circle of knowledge. Stitch by stitch, they each asserted a claim to those circles.

When I joined a small needlecrafts group through my intergenerational, interracial church a few years ago, the group resembled the stereotypes. The leader was an older white woman whose home was scattered with blankets, scarves, and tea cozies she'd fashioned out of yarn. The majority of other women in the group fit a similar demographic. Despite our shared faith, I could not have imagined I would have occasion to be in community with these women. I expected at best, a cool reception from them, at worst, Mitchell's "know-your-place aggression." I did, however, understand that I belonged in this world, that my place was not up for debate. Some of the white women were just learning to cast on or chain, while I was practised and experienced. I wasn't new to this. Instead, I was the unwitting heir of women—and men—who used their skills to create functional and beautiful objects. There were certainly moments when I was uncomfortable; I noticed the subtle surprise when I pulled an array of tools, notions, and works-in-progress from my bag. The group leader asked me what colour my kitchen was. I thought maybe she was being nosy, and I expected some kind of judgment to follow. But when we met for the next group meeting, she handed me a dishcloth in colours that matched my kitchen. She had shown me how to knit using Tunisian crochet, a technique with which I was unfamiliar, and the dishcloth used that method. It was such a small gesture, but I was really moved. I understood that handmade items represent a lot of time and energy. They are an extension of the maker. By making an item just for me, she shared our common ground and saw me as a fibre artist. Again, perceptions around whiteness and making—perceptions that I couldn't get away from—were thrown into flux. I was constantly pushing against an invisible door, and I was never sure whether I could walk right in or would have to knock it down.

Although there is significant association between the fibre arts and women of colour, in the US and elsewhere, the social definitions of womanhood have steadily whitened ideas about these activities. Like most cultural phenomena, there may be a variety of reasons. Surely, though, the erasure of Black women and other women of colour is owing, at least in part, to the framework that defines femininity in domestic terms. When *Vogue Knitting*, a niche publication that has rarely featured a non-white woman on its cover, garnered a wealth of attention for its portrait of former first lady Michelle Obama, a backlash arose. The story was meant to highlight Obama's newly acquired status as a knitter during the COVID-19 quarantine. YouTuber Kristy Glass posted an Instagram story criticizing the image—questioning why Obama was not wearing knitwear in the picture and why her wedding rings were on her right hand rather than her left.[11] If even the US first lady, a figure historically presented as the ultimate symbol of national femininity and domesticity, was not immune from attempts to exclude her, what was I to do? This was the puzzle I kept trying to solve for myself. My own positive experiences aside, I could not expect that everyone would recognize my right to an identity as a maker.

Several legacies are mine: post–civil rights movement baby, daughter of makers, beneficiary of my ancestors' ingenuity. I'm not always sure what to do with those legacies. When I claim space as a knitter and crocheter, what am I claiming? There's no *need* to use these techniques; I can buy anything I need. Although I always ask for a receipt, in case I need to prove myself, I can shop in any store I like. The purpose of my identity as a maker is twofold: first, my life deserves soft, beautiful leisure in the form of yarn—Black people have to be intentional about that kind of joy; second, the items I make are proof I've done something worthwhile. When I move stitches from one knitting needle to the other, I've been at least a little bit productive. The majority of items go to charities for babies and people whose basic needs go unmet. Like my grandma Birdie and so many others in my family and community, I can make myself. I make myself useful, and kind, and creative. If the fibre arts cannot be untangled from the domestic realm, I am claiming the domestic

11 Emily Shugerman, "The Racism Drama Unraveling the Knitting World," *The Daily Beast*, December 10, 2021, https://www.thedailybeast.com/kristy-glass-and-the-racism-drama-unraveling-the-knitting-world.

as *my* space too, as a Black woman. I am an heir, and I am continuing a communal tradition. When I pick up hooks and needles, I confirm that I know my place, and it is any space I wish to occupy.

TEXTILES OF THE REAL

RENÉE SAROJINI SAKLIKAR

PANDEMIC PIECE

My husband brings home a quilt, provenance unknown, a gift from his workplace: a large square coverlet enriched with complex designs, thin black border encasing a background of creamy-white fabric nubby with top-stitched spirals. In the centre of the quilt, an eight-point star made of narrow folded panels, dark brown with small sparks of amber-and-white flowers. Scallops encircle the straight edges, framed by a continuous series of connected loops sprouting serpentine leaves.

These finely wrought details make themselves known only in the wear and tear of daily living, by touch and by eye. Pattern bringing comfort, spread out over our sofa. Every time our hands reach for the quilt, we promise to one day count each leaf but never do. It's only after months of laundering that I notice the inscription sewn on the upper back corner. All that remains of the makers' message to us is the ghost cursives, undecipherable. It is winter 2020 and our first wave of COVID. Two years later, after cycles of wash and air-dry, the care of the makers still appears in shadow, trapunto, stuffed, raised, boutis—terms I look up on the internet. I am but a watcher who loves the feel of the worked fabric, and I wonder: whose hands gathered, saved, mapped, drew, pieced, stuffed, stitched, pressed?

THE GREY SHAWL

My mother telephones from her care facility and speaks to me about our life, settlers landing first in Newfoundland, then sojourning across the continent, from Nova Scotia to northern Ontario, from Quebec to Saskatchewan, "fetching up finally" as relatives would say, in "the town of towns," New Westminster.

My mother says she's freezing cold in her shared room. They keep the window open "because of the COVID." It's the fourth isolation in outbreak protocol. "Deekrah," she says. "Do you remember Grandpa Saklikar gave you that wool shawl? Where is it?" I mumble something indeterminate, not wanting to remind her we haven't seen that shawl in decades, and I've now no idea what's become of it. As my mother speaks, though, I can smell the Kashmiri wool, and my shoulders long for its light, strong, rough-edged texture. Or do I imagine it, a grey shawl, large enough to wrap round and round?

TEXTILES OF THE REAL

And what about all those family textiles: drawers and drawers full, kept by my mother, from India to Canada. Fabrics stored away until this past autumn, released into the air of the Goodbye Condo, dusty with age. Instead of sifting and sorting, and although I intended to curate a small extraction as a keepsake collection, when the time came and the junk-removal folks were at the door, I just gathered and packaged and turned my back on old saris and silks. In my mind's eye, my mother's fabrics are still in place in the condo that is now sold. The cloths in a textile memory bank, where each fold remains unchanged, as if in a museum I once saw in Ahmedabad: batik, silk, Rajasthani, dyed Kerala cotton, Jaipur and Dupioni silks. At night, dreaming of fabric, I wake longing to see, if not to touch, the rough-rough of silk-cotton, yards of peacock blue bordered with gold thread. Mornings, with a cup of tea placed by the computer, I click on digital artifacts from the time of my parents, Gujarati, Marathi: wall hangings, dupattas (shawls), saris, lehenga (wide skirts held up with elastic or drawstrings), and choli (midriff-baring and fitted short-sleeved tops). The real accessible only through transmittal, memory as an electric pulse, past to present. And how can I reach them, these lost objects only partially known, half-remembered ghost presences, except piece by piece?

TO BEGIN A PRACTICE

When writing, I first touch paper, my skin dry enough to require black-cotton gloves. Then I rip, cut, piece, shape, glue oddments of white computer paper from the recycling bin. Once the pieces are fixed in some fashion, either by painter's tape or by a staple or stitch, I layer on ripped cut-outs from old books, cast-off magazines. Touching paper produces dreams of my ancestors, crafts people from Gujarat and Maharashtra. They hail from the Republic of India, and as an immigrant-settler raised to be as "Canadian" as possible, it's only lately—as I make the poems that fit inside a long epic poem, whose heroes turn to making as a form of resistance, including the fibre arts of weaving, spinning, and quilting—that I think about the way craft and textile seem to sing to me with atavistic resonance; maybe my ancestors, farmers and textile workers whose later generations became doctors and lawyers, have ceded to me some faint memory of what it means to work with one's hands.

NEXT PAGE: LEFT: Renée Sarojini Saklikar, fragment of a handmade chapbook with shredded strips of paper and glue, 2014. | Photo: Renée Sarojini Saklikar.
RIGHT: Quilt with top-stitched patterns, circa 2020. | Photo: Renée Sarojini Saklikar.

Janet Malcolm
Dickinson
Bookstein
ssembled
The collag
called "The
ruction pape
spired by M
drafts of lo
Emily
olo exhibi
ollection o
d shards
son's late

BEFORE-TIME MEMORY

Many years ago, my late Aunty Nila accompanied me on a journey back to the city of Ahmedabad. Aunty Nila secured for us tickets to an exhibition, where I saw wall hangings of cotton fabric, ornate bridal outfits seeded with pearls and tiny mirrors, lengths of Dupioni silk, painted and embroidered. We spent time just looking, absorbing. The room was temperature controlled and dimly lit. We spoke in hushed whispers, our gaze on silk and cotton, stretched and framed fabric, decades old. The walls and display drawers of the textile museum evidence of an ancient craft.

Later that afternoon, Aunty Nila and I visited relatives. We travelled by bus across the border into Maharashtra, India's perennial heat and dust producing a stupor in me, lassitude overlaying so many emotions that I, normally chatty and eager to share, remained silent, jostled by the bus. Only now, decades later, I realize that my aunty also said nothing. Perhaps we both were lost in thoughts about what it means to be immigrant/emigrant, what's kept, what's lost. In the intervening years, Aunty Nila continued with her home-based craft projects. In Mississauga, we visited a Michaels, and I trailed behind my aunt, her shopping cart filled with glue guns, pottery sleeves, sequins, embroidery kits, felt pens, bags of fibrefill and five-inch tension hoops. Did she hold in her mind's eye memories of our Ahmedabad textile visit? I never asked. Something inside me kept quiet. On both occasions, olde world to new, desire for texture enlivened my imagination; my fingers longed to touch, the gesture suggestive of transgression. In Ahmedabad, I had contemplated breaking museum rules, reaching up to those climate-controlled walls to stroke the ancient fibre. In Mississauga, while in the lineup for the cashier, would my aunt have been shocked to see me rip open embroidery kits—but of course, how could that have been allowed? Mystery follows memory, the how and when of connection, what is forgotten, remembered.

LIVING HISTORY

The Paramparik Karigars who reside in the city of Ahmedabad, in the state of Gujarat, close to where my family once lived, are renowned craftspeople who create detailed painted fabric—wall hangings; veils; handstamped intricate patterns on cloth hung in doorways, hallways, outside street-vendor shops—to create holy spaces of worship to the Mother Goddess. The fabric arts of the Karigars are known as "Mata-ni-Pachedi," which literally means "behind the Mother Goddess." The phrase signifies the origins of the art: a sacred practice of the outcast castes of India's ancient Hindu class system, the so-called untouchables; dark-skinned and historically banned from worshipping inside temples, they create their own worship spaces in dusty streetside corners. The female deity usually sits in the centre of a complex architectural grid of printed and painted images from myth: singers, musicians, shamans, and animals. Birds dance and fly to celebrate the goddess. Outside borders reveal the sun and the moon in two upper corners. Much of the artwork is freehand; bamboo brushes fill in colour, carved woodblocks stamp images.

The artwork of the Karigars is now highly prized. Their signature black and red colours are made from Harada pastes: jaggery and iron to form black, and crushed tamarind seeds extracted and mixed with alum to create red ink. In order to work their fibre arts, the Karigars harvest dried dhawda flowers. This powder they mix with mordant and alizarin to boil in cloth pouches over their one-pot flames. The resulting yellow colour will glaze the cotton fabric used to create wall hangings and veils. The cotton is washed in the Sabarmati River, and the strength of the sun's rays affects the intensity of colour. The rhythm of the seasons dictates the timing of this labour-intensive process. The Karigars avoid the months of the monsoon, when flooding can in an instant destroy weeks of work. Increasingly, they must also negotiate increased river pollutants and refuse, as well as variable water levels. They spread their fabric over rocks and find patches of ground amid heaps of rubbish. They persist—careful, precise, intent on rituals and details. I long to replicate my own word-working inside the practice of my people, although I am without their skills and on the outside of their cultural parameters, save for the colour of my skin and my surname, with its signature suffix, *-kar,* denoting "craftsperson."

Nights, I click over images, reminded of the women textile workers in my family: Aunty Nila, Aunty Sushila, Grandmothers Godavari and Ayesha, and my mother. One day, will my hands learn embroidery as they learned and taught? *Smocking.* The sound of the word echoes alongside a memory of my mother, home from working in the Baron of Beef cafe at the Hudson's Bay in Park Royal, seated in a green chair in our living room, embellishing one of my blouses, her tired brown fingers gathering fabric into tight pleats. Much as she tried to interest me in taking up a needle and paying attention, I did not. In fact, I debated her usage of the word *smocking,* and she just shook her head and kept to her stitching.

ORPHANED FAMILY

My sister, whom I rarely see, is my only sibling. Once, I travelled the city to find fabric squares for her felting. She made me a felt-rose broach in sea greens and blues. Five petals, soft to the touch, the metal pin, blue thread cross-stitched to the fabric through three holes, delicate and strong enough to have survived the years.

Between us, shards of memory: one Christmas she crafted pine cones into ornaments, sewed plush red-velvet bags to hold the objects. When recently we cleaned out our mother's condo, my sister scoffed at keeping the velvet bags, but I tucked them away into a box, shoved into my office closet with all the other keepsakes rarely seen. My sister knits, sews, and bakes. I stand in front of screens. Or sit in front of screens. Or look down at hand-held screens. Or prop screens on my lap. In the dark, winter images of fabric squares, quilts, embroidery flow into my brain.

THE WAY OF MEMORY

The first and only time I sign up for a quilt-making workshop, I make it as far as the entranceway to a large room in New Westminster, the old Curling Club building. On the walls, an exhibition of quilts. In the room, a collective of women. They seem friendly. They nod and smile but don't approach me, and somehow I'm too shy, too situated in an atmosphere of not belonging, not seeing anyone else who looks like me, to initiate conversation. How to say it all these years later? Too othered, in my brown skin, to take the first step toward these white-women makers.

This feeling of otherness creates in me a nervous, distracted energy, difficult to explain. One feeling layered into another. I sense a push-pull of *welcome* and *not really*, eyes that flick up and down my baggy jeans and canvas bag. No greeting effusive enough to move into conversation, *why don't you join us in here* perhaps implied, but I don't pick up on the unsaid invitation, if it exists. Their shared processes and materials emanate a demarcation. To this day I cannot recall pattern or theme from the quilts on display. I find an excuse to drift away. It is New Westminster. It is the 1980s. In the fabric of that place and time and culture, the uninvited, an erasure. There is settlement, procurement, adaptation, and accumulation. There is the not spoken. There is outsider and insider and *how long have you lived here* and *where are you from—*

Unable to work up the courage to join, to sign up for another class, I start to collect stories about quilts. When I move away from the city, I lose the box that holds the stories.

MAKING AS A FORM OF THINKING

As a university student, I travelled the city by bus. The direction, east to west, and the mode of transportation deepened otherness. In my lap a copy of *The Norton Anthology of English Literature*, whose front cover bore the photo of not one woman writer, let alone anyone of colour. From *Beowulf* to Beckett, I saw no one who looked like me. Solace came in extra readings: books on embroidery, quilting, weaving, the history of fabrics, the connection in language with, for instance, the word *paisley*, a Scottish town where mill workers first learned to imitate the teardrop shapes of Persia and the ornate embellishments of India. In the jolts and stop-starts of the bus, my fingers traced pattern.

English classes found me mostly mute. Often, at the start of term, the professor, at the head of the room, glasses perched on nose tip, frames balanced just so, would look down at my name, struggling to pronounce Saklikar, and after a brief pause would then look back up at me, eyebrows raised quizzically—*are you sure you are in the right class?* Who can know for sure, though. Those years studying English literature, only once or twice did I search the academic catalogue to look up "Creative Writing."

Once, I found myself in a seminar with the Canadian poet Robert Kroetsch. When he read from *Field Notes*, again came that desire to make, to shape, to enter into language as material. I said nothing. The room filled with students, their questions and comments. We sat on overstuffed green couches. No one said anything to me. I still have the notebook from that seminar and in it are only a few words, almost all unintelligible, the pencil markings so faint, but alongside the words *Field Notes*, my handwriting shimmers: *make something.*

MAKING TO RESIST: THE RAJAH QUILT

Years later, one morning, when working on crafting poems, I find notes scribbled on ink-stained pages, lines for a poem about women convicts of 1841 quilting as they were transported from Woolwich, England, to Hobart, Australia, on a prisoner transport ship—a 352-ton barque, the *Rajah.*

> *Dreaming of Quilting*
> that collect of women, heads bent, fabric
> stretched, frame-taut, squares pulled, cotton batten laid
> layers stitched, touched, stories and laughter rise
> warming the air between, somewhere a bird
> whistles, sound appliquéd into silk threads
> apron and cap, scissors, thimbles, pins
> patchwork pieces by the pound—

To one day see the Rajah Quilt and all its 2,815 pieces in the National Gallery of Australia is a dream of mine. Until then, I store and rub the images, work with the text of women's labour. These outsiders, making something to survive the years: there's the nub that holds me into my own making practice, to find and sustain encouragement in the face of the world's indifference, to stay true to the original vision.

Inhabiting that tension between inclusion/exclusion, I learn to accept the shyness of my own stored otherness. How, then, to also stay open to the possibilities of making with others? To embrace community? In 2016, at the Surrey Art Gallery, I delight in the intricacies of a thread-and-fabric installation by artist Robin Ripley. My eyes linger on snap fasteners, pins, needles and needle case. The gallery commissions me to write a poem inspired by their work. Women's labour continues my fascination, obsession even, with language as material: the rhythm of a ten-beat line encompassing the text as if a fabric square, snippets of rhyme and the images of making, threads, strung and tied, linked to the memory of those Karigars of Ahmedabad.

Song Bird
Ice-fed, wet yarns felted, a loom of stars:
In the hour before sunrise, three ribbons
They will come to you, foretold the Mother.
Winged tapestry—tied strings, salvaged pieces—
Divining wheel, a thousand threads entwined
Named golden brown, she knew to snap, pin, tie
Hidden: cascara girl: camas, birch, pine,
Woman, seated at a bench, soft cloth pulled—
Woman on a platform waiting, eastbound
Time to touch, that absence fastened, cast off
Before every door, every key thrown, every gate locked
Forward, backward, a thousand needles cleaned
Our hands in the Before-Time, thread to loom:
Our eyes sparkled, names embossed, cut, held.[1]

By spending time with fabric artists, I begin to find my way back to my long poem, "THOT J BAP (The Heart of This Journey Bears All Patterns)," an epic fantasy in verse.[2] Dreams of quilts and quilt makers return. I imagine makers as resisters in a world dominated by climate catastrophe and global inequality. The resisters join with seed savers and medicant women of the wishing well. They are led by matriarch makers who teach survival skills: how to sew, to make soap, to throw mud on the wheel.

1 Published as "The Song Bird" in *Bramah and the Beggar Boy*, Nightwood Editions, 2021.
2 The imagined makers and their work appear in *Bramah and the Beggar Boy*, Nightwood Editions, 2021, pages 238–44. https://thotjbap.com.

PIECE BY PIECE

Nights, I dream of the women makers of the Rajah Quilt. During the day, I sketch out squares for a memory quilt, imagining the dead and the living seated together, making a quilt of Saklikar-Patel. On my right, my late mother, a shade who drifts in, no longer in her wheelchair, eyesight restored. She takes a seat beside me, silent, words all gone. Her long brown fingers restless. To my left, my sister, felt pieces at her feet. Opposite the three of us, the ghosts of our dead: my aunty Nila in a blue sari, and with her, my long-dead grandmas Godavari and Ayesha. Two lines of women, the living and the dead, a rectangle of making, and between us a table with a frame to pull, snip, layer, press, pull. In silence, we work fabric, threaded and together.

WOOD IS A FABRIC

Walking home, conscious of all the items on my to-do list, not one of which will require me to gather fibre, nor piece, nor make a garment, nor thread a needle, nor click needles, yarn balls at my side, I see in my mind's eye stacks of books on my apartment floor, reams of paper: files, notebooks, foolscap, bits of text. Beside me, in real time, small tight buds of cherry blossom not quite ready to flower, Whitcomb and Accolade. The trees planted over twenty-five years ago beside the Neighbourhood House.

I am outside surveying the street. I've just come from the gym, recently reopened, with its inlaid wood floor, a thousand scuff marks. That floor: where did the wood come from, when was it laid, whose labouring hands placed the wood pieces, fitted and joined, counted and cut, fibre affixed to cement? Length and dimensions, a process of measurement. I've danced on that floor hundreds of hours and only now, my mind filled with images of fibre arts, does this quest to know more about making, real and imagined, arrive again. All these things. Fabrics of the real, that I love. In the morning, I take up again pieces of paper, word fragments, sifting verbs to make a pattern, language an object itself, redolent with meaning: anxiety, anger, safety, misunderstanding, necessity, piece by piece.

THE HEALING WORK OF COMMUNITY FABRIC COLLAGE

KATHLEEN WINTER

I went back to the old town where I was born, Newcastle upon Tyne, an industrial city in the northeast of England. At the Saturday market, I noticed a busker. She had my build, my unkempt hair, and, it seemed, a squeezebox concertina like mine, on which she played the kind of folk tunes I like to crank out. Maybe she played "The Ash Grove," or "Singing the Travels." I threw a couple of pounds in her hat, ate lunch from a pie shop, meandered Northumberland and Pilgrim streets, then boarded a bus to Hainingwood Terrace, which was supposed to have been demolished, according to my dad, shortly after we left it.

On our corner stood a shop, outside of which my mam used to leave me in the pram when she went in to buy the day's minced beef and suet. The shop and the entire street were intact, not demolished at all, half a century after our departure for Canada. The shop was no longer a butcher's: through the window I saw rolls of bright fabric. The door opened, and out came a child holding yellow cloth evidently given to him by the woman inside, who looked like ...

Was she the busker from the Newcastle market?

I poked my head in. "Did I just see you—"

"Yes. I remember you. You threw two pounds in the hat."

Another child arrived; she gave him some green cloth, and he ran off. Two middle-aged women appeared and took more cloth away. Then an old man. Happiness hovered over these transactions.

"What are they doing with the cloth?" I asked.

The woman who looked something like me and lived on my old street said, "We're making a memory map. I've just had a new bolt of silk printed with cranes, and the two women are going to stitch the cranes along the river, the way they remember from their childhood."

I glimpsed the river from where we stood. I was now inside the not-anymore butcher shop whose windows overlooked the Tyne. It was true, the industrial cranes that lined the shores when my dad worked in the shipyard had gone. The busker / silk printer told me they had been dismantled and sent to Peru, which I found oddly familiar, because that was what happened to the narrow-gauge track of the railroad in Newfoundland, which was the place my family immigrated to after leaving the banks of the Tyne. Somewhere in Peru, apparently, the cranes and the railroad of my two homelands had united without me. And here I was, talking to a woman who said she was mapping memory.

Her name is Clare Satow. In the ensuing months, her community memory map would be complete; people of all ages in my old hometown would be able to see their work exhibited in a gallery: a collective-memory textile piece representing employment loved and lost, the rhubarb and pigeons of allotment gardens, drifts of vetch and coltsfoot along their back fences, streets that had changed or no longer existed, the butcher shop when it was still John Sharp and Sons Family and Shipping Butchers, and Ridley's sweet shop with its jars of licorice pipes and Sherbet Fountains.

When I was in primary school in that neighbourhood, a person came to our class one day and taught us nine embroidery stitches: blanket, chain, straight, stick, slant, two kinds of cross, spokes, and French knot. I remember hardly anything I learned in school before or after that day, but those stitches have remained in my repertoire ever since, and I have often thanked that mentor, whose name I do not know, for giving me the gift of stitchery. Years later I learned of a process called slow stitch, upon reading a book by practitioner Claire Wellesley-Smith of Yorkshire. In *Slow Stitch: Mindful and contemplative textile art*, she advocates making a stitch journal simply by stitching meditative marks from your inner or outer life. I stitched a white meandering river walk and golden grasses in snow. I began this on an old painter's tarp I saw my companion washing in the sink to prepare for his next construction job.

"Can I have that?" I asked, as he hung it to dry on the clothes rack. It had black and cream paint splotches all over it, very Jackson Pollock. "It has potential," I said.

Amazingly, that stitch journal now hangs in the gallery at the Wordsworth Trust in Grasmere, England, because I stitched many things about Dorothy Wordsworth onto the tarpaulin as I wrote my recent novel about her, *Undersong*.[1] I stitched rain, violets, ferns, and sheep from my visits to Grasmere. At home in Montreal, while writing the Dorothy book, I stitched my little white dog, knowing Dorothy also had a little white dog, much beloved. I documented the beginning of the COVID-19 saga by stitching a heron in Lost Lagoon in

1 Kathleen Winter, *Undersong* (Toronto: Knopf Canada, 2022).

Vancouver as the cafes shut down and flights home disappeared, and we had to say goodbye to all the magnolias and flee back to Quebec by road, to isolate at home. I stitched my world and Dorothy's world, which occurred during parallel industrial revolutions. My stitches were messy and emotional. My stitch journalling is not professional but amateur in the old sense of the word, meaning done for love.

In my writing practice, I sometimes have no words, and that's when I turn instead to thread and cloth and colour and image. I can stitch memory and sensation in a way that often eludes words. The practice of stitch journalling helps me to know what I'm hatching or feeling or exploring.

I learned about the importance of going beyond words some years ago, when I was invited to teach a writing workshop to Innu children in Labrador. I realized the stories they wanted to set down required more than words. They required marks that were graphic and illustrative, not only linguistic, and especially not in English. One child drew the footprints of a dog that began on the storyboard and then veered off it onto the wall and into a land out of sight, because the story was that the dog had got lost.

Later, with Inuit children and elders in the Torngat Mountains, I facilitated a textile project inspired by Clare Satow's community memory map. Our cloth scroll depicted a sealskin drying, an ulu knife working, a strand of northern lights, hunters with dogsled and harpoon, and local wild plants studded everywhere like jewels: crowberry, Arctic poppy, Labrador tea. We used sealskin, sequins, beads, thread, and paint. It became a beautiful stitchery that the artists hung in their community centre in Nain. The end product was bright and strong. But what I loved even more was the feeling among us as we gathered and stitched, and drew, and illustrated memories with fabric and accoutrements. Participants taught each other stitching or beading or drawing skills. People helped each other. We talked as we stitched. Sometimes we sang. Time went by that felt like no time at all. People stopped by to watch as we created, and they ended up staying to contribute ideas inspired by the community fabric work. The process was one of tactile creation—yes, we would have an art piece to show—but even more thrilling for me was that in the doing of the work together, we became stitched into each other's stories. This felt like an enveloping, easy fluidity: a kind of peace.

In this time following what I might call our two years of collective trauma, isolation, and loneliness around the pandemic, I have begun a new community textile project: a healing fabric collage that talks about both how we've felt in our isolation and how we might survive, psychologically and spiritually and socially. In its beginning stages, it already bears images of the ways we participants have kept our souls from perishing: a porch garden, the medicine of music and animal friends, the love of someone who chose to keep caring despite ideological differences. The work is stitched, painted, and collaged onto—again—a painter's tarpaulin. I bought a brand new one at Home Hardware this time for twenty-four dollars. It's easy to stitch and roll and transport between gatherings. I hope by autumn it will be covered in images of resilience and hope. It will not push away or deny the sadness we have all felt. But already in the group that has met just a few times, we have laughed and cried and sung together. I never feel such community when I am at home alone, writing.

Something about working on a fabric piece together makes even this broken world feel somehow mendable, partly because of the fragmentary nature of textile work: scraps, snippets, threads everywhere. In embracing fragments, we come home to an ever-shifting wholeness. Creation includes mess, dissolution, pieces assembling or disbanding into offcuts and shreds. To make the healing collage, we work where we can find space: sometimes at the United church meeting room down the road, other times at my house. Ends of fabric scatter over floor, chairs, and table. Children become attracted to the space once chaos reaches a peak of glory, and something new happens. Little Max yells, "Hey, I've always wanted to make a stuffed toy—can I make one out of this?" He fishes up a tarpaulin snippet and begins cutting and stitching a toy called Tom while his brother hauls ingredients out of my cupboard to bake a vegan lemon pie. Everything feels precarious: we could be working toward a cohesive whole, but there's always a risk our creative action might swirl awry. The story of our making could decide to break into fragments and elude us, leaving us in that old familiar place where we stand alone, trying to make sense of an undecipherable world—the way my writing self might feel when sitting before the blank page, wondering how to connect feeling, word, and image into something coherent, something meaningful, something that makes story out of this roiling tumult into which we have been mystifyingly born.

TRANSITIONS

JENNY JUDGE

A drip of paint slows and begins to coagulate. It is just at the point of hardening, still a liquid, and taking its time to solidify into an object. I sit quietly in the moment, breathe methodically. A scientist would explain this slow shift of a liquid becoming a solid as an example of phase transition, when molecules change from a high-energy state to a lower one, or when a liquid, gas, or solid changes into another phase.

I can't believe I am literally watching paint dry.

On the day I notice the drip, I am not yet ready to start a new work, and the only task I have energy for is to clean up and organize my art studio. Pieces of thread hang from the ceiling, leftovers from a previous fibre sculpture not used because they were too thin, too long, the wrong size, or the wrong colour. They are like belligerent teenagers that refused to leave; they're in my way, and I am always brushing up against them. But on this day, the day I've given up on creating anything

new, I dip one of them into an old can of white house paint that I had planned to throw away. "One last try to make you into something else," I say, forgetting that I'm supposed to be cleaning up and not concerned that I'm in conversation with a group of threads. The old paint has become heavy, so it blobs down, making yet another mess. It's probably time to give up.

1982: I sit on the floor in the hallway of the art department alongside my new work, a welded metal sculpture I wrapped in wool fleece. My peers and professors have just put me through the ringer of a third-year BFA *critique: "trivial and too feminine," "not serious enough," "just take the wool stuff off." I try to let the comments roll off my shoulders, but I feel defeated. An art history professor walks by and extends his hand to help me up off the floor. "Come to my lecture tomorrow, you won't be disappointed." The next day I am introduced to the work of Eva Hesse, Louise Bourgeois, and other women artists who work in fibre. It is a start.*

I have been here before, and I have to keep trying, to give the threads a chance, to let them speak. Out of this all-too-familiar moment of weakness comes my resolve to continue, to voice in a material that has previously been discounted by the formalist canon that was prevalent in my early artistic career.

During the second attempt, the paint drips slowly, coaxing me into experimenting further. I prepare a lighter thread, red, a leftover piece that was wound onto a wooden spool from the old sewing kit. I tie it with small objects and water down the paint to be a lighter consistency, to give it more movement and to allow gravity to carry it down at a faster rate. I dip it and wait. This time it slides smoothly, and the drip falls over itself, leapfrogging to the bottom. It envelops the small items of sewing paraphernalia I've attached along the string: buttons, coloured threads, and thimbles, small pieces of memory from my mother's collection, many of which I earlier cast

Jenny Judge, detail of *Phase Transitions*, 2023. Strings with plaster-cast sewing paraphernalia, words, and found objects dipped in paint over a period of time. | Photo: Mads Colvin.

in porcelain and glass. I've also included rusted pins, sewing needles, and metal clasps. They seemed just the right things to attach and to catch the liquid as it falls.

1967: I sit on the floor of my mother's sewing room. The mottled beige linoleum is cold on my legs but a welcome respite from the summer heat outside. She spills the buttons out for me to organize—blue, red, black, white—and I put them in categories, arrange the needles by size, and wear the pincushion bracelet on my arm. The plastic cuff is much too large for my wrist, but I am being helpful. She is sewing a skirt made from my favourite yellow-gingham fabric.

Partway along the thread, the drip slows. It passes one of the rusty pins and falls off of its very tip, encases it, changing its shape so it is barely recognizable. It carries on and envelops more attached memories, like it's trying to preserve them.

I am surprised to feel dampness on my cheeks.

This is the beginning of a new fibre-art installation that I start in my sixty-first year, not caring anymore what people may think or whether it is a waste of time to create a whole roomful of strings or not—strings that stop us, show captured moments over time, and remind us that time passes. The choice of materials, threads and objects from the discarded sewing box, is here to help me speak. The simplicity of the materials captures a simple concept and one that could easily be missed: that to catch a drip is to catch a tear, a lifetime of hidden grief.

1990: My father is sixty-one when he dies of cancer.

I do my best to hold back tears as I follow the coffin up the long nave of Timothy Eaton Memorial Church to the hearse outside, the same aisle I walked down with my father when I was married. I keep my

PREVIOUS PAGE: Long-exposure photo of Jenny Judge working on her installation piece *Phase Transitions*, 2023. Strings are being tied with plaster-cast sewing paraphernalia and found objects, then dipped in paint. | Photo: Mads Colvin.

eyes focused on my feet and catch the salted water on my black patent-leather shoes, dulling their gloss. I walk calmly, with measure, and try hard to uphold myself with dignity, as is expected in a large Toronto funeral. I am pregnant with my first child, a grandchild he will never meet.

Grief is put aside for the busy life of a new mother.

I continue to dip threads into the paint: each one in a different viscosity of liquid, each one threaded with different objects, and some dipped multiple times, over several days. A collection begins to form. The drips vary in size, freeze at different rates and in different places. I watch the physics of phase transition at work as all of the moving molecules in the liquid begin to organize and turn less mobile, though still vibrating and vying for a more fixed position. I sit surrounded by threads, in among them with their shifting entropies of liquid and solid states. The drips navigate their way along the sewing thread in a long and measured journey, just like the walk up the nave, behind the coffin, taken a generation ago. The tears I couldn't shed over time are held within the drips, the drips that work their way down the threads as they cover memorabilia, envelop them, and hide memories.

What next? These few threads do not speak loud enough, nor give presence to the intensity of my feelings. The threads and objects need to grow in number and over time so that they can capture time, time passing. But even as I ponder these plans, I wonder if the work should exist only in the instant when it captured my attention long enough to relive an event in my life that I had put on the back burner, forgotten. Was it telling me that it was time to shed my tears? Perhaps this piece should not be made, should never find its place in a gallery, because it has already fulfilled a moment in my history. It has reminded me to push on, to search and find the joy in memories that come from an earlier time. It is merely part of my sixty-first

NEXT PAGE: Long-exposure photo of Jenny Judge working on her installation piece *Phase Transitions*, 2023. Strings are tied with plaster-cast sewing paraphernalia and found objects, then dipped in paint. | Photo: Mads Colvin.

year, a year of transition; the drip would have gone unnoticed in my younger high-energy years.

My current age and slowing atoms have surprisingly provided me with a renewed strength. My unhurried gaze has allowed me to see in a deeper way, given me a heightened ability to notice and wisdom to witness the seemingly insignificant. I also know that on a molecular level my body is slowing, that my blood and life are being rearranged and will eventually crystallize, transition, just like the drips nearing the bottom of the hanging threads. Perhaps that drip was my father coming back, paying a visit to remind me both to be brave and that I have been in this place of vulnerability before.

THIS STRAND LEADS TO MY PAIN

JESS TAYLOR

WIND

I fold the end of a strand of yarn with one hand, then wrap more yarn with my other. I keep winding the yarn around and around itself. I need to make it round and even, a flawless ball of yarn. And, despite failing to make anything else in my life perfect, I succeed. When I'm finished, I take a picture of myself lying in my hospital bed. I'm wearing a blue sweatshirt—solid-colour sweatsuits are my decided uniform of recovery. I hold up the ball of grey-heathered yarn. *Behold the perfect ball of yarn,* I write as I post it to social media. My smile is genuine: my excitement over the roundness of the ball makes everything else go away.

DROPPED STITCH

I've been in hospital for two weeks now—one week in Sunnybrook's trauma ward, and now I'm at Toronto Rehabilitation Institute, where I'm scheduled to stay for five weeks. When I leave, it will be spring. The day before the ambulance brought me from where I was struck by a car as a pedestrian, there had been a blizzard. Since my pelvis was broken ("shattered," the surgical resident tells me), time has been suspended. Even when I went outside from Sunnybrook to the carrier ambulance that brought me to TRI, I didn't register the cold. I remember grey, my jacket over top of me. But mostly I remember chatting with the paramedic and asking about his life and his dreams. He was a recent grad from a firefighting program but had found a job in patient transport more easily. At the end of the year, he'd be moving to Australia. A new adventure. I gave him my best smile. I told him this experience had been good practice for the day when I'd be old enough to have hip replacement. I want to live to be old now. That is new for me, but I didn't tell him that. We both laughed, thinking about this life-changing injury as practice, as an experience that will make everything easier. It hurt to laugh, but I appreciated the distraction.

At times I feel the only way out of my pain is distraction, so I wind the ball, and I knit. I started knitting this way, as part of the adventure to untangle my mind. I couldn't breathe. A pain in my chest had formed when I was ten years old and never went away. It felt like constantly being heartbroken or stepped on or shoved so hard all the wind was knocked out. The pain led me to those experiences in actuality, and it felt like all I was doing was running a wheel along a groove, and over time the groove got deeper and the wheel more used to the way.

I can honestly say I hated myself in 2016. I hated the way I felt, hated how I disappointed myself. I didn't much hate the way I looked, but I hated that it was me in the mirror. By 2018, I'd dug myself out of that gutter, more or less, by applying myself to new hobbies, meeting new people, leaving a relationship, learning more about myself, and working each day to become more the person I wanted to be. I meditated in the morning and then again when I got home from work, creating a bubble of safety and clarity around my day. At night, I knitted until it was time for bed and my eyes couldn't focus anymore.

It felt like things were turning around.

I wanted to be alive. I was making decisions toward living a long life.

And then things turned around literally, as the world spun when I was hit by a car turning left.

MAKE 1

The way knitting can relieve chronic pain, anxiety, and depression has been well documented, and anecdotally, almost every knitter or crafter will boast of the mental benefits of their craft. Crafts pose a challenge, are an escape from the troubles of war and the pandemic, and allow people to make something when they are unable to in another way. I couldn't leave my bed independently, but I could knit at warp speed. Crafting connects people to each other and can also provide a distraction or shield in social situations. Others describe the way their crafts help them focus, boost productivity and creativity. In a recent virtual survey of over three thousand knitters, most reported that knitting contributed to a feeling of calm and increased their happiness.[1]

Aside from the mental-health and self-esteem benefits, the British Pain Society also performed a qualitative survey on the link between pain reduction and knitting.[2] One of the subsurveys involved a facilitated knitting group, and facilitators asked attendees to record their pain levels. Upon concluding the knitting group, those who normally experienced chronic-pain flare-ups after sitting

1 Jill Riley, Betsan Corkhill, and Clare Morris, "The Benefits of Knitting for Personal and Social Wellbeing in Adulthood: Findings from an International Survey," *British Journal of Occupational Therapy* 76, no. 2 (2013): 50.

2 Betsan Corkhill and Carol Davidson, *Exploring the Effects of Knitting on the Experience of Chronic Pain—a Qualitative Study* (Bath: Stitchlinks and Pain Management, Royal United Hospital, 2009).

for a prolonged time were not triggered. The study concluded that this meant knitting wasn't working solely as distraction but also had a further therapeutic impact. Several attendees credited knitting as having mental-health benefits, especially in areas related to self-esteem. They also stated knitting had a pain-relief component and in many instances said the relief was as effective as medication.

CAST ON

My mother brings me my knitting bag from home, and I continue with a sweater pattern I've been working on—my first real sweater. I can't watch TV; there's a vent right above my bed blowing loudly and, combined with the constant visitors and the check-ins from nurses, doctors, and my mother, I feel overstimulated. The yarn I'm working with is a heather-grey worsted with flecks of blue. Around the bottom and cuffs of the sweater, the grey stockinette is traded for a rib stitch in light blue with flecks of grey and white. I'm not afraid of a challenge, and I picked a somewhat-complicated pattern for my first sweater, knitted from the bottom up with an eyelet pattern around the yoke. Small holes form diamonds that, in my hands, come out more like teardrops. The only thing that frustrates me about the sweater is how slow the progress is, like my healing. A little each day.

My friend M brings me a pattern for a chunky quick-knit sweater, large circular needles, and rust-orange yarn. I switch between the two projects until I start making headway on my chunky knit, and then I'm hooked. The pain fades away, and all I care about is finishing. It works better than the hydromorphone.

Aside from pain relief, I've also found a sneaky way to remain productive. I try to do this in many different ways: calling into work meetings from my hospital bed; writing down my physio routine in my notebook; and more than anything, knitting. If someone visits me, my hands can keep moving. Downtime in my room? I'm still making a sweater. Perhaps this is what the participants in the chronic-pain study meant when describing how knitting increased their feelings of agency and self-esteem.[3] One participant said, "I can't be useless if I can knit." This is how I feel as well, terrified that I'm useless, that I need too much, that I am only taking from others and no longer am someone who works, helps, creates. Writing, a central aspect of who I am, has not been coming. It's hard to get out of bed, and even throwing out a wrapper from a cheeseburger is impossible by myself. I rely on gait aids to walk, friends and family to accompany me while moving from one place to another. Knitting is an escape from these feelings.

But this productivity creates a tension between the way knitting and crafting can relax and provide stress relief and how it feeds the ever-increasing productivity machine of capitalism, which creates the feelings of uselessness for chronic-pain sufferers in the first place. Who is to say that someone needs to produce in order to be worthy? That being in need is somehow lesser than being able to give or to make? Most hobbyists also come across those who refuse to believe that a hobby can just be a hobby; the goal must be monetization, professionalization of the craft. While meaning it as a compliment, I have suggested that a friend who is an excellent chef go into business making frozen dinners. People who (like me) say these things mean that the time and energy someone is putting into their hobby is valuable. But for those who wish to have a hobby for the sake of leisure, monetary value is not the point. The word *hustle* has displaced *hobby* to the extent that in "The Case for Having a Hobby," Jaya Saxena admits that she forgot the word while describing a just-for-fun band her spouse had joined without any goals or desire to make money attached to it.[4]

In *How to Do Nothing,* Jenny Odell explores how true leisure time has been eroded in our digital age. Social media, in particular,

3 Corkhill and Davidson, *Exploring the Effects of Knitting.*

4 Jaya Saxena, "The Case for Having a Hobby," *New York Times,* May 10, 2018, https://www.nytimes.com/2018/05/10/smarter-living/the-case-for-hobbies-ideas.html.

encourages the capitalization of all output, including anything that is done outside of work hours.[5] Influencers do not take holidays; the pictures they post of their relaxation are monetized, plug products they support, or are building blocks in creating a "brand." Crafters, hobbyists, and fibre artists are not immune to this themselves; a quick scroll through Instagram or Facebook reveals sewing and knitting influencers and others trying to monetize their crafts. When unable to make money, create, or be productive, many people lose their sense of worth. When people are not constantly generating capital, they feel they must be improving themselves in order to gain more skills and/or become mentally healthy and fit to work. In her interview with *The Guardian*, Odell mentions that even self-improvement is work, not leisure.[6] Self-improvement is just as often pushed into our leisure time. Within the chronic-pain and knitting study, I was amazed to see how many of the quotes were tied to self-improvement in addition to pain relief.[7] In many instances, not being able to help, work, or produce seemed to be a bigger concern of participants than living with pain. They described themselves as being "able to help those in need instead of being in need" and said knitting allowed them to be more creative. But there is something about hobbies outside of productivity that are increasingly therapeutic; leisure is a necessity that has been co-opted by capitalist culture, to the extent that I use hobbies as a way to never stop working.

The only person to call me out on this is a medical resident, A. "Your only job while you're in here is to rest," he tells me again and again. "If someone comes to visit you, and they don't help you, send them home." When he catches me knitting, he says, "You're knitting too? You're doing way too much." And then he sits down and talks to me about my pain and medication. Before he leaves, he asks me

5 Jenny Odell, *How to Do Nothing* (New York: Melville House, 2020).

6 Ellie Shechet, "How to do nothing: The new guide to refocusing on the real world," *The Guardian*, April 2, 2019, https://www.theguardian.com/lifeandstyle/2019/apr/02/jenny-odell-how-to-do-nothing-attention.

7 Corkhill and Davidson, *Exploring the Effects of Knitting*.

to slow down, take time to just relax and heal. To everyone else, my knitting is under the radar, trivial.

Sometimes, after I'm back at home, on nights when my pain is manageable, I reach for my knitting while watching television. I want to cheat relaxing. I'll be in a period of doing, doing, doing. My whole self will be shaking with the energy that comes from the anxiety that if I stop, I'll fall behind (behind what, I'm never able to answer). As I knit, I'll feel a headache rise through me, my eyes tingling. I'm better at recognizing this now. I'll put my knitting down. *You don't need to make anything,* I tell myself. *You can just be still.* And I'll lie down, set my head against the arm of the couch, and watch television until it's time to go to sleep.

TINK

Before my accident, I tried to teach my friend S to knit at a time when she was feeling stuck and confused. I thought knitting might be able to heal her the way it heals me. She liked working with her hands, but something about knitting didn't connect with her. We started with large needles and thick yarn, but somehow, she accidentally split the yarn. Another time, the strand snapped in her hand. We went to a weaving class together, and afterward she threw down the loom in a rage, her threads all tangled. The loom smashed, and the remaining strands, strung taut along the frame, popped off. "I'm just not *patient* like you," she said to me later.

I found that funny: my whole childhood I'd been called impatient, and whenever someone learned my star sign, they said it fit due to its negative qualities. I began to see myself this way: impatient, competitive, difficult.

Through knitting, I'd transformed pain to patience, and that seemed a reward in itself. It wasn't the peace I sought, was still seeking, but it was a start.

YARN OVER, KNIT NEXT ROW

My nerves must be snarled and tangled like this yarn—some days are smooth, and other days they snag with pain. Stitches are dropped. A hole opens up, and the yarn unravels.

The neurologist on the first floor of TRI holds up a piece of copper wire. He strips back a bit of the plastic casing and shows me the copper strands inside. He says it works as a good model of a nerve. He explains that nerves heal slowly, much more slowly than skin, than bone, even, and this is why I still have such bad nerve pain.

"Your nerves, they might heal inch by inch—that's why your toe used to feel hot and why you're feeling it in your calf. But nerve pain is different from other pains. Other pains are telling you that something is wrong, that there's a threat. Then as the inflammation goes down, new skin forms, bone heals, the pain stops. Nerve pain doesn't work that way—the nerves fire up as they heal because they are trying to work again. Sometimes they find new ways to travel, and feeling will get back to normal in an area, but often that comes with pain. But it's the nerves misfiring, sending signals to the brain that your body is in danger when actually it's healing. The medication you're on is actually a brain medication. We'll increase the dose."

"A brain medication?"

He hands me the wire, and I turn it over in my hands, look at the copper.

"It's neat, isn't it?" he says. "Better than a medical model and it barely costs anything. Gabapentin, Lyrica, those medications tell your brain not to register the pain as pain."

"But I'm still feeling pain?"

"No, your body sends the signals to your brain, but your brain can't interpret them that way."

"Oh."

I lie back on the bed, and he sticks needles into my calf and thigh and then pulses electricity through the muscles to simulate a reflex.

After the test, the neurologist traces the nerve that's damaged. He points at one of my incisions, over a large metal plate holding together the left side of my pelvis. "I think when they went in here, they cut this nerve. There is one small nerve here, connected to here." He points at a spot on my outer thigh. "The surface of your skin in that one spot will likely never regain feeling, but it's just connected to the surface, so the nerves impacting your muscles, all of that should heal. And on this spot, I don't know, you could get a tattoo saying *I can't feel this* or something."

Back in my room, I pick up my knitting, trying not to think about the needles and pulses of electricity from the EMG test. The blue strands tangle together. I realize two different skeins of blue have wrapped around each other, knotting my working yarn. I don't have the energy to untangle, to tease these strands apart. I take scissors to the yarn, watch the individual fibres splay after they are cut. *I can't feel this.*

KNIT

A colleague visits with his partner, N. They bring me lentil soup, granola, things to fill me up and help me heal. We talk about creativity and how I am not writing, cannot write. Knitting has filled that outlet, I say. "At least I'm creating." My heart aches with the lie. I don't know what it will take to get back to myself again.

Knitting does feel like a puzzle in a similar way to writing, but there can be no comparison. I would never claim to be an expert writer, as good writing requires you to admit that you are only as good as your next word, nothing more. But I am a beginner knitter, stumbling through patterns, trying things for the first time. I never know what yarn to buy. I can't make things up out of my head. There have been decades where I didn't knit at all.

Writing, in comparison, has been the only thing I could count on about myself as I grew, and when I said or did things that made me question myself, it provided me access to other worlds where I could question and reflect freely, safe from scrutiny.

N says she doesn't knit, but cooking is like that for her. She is probably the most intelligent and intellectual person I've ever met. I wonder if it's true for her, that she can combine this work of the body with the yearnings and curiosity of the mind.

Becoming involved in a hobby requires a balance of expertise and novelty; a hobby is interesting because it is exciting and new (or has built-in novelty and challenge, such as new patterns) but requires enough ease of mastery to avoid frustration. Perhaps N has reached a level with cooking that allows her a fluidity of thought that I do not have with cooking, that allows room for improvisation rather than regimentation.

While level of expertise was not measured, people who knitted more than three times a week reported higher levels of the mental and emotional benefits of knitting, in particular happiness, a sense of well-being, and cognition,[8] than those who knitted only occasionally. Frequent knitters "described the challenges of knitting, such as working out a complex pattern and exercising new knitting skills as improving their problem-solving abilities."[9] Perhaps the more I knit, the more it will begin to feel like writing for me. Perhaps I'll start to feel more like myself.

I continue to knit and learn and start to experiment with changing colours and textures in a knitting pattern. I text my brother and ask if he can bring me to the knitting store. "I need yarn," I tell him. "But I can't get the walker down the stairs to my apartment by myself."

I begin to record my knitting ideas through pictures and to jot notes in a small book. *At least it's in a notebook, even if it's not writing.*

8 Riley, Corkhill, and Morris, "The Benefits of Knitting."
9 Riley, Corkhill, and Morris, "The Benefits of Knitting," 52.

K TO END

My walker is awkward, hard to manoeuvre, as I make my way through the knitting store. I feel embarrassed immediately and want to leave. My brother helps me to find yarn and decide on the colours, and I know none are the colours I want, but I'm nervous and panic buy it so we can get out of there. I keep knocking spools of embroidery thread off their stand.

I'd imagined myself lost in a sea of colour and texture, walking down the aisle of Liberty fabric bolts as if I'd stepped into another world. My fingers caressing the different softnesses of the yarns, marvelling at how a smooth and tight yarn is soft in a different way to a yarn loosely twisted together in thick strands. I'd expected to spend time examining their weights.

Instead, I leave with my face aching from blushing and that awkward smile that both my brother and I do when we are uncomfortable. He is smiling too.

"Did you get what you needed?" he asks me, as he tucks my bag from the store into the walker basket under my seat. I want to cry, but I don't know how to express how I feel. I nod.

Sometimes while I knit, instead of trying to distract myself from my pain, physical or emotional, I think about it. My hands take a piece of yarn and create something new, and my mind takes my pain and weaves it into something bearable, interesting, inspiring of my curiosity. Why has this pain persisted? Has it always persisted? How would I describe it to another? Is it possible to describe it to another?

In *Regarding the Pain of Others*, Susan Sontag discusses how suffering, war, violence, and pain are unable to be fully registered by others who haven't experienced it, not even when reproduced in the most vivid photographic detail.[10] Instead, people are drawn to the gruesome details from a place of remove.[11] People I barely know

10 Susan Sontag, *Regarding the Pain of Others* (New York: Picador USA, 2003), 76.

11 Sontag, *Regarding the Pain*, 121–23.

message me on social media, wanting to hear the details of the accident, of what I'm doing, of whether I'm going to take the driver to court. From my hospital bed, I am unable to engage. Once I'm home, I feel even more separate from others. I am no longer the gruesome spectacle of the accident; now I am slow recovery, invisible pain. There is nothing I can say, no details I can give that will create a true sense of empathy and bridge that distance.

I can't describe to someone else something that I don't understand. How can pain only be neurons firing in the brain or a warning to avoid something, when it is often so persistent, lingering long after a threat is gone? If I'm "healed," then is it a problem with the mind? If I limp, but only I notice it, do I really walk with a limp? When I first come home from the hospital, I start to read about pain in pursuit of understanding. One of the books I read, a comic called *Pain Is Really Strange* by Steve Haines and Sophie Standing, refers to a study in *The Lancet*, which reveals that understanding pain and how it works is key to its reduction, especially for those with chronic pain.[12] And I find reading about my pain, thinking about my pain while knitting, attempting to describe it to another, does help reduce it almost as much as using knitting as a distraction.

There is a type of meditation where you focus on breath or watch your thoughts floating by with detachment. There is also a meditation of distraction, the clichéd envisioning of the "happy place" or working to manifest your desires. At first, this is what I'm doing with knitting, especially while I'm learning, constantly consulting the pattern. Distracting myself, counting stitches instead of breaths, falling into a rhythm.

After I started cognitive behavioural therapy in 2017, I started to do another type of meditation: validation exercises. I'd close my eyes, listen to my breath, and then, instead of leaning away from thoughts and feelings, observing them as passing moments, I'd lean in. I'd *feel*.

12 Steve Haines and Sophie Standing, *Pain Is Really Strange* (Philadelphia: Singing Dragon, 2015), 3.

What do I feel? I'd ask myself. Anger. *And under that feeling?* Fear, sadness. *It's okay to be sad. I still love you when you're sad.* I'd do this for five minutes when I got home each day. Sometimes I'd cry, and sometimes it would be as routine as making a cup of coffee in the morning.

I do this type of meditation while I knit, but with my pain. As my mind gets used to the pattern of knitting, so my needles' movements become like my breath, calming in the background before my mind and emotions go on a journey of interrogation. *Where is your pain? How do you feel about your recovery? What does it mean to be recovered?*

I direct my consciousness to the spot where my tailbone joins my pelvis, to my glutes, to the nerve that runs along the outside of my thigh to my calf to my toe. I let the pain wash over me. Just like with the emotional validation exercise, I go inside the pain, I am surrounded—then acceptance, relief.

CAST OFF

In *Pain: A Very Short Introduction*, Rob Boddice tackles contemporary thought on the intertwining of emotional, mental, and physical manifestations of pain, yet he remarks how medical professionals in the Western world are still taught to think along the lines of ailment and injury, pain or sickness to diagnosis to healing.[13] For me, this is true for a year. While in TRI, I see a psychologist once, and an underperforming social worker tries to help with my release, but all of the medical professionals take my upbeat attitude, the way I joke and focus on being a "good patient," following instructions and doing exercises, to mean that only my body needs healing and not my mind. Never mind my history of anxiety and depression. No one digs into this in any great depth or thinks about how some of my issues

13 Rob Boddice, *Pain: A Very Short Introduction* (Oxford: Oxford University Press, 2017), 77–78.

with social anxiety, generalized anxiety, and self-loathing might be exasperated by the accident or how maybe my jokes and attitude are a symptom of my mental and emotional struggles instead of a sign that they don't exist.

They refer me to psychotherapy that focuses on the surface of my feelings instead of diving into the core of what has happened. That I've almost died, that I want to talk about death, that I want to talk about not existing and how I now want to live, want to exist. I don't know what it means to know that I'll stop. I want to talk about my pain. How it feels. How it makes me feel alone, how it makes me feel like I need to perform, be healed, how I feel so pressured to be healed and to have recovery be linear, when each day is new to me, and some of the new days feel worse than the five that came before.

At my one-year post-op appointment with my surgeon, we talk a bit about my pain and nerve damage. While I haven't returned to rock climbing or creative writing or working the way I did before, I no longer need gait aids. He tells me that according to the X-rays, my hardware (two plates and a large screw) and my bones' positioning look great, and my mobility recovery is everything they hoped for. So, other than physio and continuing with strengthening, I'm done. Healed. We briefly discuss my lawsuit with the insurance company of the driver who hit me. "You'd be surprised," the surgeon says. "It takes so long for those things to get resolved, and I find it drags on the pain. Leaves the focus on it. Like a lot of patients, they see an improvement once it's resolved and their lives aren't about the accident anymore."

"That would be a relief. I hope so. I'm so tired of talking about it, of thinking about it. I don't feel good. I still hurt and I feel nervous, I don't know."

The surgeon pauses for a moment and then looks me in the eyes. "Do you think you have PTSD?" It's the first time anyone has asked me. Something squeezes inside my chest.

"I don't know. Maybe? It's possible."

"I'm going to refer you the PTSD clinic here. It's covered,[14] they'll do an assessment. and you know what? If you don't have PTSD, or if they think, 'Okay, we'll refer her elsewhere,' then fine, okay, but I think getting the assessment would be a good idea. Can I do that referral for you?"

And for the first time, I start getting the help I need.

KNOT

The pain doesn't end there. Of course it doesn't. Some days, I feel like the whole bottom half of my body could walk off without me and I'd be relieved. "Give me a transplant!" I joke. "Do they do body transplants from the hips down?" People laugh, and I laugh, and then on the way home, my face is still. When I get home, I flop onto the couch. With the door locked, surrounded by blankets, I feel safe. I turn on a heating pad, lay it against the side of my pelvis, and I begin to knit. I am alone, and I feel my pain, as the needles keep their rhythm.

14 In Ontario, several health services are covered by the Ontario Health Insurance Plan (OHIP), accessible by all Ontario citizens and permanent residents. Services that are not covered by OHIP are either paid out of pocket or by a private or employer's insurance plan. Psychotherapy services are not covered by OHIP, so gaining access to intensive treatments can be difficult.

READING THE BEADS

DANIELLE LUSSIER

I did not learn to bead at my nana's kitchen table, as I probably would have if the world was a different place. The world, however, is what it is. In many ways, colonial systems—grounded in law and supported by policy and countless co-conspirators in the Colonial Project that is Canada—worked exactly as designed. For generations, Canadian law criminalized our ways of knowing, being, and loving in community. This included but was not limited to restricting the production and mobility of beadwork and the knowledge that makes beadwork practice possible. Education and legal systems in particular were co-opted to assimilate us into the body politic, erase us from the historical narrative, and exclude us from the visual record. Women, beading around a kitchen table, sharing information and stories while clothing the Nation in a distinctive aesthetic, were very dangerous indeed. It was critical to the Colonial Project that we be controlled by any and all means necessary, including genocide.

Danielle Lussier, *Form a Calming Circle: A(nother) Modern Métis Firebag*, 2021. Modern and antique glass seed beads on purple melton. | Photo: Danielle Lussier.

And yet we are still here, resisting and healing in a thousand ways. Some of us, through beadwork.

From the first days of law school, Learners are taught the doctrine of discovery and some legal wizardry wherein the Supreme Court vehemently maintains that terra nullius[1] does not technically exist in these territories known as Canada, and yet, somehow, Canada magically absorbed underlying title to all land during colonial expansion.

Learners leave property law and head down the hall to criminal law, where they learn of legal tests established on facts borne by the bodies of Indigenous Peoples, of the over-incarceration of Indigenous Peoples, and of our systemic dehumanization when our lives are violently ended or when we disappear. Many Indigenous Learners, meanwhile, sit through class acutely aware of the parts of the stories not taught. Our mums and Aunties and sisters weep and retch and grieve for stolen sisters when courts, witnesses, and lawyers remind us that even in death, as Indigenous women, we are individually and collectively considered to be less than human. I will spare you the details of the violence of learning public and constitutional law as an Indigenous Learner; in many cases, the way Section 35, the part of the Canadian Constitution that entrenches our rights as Indigenous Peoples, is taught (or not taught) is more egregious than you could even imagine.

To survive this professionalization process, we must acclimatize, assimilate, and learn to speak the language of law. I have long understood the process to be, for Indigenous Learners, one of violence—an intellectual rupture. In the face of intellectual, cultural, and sometimes physical violence, some of us put our heads down, attempting to attract as little attention as possible, and try to simply survive the

1 A Latin term meaning "the land of no one" or "nobody's land," now understood as a legal principle of public international law operating to legitimize colonization.

space. Some of us actively resist racism and colonialism in the classrooms and hallways, with varying degrees of success. Others choose to walk a path somewhere in between, based on complicated safety calculations made in real time. Existing in these spaces is exhausting and often actively dangerous. In many ways, at a micro level, the process mirrors how we have long navigated the imposition of colonial systems on our communities on the whole.

I started law school two thousand kilometres away from my home territory, when I was eighteen years old. The wherefores and the whys of how that came to be constitute a story in and of itself, but the relevant bits today relate to my tender age and the use of legal education as a tool for colonizing the mind. Far from home and navigating these spaces as the only openly Indigenous person in my law school class, I chose survival by invisibility. I found spaces outside the law school, such as the Indigenous Students' Association, where I was safe enough to weep in between classes and visit with kin, but within the four walls of the law school, I put my head down and said nothing. This option was a privilege grounded in my white-coded appearance, and while it was objectively the safest course of action available to me at the time, I carried sadness and shame at my decision not to resist more fully. I graduated, was called to the bar, became a lawyer, and put my experiences in an invisible box I dragged around to every professional space I operated in for the next decade.

And then I became a mum. Along with my responsibilities, my entire world view changed overnight. Ensuring that my babies encountered less-hostile spaces as they moved through the world as Indigenous people became my first priority. Survival and safety calculations became infinitely more complicated and more simple at the same time, and "head down" was no longer an option as I carried (literally) tiny humans on my back. The moment I grew up and let go of my efforts toward self-preservation, I turned my mind to the generations that would follow, determined to be a better relation and advocate for young ones. While I could not effect change in every space they would enter, I seized the opportunity to reframe my past decisions by re-entering the academy to pursue my PhD with my head up, deeply motivated to resist.

I could lie and tell you I began my doctoral studies with the intention of prompting a beadwork revolution in legal education, of teaching countless Learners to bead in law schools across several provinces, and of recentring Indigenous ways of knowing and sharing information in my own learning practice. I could tell you I set out with the intention of reading the beads and thus changing conversations. It would be a nice story, but it isn't true.

I *was* determined to resist racism, colonialism, and the erasure of Indigenous Peoples, and to do it in beautiful and loving ways, but my mind had suffered significant colonization through my interactions with legal education and the legal profession. Survival, as I understood it, depended on thinking and speaking and presenting as an agent of a colonial "justice" system. Colonial systems put in place to disrupt Indigenous ways of knowing and being are incredibly effective. Reading the beads was not, as yet, part of my vocabulary.

The true story of how I came to bead a chapter of my doctoral dissertation in law is far more circuitous, as some of the most important stories are. A series of events, some fortunate and some unfortunate, none of which I could have strung together into a cohesive narrative at the time, ultimately came together. A potent combination of time, space, hindsight, and healing allows me to tell a piece of the story today.

When I began my PhD, I had, in fact, never laid hands on beads before. Beadwork came into my life in what I would later recognize as a moment of crisis, smack in the middle of my doctoral program.

Despite my best intentions to build something beautiful as a legacy for my children and their children, my desire to resist colonialism in legal education got lost along the way. Somewhere between difficult classroom experiences, comprehensive examinations, birthing my third child, and accepting a full-time position working within the faculty, where I studied slowly and in stolen moments in the wee small hours while the children slept, I fell into my old patterns. I found myself ducking for cover, lowering my voice, and closing myself off from the world. The need for calm, to be grounded in culture and to come back to the purpose and intent of my graduate studies, was strong around the moment when the beads found their way to my table.

A trip to a local Indigenous-owned store to purchase sacred medicines changed my life. That tiny pocket of safety in the middle of downtown Ottawa, where I did not, as a member of the Red River Métis diasporic community, have harvesting rights, also sold beads. I entered with a little disposable income in my pocket, and I left with all the treasures needed to reclaim a practice that had not held space in my family in living memory.

My first tentative stitches calmed my mind and body, and my practice developed at a pace that left me in no doubt of ancestral memory and learning. My thumbs and forefingers worked needle, thread, and melton tradecloth intuitively, coaxing the beads into curves and tacking them down without buckles or gaps. I beaded mice, turtles, and hummingbirds for the children, astonished at the strength and capacity of my hands. Eventually, I began to dream in beads. Literal dreams grew into a figurative dream of building something new, decolonizing learning spaces, and healing community.

While my scholarship had stagnated as I struggled both to maintain a precarious balance in my life and to forgive myself for not resisting the subjugation of Indigenous knowledge within the academy as robustly as I should, my body immediately understood the inherent therapeutic power of beadwork. I introduced it into the law school, gently, in hopes it might sustain the community I was part of and had also been hired to support. I gathered with Learners, colleagues, and professors to sew regalia, bespoke beaded stoles and hoods created in consultation with Learners and their kin, to honour our graduates at convocation. We beaded orange shirts to mark Orange Shirt Day in September—now the National Day for Truth and Reconciliation—poppies for National Indigenous Veterans Day on November 8, and women in red dresses to honour the work of the National Inquiry into Missing and Murdered Indigenous Women and Girls. Each new lapel pin, graduation stole, and beaded yoke supported learning and unlearning in community, all along the way.

As our collective skills improved, the patterns created for the beaded stoles and convocation hoods became increasingly complex. What began as beadwork patches, three inches in diameter and gently stitched to tradecloth stoles, evolved into fourteen-inch vines stretching from shoulder to waist and beaded directly on long strips of wool that were later professionally finished by in-house talent: professors and associate deans who moonlit as seamstresses in the lead-up to convocation. Eventually, our community collaborations required a year-long process for each future graduate involving thousands of beads and hundreds of metres of thread. Those around me would term it a "beadwork revolution" and a "transformative experience" for our little corner of education. But my research remained stuck as I continued to personally struggle through incidents of racism and anti-Indigenous violence that plagued even these slightly reimagined spaces.

Years later now, when I serve as lead educator in a co-learning space, my Learners will be the first to tell you that when things get tough, I reach for the beads. Like many beadworkers, I recognize that my practice carries therapeutic power for individual beaders and for communities on the whole. One of my former Learners, Natane Allison of Bkejwanong (Walpole Island) First Nation, once described beadwork as a practice that brings "inner peace."[2] It is a slow, meditative, and contemplative art, one that cannot be rushed. Lisa Shepherd, Métis artisan, explains: "There's no instant gratification in beading. There's life, and there's a breath in the work that you are doing. And you have to slow down, and your heart rate slows down, and your breathing deepens, and there is just this connection that happens."[3]

Thousands of stitches and zero pages of progress toward my dissertation later, COVID arrived in North America, and the world seemed to stop. During the first wave of stay-at-home orders, I was faced with a choice, one faced by many who found themselves caring for children while working remotely full time, locked in houses with parents, spouses, and pets they likely never anticipated spending twenty-four hours a day with when they designed their lives in a prepandemic world. While juggling all the priorities, trying to keep families safe and healthy, many of us had to decide which balls to let drop. The academic calendar told me it was time to conclude my PhD journey, and the choice was stark: attempt to maintain the precarious balance and complete the work, or put the dream of a doctorate to bed.

The timing was difficult, but the calculation was easy after speaking with my children. Having dragged two toddlers to classes in a double stroller, having given birth the day after completing my final coursework, having taken only a few months' leave before returning to campus with the same two toddlers and a nursling in a baby carrier, the sacrifices my family had made to bring me to the cusp of the dissertation were too many to ignore. The right decision for my family in that time and space, and what I felt I needed to do to honour their sacrifices, was to continue on and close the circle.

2 Tawny Jade, "A particularly hysterical phone call later," Twitter, July 10, 2020, 8:58 p.m., https://twitter.com/_tawnyjaaade/status/1281754637205463040.

3 Parks Canada, "The Flower Beadwork People," YouTube video, 4:41, May 25, 2016, https://www.youtube.com/watch?v=54ipBLZJ6L4.

NEXT PAGE: Danielle Lussier, *Law with Heart Honour Shawl*, 2020. A rufous hummingbird, tireless prairie pollinator, hovers above the good medicine of buffalo berries, blueberries, and saskatoons on the front of the shawl. Beaded in size 10, 11, and 15 glass seed beads. | Photo: Danielle Lussier.

The commitment to writing began with ten minutes a day, all I could manage in the throes of the crisis. Momentum took over, and I found myself drafting whole chapters in the Notes app on my phone, seated on park benches watching children slide, or in a blue lawn chair my nephew bought me to facilitate backyard supervision of digging a hole to the core of the earth, or on the front step while sidewalk chalk filled the driveway. I would jump up in the middle of dinner and scribble paragraphs on bits of construction paper to later translate into academic speak from nine at night until three in the morning, with fingers crossed that my youngest would sleep through the night.

The children watched in real time. One afternoon, one of my girls asked, in the honest way of a child, what exactly I was working on and when I would be done. I stumbled through an awkward explanation of asserting intellectual self-determination and making space for Métis ways of knowing in law and learning. I talked about legal orders and learning law and how I thought beads would help bring love and kindness and some of our ways into spaces not designed for us or by us.

She gently interrupted my rambling peregrination and asked when she would be old enough to read my thesis, because I was confusing her, and also, Mama, why are you writing about beads but not sewing any?

This work I was engaging in clearly wasn't being written in a way that my children would understand. If the work was *for* them, as I intended it to be, then I was being a bad relation in not properly translating the work so they could comprehend it. I owed them better; I finally understood what needed to be done.

A dissertation full of theory and analysis and million-dollar words might help support other educators who were working to build safer learning spaces. This, by extension, would support the children ... eventually. Beading a mnemonic device to translate the stories I was trying to tell would bring them into the process now. And so, I set aside the words and put the beads where my heart was. The honour shawl born of the process ultimately served as a macro demonstration of beadwork as a tool for creating space for Indigenous pedagogies in law learning, and it became a legal love letter to my children.[4]

The front of the shawl, beaded on purple melton tradecloth, carries a rufous hummingbird, prairie pollinator, and clusters of buffalo berries, blueberries, saskatoons, and strawberries. Each cluster can be read in multiple ways, with the stories and knowledge carried in the shawl evolving over time as the children grow.

The back of the shawl carries my family, beaded as a herd of buffalo that each bears a different set of teachings on their back. One speaks to Nation-to-Nation relationships and stories of Métis resistance; one carries the Laws of the Prairie; a third embodies teachings of humility and nationhood; another still hints to the bardic tradition of the Métis Nation and law held in songs.

A fotonovela engaging with the shawl and her teachings formed the penultimate chapter of my dissertation, which was ultimately awarded my university's prize for outstanding thesis across all of the humanities. More importantly, in my mind, the shawl itself hangs in my closet and offers an opportunity for continuous learning and growth. When I dress in it now, without fail, one of my children will stop me to run their hands over some berries, or a buffalo, or the Red River that grounds the beadwork. As they grow up, the beads remain unchanged; but the dialogue around them deepens. They speak of what they remember of the time when the beadwork was born and ask increasingly difficult questions about land, law, learning, and home.

In the garments I have created since I first beaded law, I have translated other teachings, stories, and research for the children. Using beads to capture ideas on everything from traditional plant use to kinship structures to their ethical obligations as Métis people,

4 Danielle Lussier, "A Legal Love Letter to My Children: If These Beads Could Talk," *Indigenous Law Journal* 18, no. 1 (2022): 1–26.

NEXT PAGE: Danielle Lussier, *Law with Heart Honour Shawl*, 2020. An obstinacy of buffalo sewn in glass seed beads adorns the reverse of the melton shawl. | Photo: Danielle Lussier.

I am creating a new visual record. I hope this will make the children stronger, rooting them in our ways of knowing, loving, and being.

And as I sew, the children are with me around the kitchen table. It is a privilege that many generations of Indigenous Peoples have been denied, and we treat it as such. We share both stories about community and teachings about handwork technique, debate pattern and colour choices, and work together to help the beads find their voices and carry our stories. The older they grow, the closer the children come to entering the spaces that are not always kind to Indigenous people. I know that there will come a point when I will not be able to protect them, and I worry about this a lot; this is the way of motherhood, Auntiehood, and caring for community.

While I hope to have altered some spaces, if only a little, with my love and my beadwork, nothing in life is certain. I know in my heart I have done the best I can to stitch the threads available to me at this time. As I continue to imagine brighter futures and to resist our erasure by quietly stitching at every table where I have a seat, I know that I am giving not only my children but also those who hold space at our shared tables the tools they will need to be able to read the beads. It's not enough today, but I am hopeful for tomorrow.

BECOMING SWARM

ANDREA REXILIUS

HEM

We are our repetitions. We are our repetitions.

A text is woven ritual. A textile of thought.

A *hem*, an experimental performance of duration, was built out of a single gesture. I stood for an hour meditating, attuning myself to the nuances of my body, and at the end of that hour noticed a slight movement. I spent the next hour exaggerating this movement throughout the performance space. My gesture was a rubbing of thumb and forefinger. I exaggerated this movement of plucking an invisible thread from the ground and extending it into the air. In my writing I found the disparate gesture of the bird cultivated. Found influences (twigs, threads, moss) in the curation of the nest (form, ascension, boundedness). I extended this metaphor into writing: the way in which textual threads (sentences, insights) develop across the page.

I thought about gravity and ascension in a piece of writing and drew the following mark: ^^^^^^^^. The hem.

When I researched the etymology of the word *hem*, I discovered the word *home* embedded beneath it, in its root system. And the word *selvedge*, first named a "self-edge." From there I saw the thread (as a form of linguistic migration, or as a form of sentencing) and the nest (language as a dwelling place, or a refuge for disparate migratory elements). Performance, stitch, led me on a path of poetic discovery from a movement my body signalled: a hem, directing my mind toward what it could not speak.

The poem is the body's speech. The poem is the silent body. The severed tongue. The poem is the pointing. The poem is what directs you. A poem is choreography.

Performance lets me view my own body/page. It lets the body speak, in its own non-verbal, non-narrative, untranslated language. A conversation happens. The throat is reformed. The body announces. The vocal cords pronounce. The habitat of the poem becomes the relationship between the page and the body. The habitat of the poem, a refuge.

The tongue, a small snake, is rooted in the mouth (a cathedral). It is both imprisoned and free. The teeth bite and bare the tongue, hemming the tongue to its home. A snake has a forked tongue. To make speech multiplicitous (literal and metaphorical at once). This fork makes transformation possible. It brings its speaker to a crossroads where two realms touch (inside and outside, silent and spoken, latent and manifest). Each speech act is an act of divination, emerging from the cathedral, placing flora/lingua at the altar. Swallowing back. Cecilia Vicuña's *Spit Temple* is this mouth.

To repeat is to open oneself to a form of prayer; your words, thoughts, actions create patterns, develop grooves, call out to what is invisible. To see what we have been petitioning.

I hung four white bedsheets around the four sides of a wooden scaffolding. You could see inside the space built by the four sheets, where I balanced on my stomach on the ladder of the scaffolding stitching *text* (migration patterns of narrative is what I called it) through the front and back of the white cloth. This performance lasted for an hour, and while the external view (a line of black or red thread moving through to the front of the sheet) looked extremely minimal, the acrobatics on the inside of the sheets—I spent the entire hour in the air, hooking my arms and legs in various configurations onto the ladder—were physically excruciating.

When I come to the page, to narrative (I define narrative as the trajectory or propulsion of a piece of text), I think in terms of a front stitch and a backstitch, or as having an undercurrent of movement (an unseen or unsaid intensity—what happens between the sheets). As a reader, I consider both the front stitch—what is said in a text, the conscious parts—and the backstitch—the secret narrative trajectory, the current that is unknown or known only subconsciously to the writer during composition.

In the summer of 2003, I gathered old maps, sewing patterns, sea charts, knitting needles, a spinning globe, and a long black ribbon with the word *air* stitched onto it. I was interested in the relationship between the knitting needle and the compass, the parallel of sea charts and sewing patterns, the gendered orientation of travel and exploration, the "magic trick" of breathing onto the ribbon, flipping it over for the audience, and finding it labelled *air*. The breath as air. I stitched four white bedsheets together and covered them in sea charts and sewing patterns.

I came to recognize the hem as a display of mapping: how a bird maps its migration (the needle poking through the sheet as its beak), how navigators map a landscape (physical cartography), how the fabric patterns themselves map an outfit (or continental drift), and how words map a sentence (the thread generally moving from left to right). I thought of a poem as a demonstration of call-and-response, of region and localization, of echo and refrain. And the architecture of the hem as continents, dresses, sea charts, and navigations, in recollection.

Repetition is an act of duration. We repeat a specific gesture for long periods of time, one hour, two hours, to see what new sparks arise from our sacred petitioning. As sound or action progresses, the thump or drone of the repetition begins to bind us to a new experience of space and time. Individual boundaries dissolve as performers/readers/speakers merge into one acting animal, bound by our collective rhythms.

To stitch: to pull something together in context, to combine two unlike things in association. A stitch as metaphor, the near and far touching, tentatively. A temporary outpouring of relationship. As long as the stitch will hold.

BREATH AS PASSAGE

I think of writing as part seance.

I think of writing as part architectural nest building.

I have gathered the threads. I have gathered the circumstance. Now I am knee-deep in the reeds. Now I am covered in milkweed fluff. Now I am a witch drowning. Now I am a goddess rising.

Now I am a witch casting a spell.

I made my descent into the underworld, into the understitch, under the tongue, grief stricken, silent. I made my descent beneath the veil. I sought my sister there.

When my sister passed away in 2017, I went back to my hometown to her mother's house to help sort out details for her funeral. Her mother monitored my every move, asking if I needed water, tea, coffee. Asking if I was too warm, too cold, too tired, too awake. Asking if I wanted the window open, a blanket. Wondering if I was pregnant (no, just in my forties with thyroid disease). Wondering if I was experiencing early menopause. Telling me how I would regret not having a baby, how I would be haunted by my loneliness in old age.

I sought the wisdom of women, the alchemical chamber of the body. I went inside the cavern of the mouth, cavern of the earth, cavern of the womb, cavern of the hive, the dark space where creation becomes. I became a lady of the animals, a pythoness, a bee. The threads knotted in my throat. Each dream I had was an embroidery.

I stitched to talk to thunderstorms inside my sister.

I stitched to gather an aesthetic. Kate Bush in her red billowy-sleeved dress. Marshes. Floods. Marie Redonnet's *Hôtel Splendid*. Marilynne Robinson's *Housekeeping*. Train tracks. Train cars. The dream of hopping on and racing toward a new horizon, a certain kind of loneliness. Existential loneliness. And independence. The exhaustion and resourcefulness of deep silence. The train tracks just across the street from my childhood house. The trees there too.

After her death, I found a small safe broken open inside my sister's bedroom. The paramedics had searched for heroin there. But the core of her was not drugs. The core of her was an image of kittens. A purple pouch full of gemstones. My sister was a lock of hair. She was Hungarian tarot cards. She was a picture of her parents on their wedding day. She was a burlesque matchbox. She was a collection of stamps.

I found a flight pattern, a ritual, a trace, a beehive, an infinite knot, a way to write and revise and revise again. A way to resentence the sentence my sister and I had been handed. To change the story is to tell the story. To enter a wound. To face it again and again until

NEXT PAGE: Andrea Rexilius, detail of *Plant Lady*, 2019. Collage with thread and paper. | Photo: Andrea Rexilius.

we are transformed by it. Until we see it clearly and move it through our body.

My sister and I are not related. Not by blood. But we are the same age, and we are both named Andrea. Her mother and my father married when we were ten. I always thought of her as part doppelgänger, part mirror image. I was jealous that her mother had fled with her in the night, brought her to America. For me, it was the opposite. My mother fled to California but left me behind in Chicago with my dad. My sister's mother is dramatic, emotional, talkative, whereas my own mother is pragmatic, quiet, and emotionally reserved.

I began stitching lines instead of writing them.

A line is a descent, an expedition into the underworld, into the root system of language.

It marks an act of sensing, of perception translated by the realm of the mouth.

I titled the stitches *Séance of the Bees.*

I think of bees as the narrative force of the stitching. The voice or sound or energy that marks the flight pattern of my asemic lines.

I modelled the lines on bee flight patterns. Figure eights and other erratic movements to and from the hive. I traced a field of flowers inside the roof of my mouth as sentence. Felt its bloom. The drops of dew. Blood and other eroticisms of fluid. The nectar of the line.

My sister died three days after her thirty-eighth birthday. She overdosed three times and was saved before the fourth and final overdose, which took place in the middle of the night in front of her bathroom mirror. She was covered in water.

I think of Emily Dickinson's "certain slant of light." How it falls across the page, or cloth, as insight.

This is an act of seance. How an essay calls embers to surface.

I began to think about viruses in narrative. How various hatreds or phobias arise from and spread through the spell cast by a single sentence or story repeating and replicating itself throughout a culture, how origin stories, mythologies, and fairy tales unfold to reinforce cultural ideologies.

I thought of my sister. An immigrant. Without access to adequate mental health care. At the receiving end of her mother's co-dependency. A woman alone and in pain.

The channel we travelled to meet each other. Our bee flight path. International, over an ocean, across electricity, a storm. Against an abyss of language. Our bodies tightly woven in shared clothing and bedrooms. Our tongues unacquainted with one another's syllabic sounds.

A divide. That which severs. That which disrupts. Passage as a rupture or reworking of a wound. A mark, as in a scar. A suture. To see the passage as intermediary zone.

In Engadine mythology, the human soul is said to turn into a bee upon death. I began to create embroideries as a way to speak. To grieve for my sister and to grieve for the bees, becoming silent, becoming swarm.

Thread pierces the front of a piece of cloth, severs the mark between what is seen and unseen, as it resurfaces, gathers a bit of what is invisible. This backstitch is how a line loops the ineffable into what it speaks. A gap, hesitation, caesura, wound, lacuna, tear, marked by this piercing.

Andrea, with whom I was thrown together under such bizarre circumstances, knows my heart's home. Just as I will always know and recognize the heart of her.

A row, a doctrine, a division, a limit, a gesture, a mark, a horizon, a lineage, a tongue. Multiple lines becoming maps, nests, homes, patterns, rituals, boundaries, containers, passages, rooms.

B
Beatrice

The palm of the hand is a map of lines. Two sisters speak not in tongues but in double helixes. Patterns of movement. Passages from foreign-language textbooks. Tethered. Doubled to a mirror image, an Andrea, our DNA.

All language, but perhaps especially poetic language, contains a front stitch and a backstitch. The wound and its utterance.

Light enters the wound. The door of one sentence closes, and the door of another sentence opens. The period as a point of puncture. An entry wound between one realm to the next.

The mouth acts as nest to bind together the threads of being. The self (or I) as needle, which pricks the air with sound. *I*, a bird's beak, a boundary. The mouth, continent of self, and all that remains outside of the self, as other, as air. What is swallowed versus what is sung out.

My sister, a woman from Budapest, Hungary, intercepted my flight pattern, my lifeline. Sang out inside my mouth. Sang out as a twinned self. As my name. As another being that was my being.

A sentence, an embroidery, a lineage, a rhizome, a thread, a divining rod, a root, a branch, a wingspan, a twig, a nest, a woven structure, a pattern, a repetition, a ritual, a metaphor, a eulogy, a song.

I resurface. I return from the underworld. By way of this line.

Andrea Rexilius, detail of *Lady Death*, 2019. Collage with thread and paper. | Photo: Andrea Rexilius.

A NEEDLE AND A VOICE

JENNY BARTOY

I poked myself with the needle. The blood beaded on the soft flesh of my index finger, a perfect dot the colour of my embroidery thread. I sucked on the wound and kept quiet.

At my Catholic elementary school in northern France, girls and boys had been separated for a craft session. In the back of the classroom, the boys each nailed together a bootjack from short planks of wood. By the wall of windows, the girls each embroidered motifs on a square of white canvas stretched in a wooden hoop.

My teacher, in a taupe turtleneck and dowdy wool skirt, a "spinster" we still said thirty-some years ago, leaned over my wooden desk and showed me how to lick the floss to thread it through the needle's eye. Fixated on her saliva coating my thread, I attempted a few awkward stitches under her watch.

The idea of drawing with thread on fabric appealed to me, but it was slow, torturous work, the needle stabbing my fingers as often as it did the cloth, the resulting crooked stitches far from the straight lines I desired. I eyed the boys hammering with gusto, rowdy with the pleasure of bringing home an instrument to use through the muddy season. Around me, hunched over their hoops, the girls murmured. I stared at my fabric and felt the distance between our genders. What was the point of learning to embroider, except to sit still?

My maternal grandparents' flat in Lille hosted a collection of embroidery samplers. Dating back to 1864, they showcased the needlework of my grandmother and every woman in her maternal lineage, up to her great-grandmother. Alphabets and decorative borders in delicate faded stitches on crisp linen were framed in white and grouped on the fuchsia wall of the playroom.

On the bottom line of each sampler, an embroidered name, city, and date underscored the design. *Age 8, age 7,* the stitches proudly spelled. Through their mastery of embroidered lettering, these girls had been permitted to shine. I imagined them stitching through the decades, hair neatly brushed and adorned with ribbons, starched pinafores and lacy socks, legs that dangled from uncomfortable chairs in which they sat straight as a stern teacher walked the rows of bowed heads, surveying their work and shushing chatty rogues.

The samplers provided material evidence of my ancestresses' self-control. The unattainable precision of their work both awed me and sparked my reluctance. I didn't yet possess words like *feminism* or *patriarchy,* but I knew I didn't want to belong to a world that expected girls to perform such perfection.

In my family's house in rural France, a sewing machine reigned atop a repurposed dining room table in my mother's room. Most of my childhood memories feature her sitting there, black mane framing her intent face, bright eyes focused on a project. The rest of our house—where my father received his business prospects and my mother served gourmet meals she cooked while she oversaw homework and teetering toddlers—shone, posh and presentable. But her sewing room was everyone's favourite.

Cold and drafty, the space had once served as a grain-storage workroom, the walls still raw red brick. A patterned sisal rug, found in an acquaintance's attic, covered the cement floor. My younger brothers and sister and I often lounged on the pair of brown-corduroy couches my parents had bought when they first married, or we practised on the hand-me-down piano. In a corner, my mother stored her fabrics on industrial metal shelves rescued from a failing business—fluffy fleece and a rainbow of coarse linen, batting thick like blankets, and silky linings. Buttons and zippers rattled in the metal of Danish cookie boxes, stacked in a tower against the wall. Her pins and needles lived in emptied mint tins. My mother made do. No allowances were made for the comfort of her space.

My father doled out cash like rations. Each month, he came into my mother's room and demanded she show him her accounting records. Dutifully she would march toward him and, as his lanky frame towered over her and a frown creased the space above his tortoiseshell glasses, she presented the notebook in which she tracked her every expense: food, bills, the occasional pair of shoes for a growing child. I had overheard my father tell my mother she was useless. "Who would ever hire you?" he had mocked when she proposed finding a job to allay our family's finances. Looking over her orderly lines of numbers, he always found an expense over which to grill her. "I'm not made of money," he would snap, and my mother clammed up.

Strangely, my father never singled out purchases of fabric or yarn. My mother knew better than to spend a fortune on extravagant yardage, but there was a lightness to her when we walked into the small shop in town crammed full of colourful bolts, rows of ribbons, and boxes upon boxes of pretty buttons. Perhaps my father found this domain appropriately domestic or else too foreign to police.

At the mercerie, I dipped my fingers in bowls filled with iridescent mother-of-pearl buttons, caressed the display of toggles, shank buttons, and snaps, and watched as my mother felt the heft of cloth, checked measurements she'd jotted on a scrap of paper, and assembled the notions she would need. I knew that, from the assortment of items in the paper bag the merchant handed to her, she would concoct a perfect garment as if by magic.

I remember telling my mother about the bootjacks, about my envy, although the details of what happened next have frayed. Perhaps she took me to the barn behind our house to find a piece of wood. She may have helped me saw a *V* into that bit of two-by-four and attach a resting stand with the vigorous bang of a hammer, nails pinched between her lips like the ball head pins she used for hems. Or maybe she did it herself, her focus on efficiency and accuracy rather than on the fumbling of my small hands.

Vivid in my memory is the bootjack, on the floor of our mudroom. From nothing, my mother had created the object of my desire. My mother could do anything—except stand up to my father.

During the week, while my father worked and we kids were at school, my mother hosted a stitching circle in her sewing room. She showed these women how to sew flannel pajamas, how to cut the tissue-paper patterns she had unfolded onto the floor after sweeping aside baby toys and matchbox cars, how to assemble a lamé acrobat costume or a tulle-and-satin princess dress for the school's Mardi Gras carnival. She taught them how to patch a tear, to knit and purl, to make buttonholes. In this group, my mother offered a preview of what she would later become: confident, expert, disarmingly charming, funny through self-deprecation—attributes that proved dangerous around my father.

For my eighth birthday, I'd received a tiny Singer sewing machine, and she showed me how to make a beret. Together, we traced in chalk and cut two plate-sized circles from a remnant of navy boiled wool, one with a smaller circle carved out like a donut hole. I basked in this rare intimacy with my mother, who was usually absorbed in my younger siblings or chores. She guided my hands as I fed the pinned layers of fabric through my little workhorse of a machine. Following her instruction, I flipped the fabric inside out and marvelled at the result: a functional hat. On my own, I made more berets in plaid woven with a stripe of forest green. Blushing, I gave one to each of my grandfathers—my father didn't want one.

My mother allowed me to select a dusty-pink-and-maroon floral print from her shelves so I could sew myself a skirt. I fashioned a large tube, hemmed the top and bottom and, with a safety pin, ran some elastic along the waistband. The skirt brushed my toes. Donning it over my jeans, I paraded around the house and into my mother's sewing room. She must have expressed pride at my success, but I remember only her frown as she looked up from the seam ripper, with which she jabbed at some half-sewn pants. "That's fine for dress-up, not for wearing in public." Rather than motivating me to hone my sewing skills, her declaration—and its implication of imperfection—crushed me. I lost interest in my sewing machine.

In the evening, I often heard my parents fighting in my mother's sewing room. My father cornered her there and locked the door. When I knocked at dinnertime, he simply barked, "Your mother is busy," before slamming the door in my face. If I argued that it was late on a school night, that my siblings needed to be fed, he ordered me to stop talking.

The more my parents fought, the more I escaped into books. I loved fairy tales, particularly Hans Christian Andersen's "The Wild Swans." After eleven brothers are turned into swans by an evil stepmother, their sister takes a vow of silence and collects stinging nettles, from which she secretly knits sweaters that will save her siblings from the curse. Nettles lined the path of the orchard next to our house, and I had felt their sting on my ankles, soothed the white welts with icy water. For many years, I would recoil from learning how to knit—my mother briefly tried to teach me—because it seemed inherently painful. Reading the fairy tale again and again, I imagined the sister's defiance. Stitch after miserable stitch, her quiet hope sustained her, that she could save her brothers.

As my heart pounded for my mother's safety on those nights, I would smile and tell my little brothers and sister that we could have a cereal dinner. By insisting on normalcy, by refusing to cower or turn despondent in the face of dysfunction, I performed my own act of defiance. I sensed that, regardless of any pain, I too would knit nettle sweaters for my siblings, for my mother.

Back then I often spent part of the summer in the south of France with my paternal grandparents. I can't remember my father's mother ever not stitching. Her single mother had been a seamstress, the job a lifeline for the two of them during World War II. My grandmother, her hair up in a strict chignon, a long cigarette balancing from her lower lip, would squint at intricate crochet or lace projects. Perfection was her hook.

My grandparents bickered, sometimes explosively. They had agreed never to separate, having both been children of divorce and stigmatized for it. At breakfast, my grandmother would brew Earl Grey tea and cover the teapot in a cozy she had sewn from floral toile. On the dark oak table where my grandfather sat in his terry bathrobe, she set a teacup on a dainty saucer with what looked like two aspartame pellets. I eyed the pills suspiciously. I had overheard that she gave him Valium without his knowledge, because it quieted him. "He's just unbearable without it," she had told my mother, who for a moment stood unblinking.

At lunch during those summers, my grandfather would slice a baguette and, across the Provençal tablecloth, hand a piece to each of his four granddaughters with a wink. But if our noise level irked him, he boomed, "Children should be seen, not heard." My cousins, sister, and I straightened on our cushioned dining chairs, lips tightened in obedience, not unlike my grandmother at the end of their arguments.

After the meal, my grandfather would nap in a lawn chair under the cherry tree, a book splayed open on his chest. We were admonished to stay out of the yard and to be quiet. During those oppressive hours, when the sun glared and the cicadas grated, my grandmother would pull lanyards, paints, and puzzles from the closet, and we girls stifled our giggles lest they wake up our grandfather. In the shade of the patio, I discovered beadwork and loom knitting and began an elaborate cross-stitch landscape I would never complete.

Decades later, I found the unfinished design crumpled in a storage box, the threaded needle still pinned to the calico fabric, a ruby line of floss meandering its creases, and the heat came back to me, the stillness of those afternoons. Like my grandmother with her pursed lips and arthritic fingers hooking yarn into compliance, I had gravitated toward stitches as a channel for the noise within me.

If intergenerational trauma can alter our gene function, as scientists now believe, can the muscle memory of many thousand hours spent stitching in quiet also be passed on? Maybe my father overlooked my mother's fabric purchases because the act of putting needle to fibre ran in his own blood, sacred.

Years after I had become an adult, my mother's fortitude finally overtook her fear. She left my father and found a job in upholstery to make ends meet, her sewing skills leveraged to keep a roof over my youngest brother's head. Not long after, I became estranged from my father, my silence a better boundary than all my attempts to be heard.

From my teens to my thirties, I hadn't touched a needle, choosing to escape in writing and drawing instead. But when I became a parent and quit my job to focus on my two sons, I pulled from a closet the Singer machine my mother had offered me years before—another birthday gift, full size this time. I sewed napkins from fat quarters and aprons from thrifted linens, pouches and purses and potholders and myriad burp cloths for the babies born in my circle. Sewing allowed me a form of expression while I tended to my children, a tangible act of presence despite my absence from the workforce. Once again, I had gravitated to stitches to channel the noise within me.

My sons grew up to the hum of a sewing machine, as I had. Was I turning into my mother, I wondered? I had become dependent on my breadwinning husband and resented it. "I am not your father," my husband reminded me in our disagreements, the pain in his voice underlining the sting of my accusations. Whenever we faced an expensive dilemma, he told me, "You decide," since I ran our bank accounts. He expected me to speak up and supported both my returning to work or my staying home. "You decide," he said.

For my mother, stitching mastery had compensated for the lack of control in every other aspect of her life. I'd been privileged to make a choice—to focus on my children for a time—but my unease remained; perhaps I had erased myself and opted for fabric and thread to fashion an excuse. While my domestic challenges did not parallel my mother's, in my mind sewing remained fraught with layers of subservience.

My boys learned to stitch at a young age, experimenting with simple embroidery and designing their own Halloween costumes. Side by side at the dining room table, we assembled the fabric version of the dolls they drew on printer paper, and as their little fingers stuffed fibrefill into soft crevices, their eyes lit up at seeing their imagined creatures come to life. While I delighted in their creative bliss, mine had slipped out of reach.

I had launched an online shop to sell the modern household textiles I sewed while my children coloured or played with Lego at my feet. For so long I had equated the memories of my mother at the sewing machine with her subordination and loss of agency. I fretted—could I separate stitching from silence when the two were so tightly woven in my DNA? I felt compelled to rip up inherited patterns, and work seemed the solution. My cutting mat held centre stage in our home, piles of bright cottons littering every surface, threads curling across the rug like some hairy invasion as I built inventory and, with obsessive attention to detail, fulfilled custom orders.

But untold hours at the sewing machine didn't net me much of an income or soothe my anxiety. My moral ambivalence about sewing had transformed a gratifying creative outlet into a chore. Turning my turmoil into a tiny business hadn't shaken my discomfort—it had only unravelled my joy.

A few years later, my husband and I left our sons under my mother's watch and travelled to New York for a conference he would attend for his job. I was pregnant again, this time with a daughter. I had longed for this pregnancy, desperate for a girl to join our family. My need felt visceral, tugging at me from within. I planned to keep working after the birth—freelance, so I could be home. Before my youngest son began kindergarten, I had decided to return to editorial work.

At the Museum of Modern Art, I stumbled upon the Louise Bourgeois exhibit, a retrospective of the French American sculptor and printmaker. A massive bronze spider anchored the museum space, an ode to Bourgeois's mother, who'd been a weaver of tapestries. The artist had sketched and sculpted pregnancy and motherhood in various iterations, often with a baby suspended over its mother, leashed to the womb with the umbilical cord like a balloon string. Bourgeois's trademark crimson ink and thread hinted at both the passion and violence of the maternal body. As I strolled through the muted-grey rooms of MoMA, I cradled my burgeoning belly and vibrated with astonishment at every drawn curve, every carved form, as if the artist had manifested visually my most private considerations.

In a section entitled "Fabric of Memory," I discovered Bourgeois's fabric books, which, deconstructed, appeared like patchwork on the museum's walls. As she neared death, the artist had repurposed her old garments and household fabrics—and the memories attached to them—for her art, hanging or stitching this cloth into sculptures, using it as background for her printmaking, even embroidering it with subversive messages and angry squiggles not unlike the tangle of arteries linking my baby to me.

As visitors admired Bourgeois's stitched work, leaning in to examine the cloth, studying the curator's descriptions, I glimpsed how the wrestling of fibre into object, into art, could transform quiet obedience into clamour. From something as mundane as stitched kitchen towels, Bourgeois had brought an international audience to consider her lived experience. Her voice and memories were woven through the fabrics on the wall for us all to ponder and absorb, so we would then remember her.

Textiles and needlework had impacted the mothers in my lineage both as a silencing and an awakening, a tether to the home and an emancipation. This thread connected our generations more than blood ever could. Sitting still with cloth and needle, we had all made something out of nothing so we could be remembered.

After my maternal grandparents died, their belongings were split among family members. My mother ensured the collection of embroidery samplers came to me. "You care about them the most," she said.

I cut linen mats and framed the stitches of my ancestresses in black. In the small bungalow I called home on a hilltop in the Pacific Northwest, the samplers came to adorn the walls of our loft—the space served as both my office and a playroom for my three children.

A quilting magazine had become my primary client, for whom I edited articles and patterns. Like my mother, I had funnelled my sewing skills into sustenance. I adored the editorial work I performed from home and became smitten with the craft itself, a rebirth of my creative spark. I dreamt in log cabins and flying geese and assembled quilt blocks like textile puzzles. Before gifting my patchwork creations to friends and family, I embroidered personalized labels—cursive names and dates in backstitch on a corner scrap—and felt gratitude for this skill that allowed me to etch my love in thread, to leave a trace for memory to find me.

After our family had moved to the United States in the 1990s, my father returned to France alone to pack up and sell our old country house. He gave away all the children's costumes my mother had sewn, even the carnival ones she'd hung in her closet, those that showcased the fanciest sequins and raw silk, those that had required hours of steady handwork. "Gave away" was what my father said with a shrug, but I wondered if he'd just stuffed them in garbage bags along with broken toys and stacks of old homework he'd unearthed from our drawers.

More than his blows or his financial abuse, in the pantheon of my father's offenses, his jettison of the costumes may have wounded my mother the most. I understood her bitterness. The loss seemed unquantifiable, the discarded heirlooms as precious as the hope and joyful escape involved in making them.

On a wintry afternoon, my daughter saw me knitting at my desk. To help myself focus on the manuscripts I edited, I made garter-stitch blankets, large stripes of colour in uneven rows, rote stitches that didn't require thought. The bilateral hand movements kept me from fidgeting, from grabbing my phone when the work challenged me, when my brain wanted to quiet the struggle with distraction.

"Will you teach me how to knit, Mommy?" Louise asked.

"Maybe when you're a little older," I said. She was only three. Her slender shoulders slumped, and disappointment veiled her face.

The bottom drawer of my daughter's dresser, which I'd painted fuchsia, with mother-of-pearl knobs, was lined with a jewel-toned rainbow of sweaters knitted by my mother. They arrived in the mail every few months, with pristine stitches and intricate cables, and my daughter rejoiced, even though she rarely wore them, preferring to run wild in a T-shirt in frigid weather.

My mother also sent dress-up costumes she'd sewn: bee, ladybug, tiger, firefighter. She'd done this for every one of her grandchildren. They knew to ask her for their most far-fetched wishes. She'd built a grandfather-clock costume for Halloween, molded medieval swords and armour from latex foam, and sewn clothes for their favourite dolls. This grandmother that my children knew could do anything. They had no inkling that she had stitched herself whole from scraps.

Her knitting desire rebuffed, my daughter shuffled to the dress-up trunk and emptied most of its contents onto the carpet before choosing a glittery unicorn horn. She twirled in my peripheral vision, a blur of neon cape.

I relished the privilege of being available to my children as I free-lanced, but my computer absorbed me, pages of words unravelling in front of my eyes, demanding my attention. I often shushed my children. "Find a quiet activity," I begged, frustrated. Guilt needled me—I was not present enough, my children should be allowed to make noise.

"What's this?" my daughter asked that night, about the spindle in "Sleeping Beauty." For our bedtime ritual, she often picked a book of fairy tales reimagined for the preschool crowd. I provided a rudimentary explanation of a spinning wheel, how it could turn fibre into yarn. As we cuddled, we read about the princess's curse and how this vivacious girl has to behave herself and never touch a spindle, lest the whole kingdom fall asleep for a hundred years.

A spindle typically consists of a simple wooden rod, not sharp enough to prick anyone. Yet the independent princess manages to poke her finger and ruin everything. In this cautionary tale, a girl is only good when silent and still. I inhaled to loosen the knot of anger in my stomach. No matter how often girls might be shushed, our defiance could not be snuffed out. It had always been the thread we could tug to pull ourselves forward.

But the concept seemed foreign to my daughter, that a girl would be punished for her curiosity. Nonplussed, she swept a strand of uncombed hair from her face and turned the page. I examined her inquisitive frown, the translucent skin on the curve of her nose, and I could see the marching arrival of a future in which she would soar, her own person, no longer needing me or our nightly cuddles.

"How about we try embroidery tomorrow?" I suggested then. The desire surprised me, lurking within, to sit quietly with my daughter and teach her this skill.

"Yes," she gasped. Delight danced in her dark eyes, more at the thought of doing a project with me, I suspected, than at the excitement of playing with needle and thread.

I sensed a remnant of my old reluctance, which hadn't surfaced when I showed my sons how to embroider, focusing instead on their tactile experience and fun. I shook it off. Louise could use burlap and a yarn needle so she didn't hurt her fingers. She would stitch whatever she wanted, the process an exploration rather than a punishing prescription.

I wanted my daughter to be loud. To be heard. I wanted her to demand to make the bootjack if all she was offered was the embroidery hoop. I wanted her to know she could do both—she could do anything. And if stitches appealed to her, I hoped she would embrace the quiet, knowing she could find force and a voice there.

My mother and I agreed to embroider our own samplers to join the collection on the wall of my loft. Instead of *age 7*, the numbers 66 and 43 would accompany our names. We both opted for designs that broke with convention: she picked a gothic alphabet vined with colourful flowers; I chose to stitch modern typography with white floss on natural linen.

In honouring our matrilineal tradition, we would also celebrate our individual voices. Maybe one day Louise's sampler would join the lineage on the wall—she would decide.

BREATHE

JAN WADE

Born in Hamilton, Ontario, in 1952, Jan Wade is a Vancouver-based mixed-media artist whose career spans over thirty years. In 2021, a retrospective of Jan's work titled *Soul Power* marked the first solo exhibition by a Black female artist in the ninety-year history of the Vancouver Art Gallery. The penetrating political, social, and spiritual commentary embodied in Jan's mixed-media paintings, assemblages, and sculptural objects, many of which involve found objects, is exemplified in her embroidery masterwork, *Breathe*. What appears below is a collage of Jan's writing, images from *Breathe*, and an excerpt from an interview between Jan and interdisciplinary artist Deanna Bowen. We are grateful to Jan for her new writing on *Breathe* and to the Vancouver Art Gallery for allowing us to excerpt from *Jan Wade: Soul Power* (Vancouver Art Gallery and Information Office, 2022), a book everyone should own.

BREATHE

The journey of an artist, of any human being really, is never a straight line. We zig and zag and, within our journey, we fall, hurt ourselves, hurt others, and then either get up and learn from our mistakes or stay down. Words are something that always helps me to see myself, and others, and the world more clearly.

Magic, under the moon; her light penetrates us all, tossing us who knows where.

The Emancipation Day Picnic—known to me, my siblings, aunts, uncles, and cousins as the "Coloured Picnic"—was a real highlight of the Black community in Hamilton and the surrounding area. We all gathered in a park (I wish I could remember the name) on Lake Ontario. Lots of cars, barbecues set up, picnic tables in the woods, and a giant old wood pavilion where you could get ice cream and lemonade until you were fit to burst. There were games: three-legged race, pin the tail on the donkey, horseshoes. All the men—Dad, and uncles, and friends—sat drinking beer, telling tall tales and laughing, while the ladies—Mom, aunts, and friends—chatting and getting potato salad, fried chicken, etc. together for the big feast.

All the cousins hanging out and checking out how each other had grown in a year, little cousins checking out teen cousins, laughing, admiring fashions and hairdos, and after the picnic feast, all would gather in the old wood pavilion and dance the night away, showing off the moves, shaking down, celebrating the sun and fun of the freedom day.

I was always drawing and very visual as a small child, and that has never changed. I think the first real artwork I ever saw was a Japanese kabuki print. On the few occasions that I had a babysitter, her name was Lorna, and she was Japanese. She took me to her family home, which had a very large closet door. When you opened that door, there was a poster of famous kabuki actors on the inside. That is the first art I remember seeing. This made a huge impression on me. My lifelong love of Japanese prints began.

Otherwise, I was most likely the first person in my family exposed to art at the Art Gallery of Hamilton, when it was out at McMaster University. I went there on a couple of school trips. I doubt anyone in my dad's family had been there—an unwelcoming "white space." My family in general were not into visual art per se, nor that world. They were into music, though. My dad and I especially shared the love of music. And all of my dad's family sang.

I was born an artist, as far as I know. The visual was always of interest to me. I was drawing before I spoke. I was a late talker. My mom says I did not talk baby talk; they were beginning to think something might be wrong, but then one day, I just started to talk like I had just been observing and waiting until I knew how it was done, then out it came. And this makes sense—out is a big part of my process. I look and watch. I read and research. I meditate and see. And then, all of a sudden, something pops out. I don't always understand it at the moment, but I do not like to censor myself. I know it will become clear, either right away or eventually.

I don't know if it did not occur to my parents, or they might not have seen being an artist as an option for me. I was Black and female. It might not have been the sort of thing they could see as a possibility for me. Sad, but true.

I have been working on the pieces for *Breathe* since about 2009 or so (and other embroidery pieces before this). At first, I was just following an instinct, a whiff of an idea. I only had time to work on these pieces as opportunity permitted, and then they became, more and more, a necessary meditation practice, a frantic prayer.

NEXT PAGE: Jan Wade, *Breathe*, circa 2004–20 (from the exhibit *Soul Power*, Vancouver Art Gallery, 2021/22). Embroidery on linen. | Photo: Ian Lefebvre, Vancouver Art Gallery.

Textiles have always been a part of the creative language spoken within Black cultural traditions. I grew up surrounded by quilt makers in particular. I do not quilt myself, but my embroidery works are heavily influenced by quilting and the rhythmized textiles of African and African American / Canadian textile traditions. I have also been influenced by the works of the Indigenous Peoples, beading and basketry and weaving in this country and the Americas. Jazz and modern art, heavily influenced by Africa and African American arts, have also been a huge influence in my life and work. The Southern Black aesthetic was the first and greatest influence in my life and work. My great-grandmother and grandmother (both born in Danville, Virginia) were my first teachers. It led to my interest in the traditions of making, handed down from generation to generation. This is how I came into art and making.

I view the embroidered pieces I am making for this project as a form of medicine, almost an incantation. They are a meditative balm; they calm my heart and mind. They help me to stay in touch with joy in these times of stress and social change. We seem to be walking into the unknown. I also feel linked to my ancestors in their struggles and their lives.

But like the best magic, this work helps me to hold hands with them. In the times of our greatest despair, we must look inside and find a source of an almost radical joy that will keep us lifted and ready for battle. A joy that will help us survive and thrive. This has never been truer than this moment. It is a visual poem.

In my formative years, I was familiar with the fear and sorrow of racism and hate and the role this sort of energy played in my own community and family. My father's family came to Hamilton, Ontario, at the turn of the century as part of the Great Migration. There was always segregation and racial violence and unjust social practices to contend with. These were things that grown-ups in our community rarely spoke of to children. They did not want to scare us. But children know. We hear of things and usually suffer through our own generational experiences of bullying (by other children and grown-ups alike) and the social rituals connected to race relations here in Canada in particular and in the world in general.

I started by working on pieces of spare cloth—nothing goes to waste in the homes of poor Black people. It is a form of generational ecological consciousness practised by the disenfranchised. I began creating very colour-infused pieces that helped to steady my nerves and resolve. It kept me in touch with my Beloveds.

When Eric Garner was killed by the police for selling individual cigarettes on a sidewalk, he kept saying, "I can't breathe." And from then on, I thought of these pieces as breathing, as breath itself, every stitch a mantra of the unacknowledged joy of breathing. A calm, moment by moment, breath by breath, stitch by stitch—a mantra, a spell-poem that would and could help sustain my own life. And our right to life.

NEXT PAGE: Jan Wade, *Breathe*, circa 2004–20 (from the exhibit *Soul Power*, Vancouver Art Gallery, 2021/22). Embroidery on linen. | Photo: Ian Lefebvre, Vancouver Art Gallery.

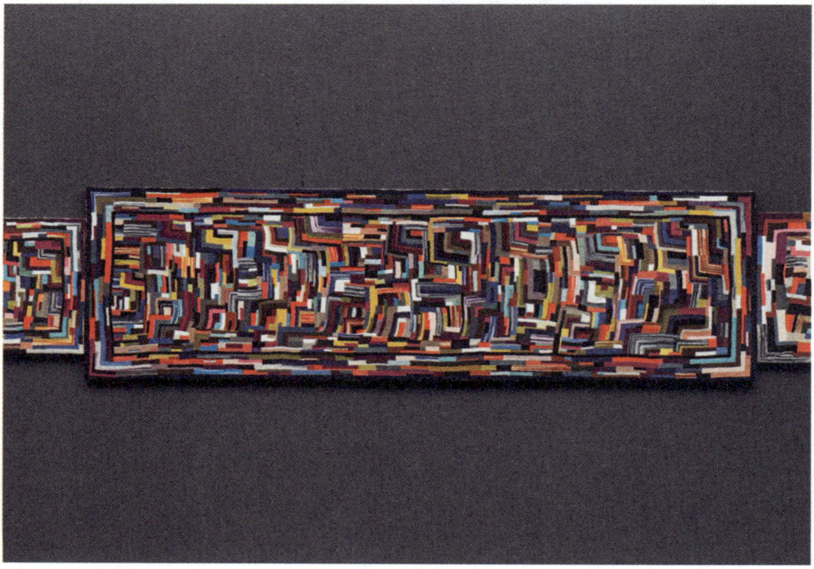

Jan Wade, *Breathe*, circa 2004–20 (from the exhibit *Soul Power*, Vancouver Art Gallery, 2021/22). Embroidery on linen. | Photo: Ian Lefebvre, Vancouver Art Gallery.

DB: So, tell me about the process for the *Breathe* work.

JW: I started working on these pieces years ago. And at first, they were much more like the formal quilt patterns rooftop and log cabin—and they did have a sort of nostalgic power over me, like a bit of a spell.

Everybody has grown up with a quilt of some kind that came from their grandmother, their great-aunt, or their mother. They're almost shamanistic, that energy of women, of the family—a protective energy.

And, as a matter of fact, I had given one years ago to artist Mina Totino. So, I said to the Vancouver Art Gallery, "Mina got hers stretched, and I love the way it looks." So, they replicated that for this installation.

The first time I saw them stretched was when the gallery acquired seven pieces for their collection. I walked into the gallery, and they were leaning upright against a grey wall, and together they looked like a giant abstract painting.

But the whole point was that I wanted them to have rhythm so that when they come together, it looks like a flowing river or the fluctuations of breathing. I wanted them to move. So, after making them for years, this was the first time that I saw I had succeeded. Before, I'd only seen them in my lap.

DB: Yeah, that's cool.

JW: I decided at some point after Eric Garner was killed that I wanted them to resemble painting a bit more, so I switched to this abstract patterning and decided to call it *Breathe*. I wanted them to look like paintings. There are twenty-eight hanging in the exhibition, but I've actually made seventy.

DB: They remind me of Jacob Lawrence, Gee's Bend, Betye Saar—

NEXT PAGE: Jan Wade, *Breathe*, circa 2004–20 (from the exhibit *Soul Power*, Vancouver Art Gallery, 2021/22). Embroidery on linen. | Photo: Ian Lefebvre, Vancouver Art Gallery.

JW: Yes. I started doing these before I even knew about the ladies from Gee's Bend.

DB: How did you come to embroidery?

JW: When I was about five or six, I was in the kitchen and my grandmother was embroidering daisies on an apron. I always wanted to learn how to do whatever she was doing. So, I watched her do it a few times, and then I tried it myself. And then I didn't use it for years and years.

When I was older and attending a comprehensive arts high school, all of a sudden, I bought some embroidery thread and started making things. I also worked with embroidery when I was in art school, but after that, I didn't embroider anything for years. When I got my first Canada Council grant, I went to the fabric store Dressew in Vancouver, and they sold embroidery thread for ten cents a skein, which if you're an embroiderer, you know that's like being a goldsmith and finding gold on sale for fifty cents a pound! So, I ended up spending four hundred dollars.

DB: What is that, like four thousand skeins?!

JW: Yeah! I carried them in a green garbage bag, and on my way home, I almost started to cry, because I began to regret spending so much money. And the skeins sat there for about a year. Then Dressew had a sale on linen. When I learned how to embroider, they said never embroider on anything but linen or silk, right? So, there was the linen, and I just started to embroider. Some of the things I embroidered are huge, and then I started the narrower patterns, traditionally patterned pieces, and then eventually—maybe about 2002 or 2004—I began the more abstract painting kind of things. At first, I just wanted them to look more like painting than textiles.

DB: When are you going to do a painting like this?

JW: Well, I think I already have. I don't necessarily feel like I have to paint like this because I embroider like this; I think of the embroidery thread like paint on thread. I always saw the connection between African American quilt making and abstraction, and never more than when I saw the generational work of the women of Gee's Bend, whom I call the mistresses of modernism. They are incredible; their work is full of mastery. I don't think I was particularly interested in the masculinity of abstract art, as I feel every being has a combination of the masculine and feminine, but of course, the accepted histories of art are about a historically dominant male art practice. Perhaps subconsciously I was expressing my own version of a female abstract expression, one that has traditionally existed within the confines of the home, to bring it to a place where it can be seen just for what it is: powerful and full of colour and flowing space.

DB: You know, when we're thinking about painting or drawing, we often talk about the hand of the maker. I'm wondering if you're thinking about that beyond any other concerns around Gee's Bend, abstraction, the ways in which Black—

JW: I'm just thinking about what I bring to it. You can get insights and ideas from other people's work, but I'm not interested in mimicking or emulating. If I take it on, it's got to be interesting. I think, *I would like to play with that a little bit.*

I'm always challenging myself to break up whatever I've known before, to destroy and make something else, do something else with it. And I guess that's what I mean. I can look at the ladies from Gee's Bend, I can look at anybody, but I'm not interested in copying their work. I'm interested in what I can bring to something they've shown me a pathway into. I think that many artists do that—a lot of art is transformation, really.

KNIT INTO BEING

LAURA COK

I had not yet started knitting for the baby when I miscarried. This was fortunate: no half-formed booties for nonexistent feet; no needles I could never again touch, stranded mid-row in an eternal limbo, which frankly was just too on the nose for my situation. But without a project, I was left with nothing to do with myself. I had no way to channel my grief, which was an immense love wheeling around in space, formless and without pity, filling every corner of every room yet having no shape. Nothing I could pin down and locate.

"If this happens again," I said to my husband—naive, then, to think that I'd so easily get pregnant, even if I lived in fear of its loss—"I can't have a project for it. I have to knit something new now, when there is no baby, for the general idea of a baby." The ur-baby. As if, like in certain theologies, my baby were floating around somewhere miles above our heads, ready to slot down pinball style into our lives. In my worst moments, it still felt like this: as though my baby were out there somewhere, alone, and I could not get to her.

So, I started knitting a blanket. I found a naturally dyed yarn in a yellow similar to the blanket I'd had as a child (and still have somewhere in my closet, the edges long disintegrated). I made an error early on but discovered it too late, and the lacy zigzag pattern was too difficult to pick back. This meant I couldn't turn the blanket into a gift, should my own baby never appear. I could not hand over a misshapen object, even though it was the kind of mistake, like certain private forms of pain, that was visible only to me. A child, certainly, would not notice.

Knitting for children is a frustrating prospect, because everything needs to be washable. You can't use the fancier wools: the natural fibres, the cashmeres, the hand-dyed silk spun with alpaca and wound in the next town over. You lose the tactile pleasure of knitting enhanced by the small inconsistencies, the occasional unevenness in your hands suggesting a human being at their spindle. But babies throw up; they dribble and leak fluids from every orifice. It's all very well to spend hours constructing a sweater out of the softest alpaca, with a raglan collar and colour-contrasting cuffs, but if I give it to a newborn's family with the admonition that it be gently hand-washed, it will end up as closet decoration. I went through a lot of superwash, which could go in the washing machine and air-dry. This felt like a reasonable compromise to me, but then, as established, I didn't have children.

On the other hand, children are small, which means knitting for them is immensely satisfying. You can finish a sweater in a matter of weeks, a pair of booties in an afternoon. When I was learning to knit, I made several tiny hats with rolled brims and little bear ears and gave them to the first cohort of my friends beginning to have children. Swap out the colours and swirl the top, and I could have a blueberry hat (for my cousin's child), or a pumpkin (sent through international mail to my childhood best friend). I made mittens and booties to match, though I stopped making the former when my pregnant co-worker gently informed me that the latest research did not recommend covering babies' hands. I'd thought we were still protecting them from scratching themselves, but apparently this interferes with development. Well, I was younger then, and there was a lot I didn't know.

When my first niece was born, I threw myself into projects. During long car rides, I made her a cardigan in a beautiful purple-flecked taupe, with a professorial collar and slightly uneven plastic buttons. She could be up there at the baby blackboard, giving the other babies homework assignments in chalk. She could hold office hours with her stuffies. I bowed to the necessity of acrylic for a striped sweater when she was six months old, but I didn't have a strong sense of babies' proportions, and the sleeves were comically long even on my lanky Dutch niece. It's the bellies that throw everything off, determinedly rotund. By the time her sister came along, I was over a year into a very depressing story of needles (for drawing blood rather than knitting), invasive ultrasounds, mood-altering hormones, and failure after failure. She would have to wear her sister's hand-me-downs, though I did have my eye on a pattern with colour-worked ducks around the collar for her first birthday. There were just so many steps required to begin again.

But the blanket. I had not forgotten about it, half finished in a beaten-up Ziploc bag. I had begun it at a time I knew I was not pregnant. Two weeks out of every month, I have that blessed, hateful clarity; the other half of the month is limbo, potentially pregnant but more likely not. Schrödinger's pregnancy for half the year. In theory, creating this for a generic baby would mean that, should I become pregnant and miscarry again, the blanket would not be tainted by the failure, since it had not been begun with that baby in mind.

The pattern was a car-seat blanket, meant to be lovingly tucked around one's securely fastened child, not dragged around, worn as a cape, trodden upon, covered in vomit, demanded, or too well loved. An unfortunate irony, given that the whole point is for the blanket—and the child—to be well loved. I could have knitted a square in garter stitch, used chunky washable yarn in colours never found in nature. But that would have been too easy, and the point of this exercise was not to be easy. It was to prove myself worthy. It was to do the difficult thing.

The difficult thing dragged on. Failures stacked up on top of each other. The statistics (90 percent of couples conceive within the first year!) and anecdotes (someone's cousin went on vacation and finally relaxed!), once mildly annoying, became actively antagonistic as we found ourselves on the wrong side of the story we'd been telling ourselves, a story with an easy start, hand-knitted teddy bears and tiny clothes piling up by my side. My mother was on bedrest toward the end of her pregnancy with me, and while pinned in place, she'd cross-stitched the Christmas stocking I use to this day, turning the abstract idea of me into something tangible. She'd had a difficult time, her own losses stacking up, so I suspected it might not be easy for me either, and yet I always knew the end of her story: three living children. If I could see the end of my story, the middle of it would be easier to handle. But I couldn't face coming to the end of the blanket, weaving in the ends and blocking it in place, only to stuff it in the closet with a handful of children's books acquired in more hopeful times. Pausing meant it was still in progress, still chugging glacially forward. At any moment, I might take it up again.

The blanket had been languishing for a while when I got the inevitable news from a friend. When you are a woman of a certain age, and especially when you are a woman of a certain age struggling to conceive, the world around you bursts with fecundity. Rabbits hop across the landscape. Green shoots peep above the March mud, relinquishing the fallow season entirely. Ducks waddle, followed by their trail of yellow fluffs. And every friend, neighbour, co-worker, and former classmate gets pregnant.

She was a close friend, one I'd had for over a decade, which in my peripatetic life meant more than most. I didn't have kindergarten friends still hanging on; I didn't have a high school posse languishing into adulthood, reliant on reminiscences of bad behaviour. She and I had had innumerable brunches together, had cried over grad school classes together; she'd seen me through bad boyfriends, and I'd seen her through the guy who got drunk and peed in the corner of her bedroom. But our lives were never going the same way at the same time: when she was happily in a relationship, I was single and lonely; when I was flush with my first full-time job, she was miserable and earning $28K a year. When I moved in with my now husband, she was breaking up with her long-term boyfriend. And just as my doctor let us know that we should start thinking seriously about IVF, she was pregnant. After only a few months.

When she told me, I texted back a string of emojis, unable to form words. I managed, barely, to resist throwing my phone across the room. It took me almost four months before I rallied enough to ask about the due date. She told me then quickly and kindly changed the subject. She let me know that she would understand if I couldn't come to her baby shower; she did all the things infertile people hope our friends will do. And I was still paralyzed by grief.

I assumed I would need some time to come to terms with the situation and be able to properly express my joy. I did not think I would need *that* much time. Other friends affirmed that I should do what was right for me, that I had a right to my feelings, and if she were a true friend, she would understand. And I agreed, to a point; she did know what I'd been through, and she understood the reason for my silence. But that didn't mean it wasn't hurting her every time I failed to ask how she was feeling, if they'd thought about names, or whether I could see an ultrasound. I'd thought I could be a better friend; I'd thought I would be stronger. I'd thought I would be further along, in more ways than one, but the cyclical nature of grief meant taking a few feeble steps toward stability only to end up right back where I started.

Throughout this silence, I started IVF. Added to the near-weekly internal ultrasounds and blood draws were multiple daily injections administered by my husband, who always brought me a fistful of

M&M's afterward. I ate them with one hand, the other holding an ice pack to my bruised belly, which was beginning to bloat enough that I feared someone would ask if I were pregnant. But the physical aspects of treatment had an unexpected benefit: suddenly we felt like we were making progress. These were tangible actions we could take—my husband concocting the medication at our dining table like a mad scientist, me crossing each dose off our calendar—that meant we were doing everything we could.

There were more statistics: How many couples have success with a given treatment. How many embryos it takes to create a child. None reassuring when you've found yourself on the wrong side of them at every previous juncture, but hope was not required. Positive thinking was not required; baby dust and sticky vibes, those sentiments so popular on internet boards, were not required. Only the physical actions counted: showing up to my appointments, taking my vitamins, injecting a medication that left red welts on my skin if any spilled out of the needle. Now I had the freedom to be as depressed as I wanted, and the only acts of hope I needed were the visible ones. Saved not by faith but by good works. So much was out of our control: how many eggs I could grow, how many embryos would survive, and whether any of them would lead to a living child. But this work of our hands was ours.

The other weekend, looking for distraction, my husband and I drove to a small town half an hour outside our slightly bigger town. We went into a yarn store, one of us a fair bit more excited than the other. I bought some washable yarn in soft, gender-neutral colours that I thought my friend would like. Later, I cast on a sweater, something suitable for a very small person in the very cold months.

Every mistake I make, I carefully pick back and correct. I think I will make booties in contrasting colours. With every stitch, I am caring for her, for the baby, for our friendship, even if I'm doing so in silence. I hope they will keep the baby's feet warm. I hope she will understand what it means.

CARRY THE LAND

BETTINA MATZKUHN

Camped by the Yukon River, I watched its great satin ribbon unspooling. It was seamed with overlapping spirals, upwellings and undertows, ridges of ripples, and mysteriously smooth circles. As an artist who works in fibre—embroidery, fabric collage—I translate the world through the surfaces of thread and cloth. I found it hard to look away from the river's surface. It had such intention that even as I stood in or floated on it, I became part of its agenda en route to the sea. I grew up by the ocean and know that sometimes the ocean holds still. On a calm summer evening, it holds quite still. But it can change its mind, balancing only briefly between active and quiet, when the tide turns or when the wind veers around. The river has a different certainty: continuous motion. The river doesn't change its mind.

In 2019, I was thrilled to be selected to participate in the Canadian Wilderness Artist Residency: twelve artists in six canoes, paddling over seven hundred kilometres of the Yukon River. In my sixties, I was the

oldest by several decades, but I found my co-paddlers to be talented, thoughtful, perceptive, and sublimely good natured. I especially found it comforting to be in the presence of so many creative people. No one seemed to think it odd when I stood up to my knees in the current, drawing the shifting patterns on the surface of the river. Drawing imprinted the intersecting lines more deeply than a snapshot; I traced glimpses of the water's passage by hand.

I also became interested in drawing the outdoor gear we used on the trip: the buckles, snaps, drawstrings, and cords. We set up camp every evening and took it down the next morning, folding tent poles, wrapping up equipment, stashing our own items in waterproof bags. Everything was compact. Our camping outfit was sturdy, practical, and made from synthetic materials, stuff made out of non-renewable fossil fuels. I thought about how my fondness for being warm and dry was permitted by this extensive technological padding. Neoprene, nylon, Gore-Tex, polyester fabric with a thermoplastic polyurethane coating, moisture-wicking synthetics kept me snug. Over those weeks, I became more aware of this dichotomy as I drew the water, land, weather, and flora along with aspects of our equipment. It became the seed for my textile series *Gear*.

Like many craftspeople, I think best while engaged with materials. Back in my studio, I asked hiking friends if anyone had an old backpack they might part with. I received two packs that were beyond repair and found a few more online. I removed them from their frames and separated pockets, straps, and belts. The packs were vertical forms, echoing the human body. Some pockets had openings like mouths. Shoulder straps formed wing-like arcs. Belts hung limp or held padded tabs out in invitation. I lived with them, tacked to the wall, for weeks. Paper drawings pinned onto the assorted parts allowed me to think through how embroidered imagery might fit into their forms. I began to see how the stitched pieces could be incorporated: literally strapped onto the packs, inlaid between

Bettina Matzkuhn, *Avalanche Lilies*, from the series *Gear*, 2022. Hand embroidery and paint on linen, used backpack. | Photo: Ted Clarke.

Bettina Matzkuhn, *Sunsets*, from the series *Gear*, 2022.
Used backpacks, hand and machine embroidery, fabric collage, paint. | Photo: Bettina Matzkuhn.

webbing, stuffed into pockets. I wanted the tough nylon packs to lug fragile ecosystems.

Embroidery has always been my creative language. It is opulent, and I cherish it for its capacity to reflect the natural world. My embroideries are largely created with natural materials—silk, linen, cotton. Yet I understand that "natural" is riven with human impact. Working by hand with fibres is an ancient technology, but textile production has new complexities both in its manufacture and its significance. While the cotton embroidery thread I prefer is from a company that adheres to Europe's Oeko-Tex environmental standards, I don't know the specific provenance of the linens I work on, the novelty threads I find at yard sales, or the silk and rayon threads I enjoy. I sometimes use unbleached cotton for painting the ground I will embroider, but I can't tell how or where the cotton—a crop notorious for voracious water and pesticide use—was grown. And then the fabric paint, albeit used in small quantities, is acrylic, a polyethylene-based plastic. The contrast of natural and synthetic seems clear but is more complicated than the two terms might indicate. If one of my *Gear* pieces is tossed into the dump, the silk and linen will decompose, but the pack itself will be an artifact far into the future. I am not making art to keep these objects out of the landfill. A few repurposed backpacks have no impact in that sense. But they may open other conversations.

By incorporating landscapes into backpacks, I wondered about what it would mean to carry the land. Perhaps to not take it for granted or see it as simply available for human pleasure. I silently chafe when I hear people talk about "doing" a trail; it strikes me the way a lout brags about "doing" a girl. I understand this is jargon, a mere expression, yet language carries cultural attitudes. I prefer to visit, explore, encounter, or, best of all, to revisit a trail. I have no bucket list or boxes to check off; I am content to walk the same trails many times. I carry the memory of a ridge in a certain light, flowers fragile in a breeze. More recently, the memory of slopes full of pine beetle–infested trees, or cedars and berry bushes turning brown in heat waves. Could the packs carry these recollections?

On the Yukon residency, I looked at unfamiliar landscapes—aspens dangling roots from an eroded riverbank, tilting trees—and wondered how much of this was just the normal hurly-burly of the land reforming itself in the constant geologic dance of weather, water, and rock. Or was what I saw accelerated by climate change? Was this enough snow for that time of year? Was this small rill overflowing from a glacier's too-rapid melting? Were the wild-strawberry leaves turning red from frost or because of drought? I can see symptoms of stress in familiar landscapes, so I assume it has spread.

Since outdoor materials are sturdy, I wondered about designing works that people could handle. Art galleries do not usually want viewers to touch the art, but I have made interactive work before and found people to be keen and respectful. It is a way to literally engage the viewer. *Choke*'s compartments unzip to reveal fire and increasing smoke. *Burn* opens to glimpses of fireweed seeds, flowers, and leaves as they begin to heal the smoking ground. *Early Melt* is overstuffed like a round yellow sleeping bag and contains the turquoise ring of a thawing alpine lake. A friend told me how the sound of a zipper makes her think of a tent opening and prompts the happy anticipation of a view. But what sort of views will we unzip in five, ten, fifty years?

I designed some small works for children, installed lower to the ground. These pieces open to reveal a hook-nosed spawning salmon or a reclusive pika—both species directly affected by global warming. The salmon because of a lack of water in spawning areas or water that is too warm. The pika, who lives in rockslides high in the mountains, is accustomed to cold; she cannot regulate her body temperature if the environment is too hot. She can move up the mountain gradually, but 2021's heat dome in British Columbia irradiated even the high alpine with forty-degree temperatures. I sewed the pika in her habitat, mouth full of grasses to dry for the winter, and hoped that the dark corridors in the rocks afforded some relief.

Bettina Matzkuhn, *Oceanus* and detail of *Oceanus*, from the series *Gear*, 2022. Used backpack frames, hand embroidery, and paint on linen. | Photo: Ted Clarke.

I understand that these works contain experiences of places I have visited but not where I dwell. I visit trails, mostly in parks, which have been removed from other human uses but reserved for recreation. I am glad that I won't find an open-pit mine in my favourite park, and yet I understand that Indigenous Peoples lived here, took care of the land, and were part of it without decimating it. Perhaps that is how I can think of "carrying" the land: to have a reciprocal relationship, the carrying and treading in balance. I am not part of the land in the sense that I live in a large city and do not make my living directly from it. Yet I am of it in that I miss it when I am away. The smell of low tide and the shapes of the mountains orient me. I am of it in that I owe it my respect and attention.

The hiking trails near Vancouver have seen an explosion of foot traffic, especially in the COVID-19 era, when being outdoors is seen as good for mental and physical health. I have cherished time in the backcountry, seeking escape from the lockdowns, like many others. Yet I see and worry about tree roots that have been so travelled they are eroding, trampled shortcuts, the sheer numbers of feet widening and expanding trails. "Viewing nature as optional—as always elsewhere or in the past—denies us, or spares us, the work of caring," writes Kyo Maclear in her book *Birds Art Life*. She describes noticing and appreciating nature on many levels. My hiking companion and I carry a spare garbage bag, in case we notice garbage on the trail. We pack it out—used diapers, takeout containers, bottles. It is a small gesture of care. I think of embroidering more backpacks and wonder how I could carry out other kinds of damage: a clear-cut, a tailings pond, or an oil spill?

The frames I removed from some of the backpacks sat on my studio table, lashed together. I thought about what they might support. Paddling the river, it is easy to imagine it as a great flowing circle. It literally is part of one, not on a horizontal plane, but in the great hydrological gyre of ocean, evaporation, clouds, rain, tributaries, and river running down to the sea. In reproductions of old maps, I have sometimes seen a river drawn around the parameter, containing the world. "Okeanos (Oceanus), him who with his sleepless current encircles the whole earth," Aeschylus writes in *Prometheus Bound.* I tethered the metal frames to each other in a circle and embroidered a river full of the patterns I had drawn in my sketchbook while standing in the Yukon River's flow. The ripples and spirals flow throughout the cycle of a day. The structure is tenuous, with bits of rope and fabric tabs and snaps holding it together. My *Oceanus* flows around some cobbled-together hardware instead of the whole world.

"Rivers are the open veins of the Earth," in Wade Davis's words, and the Yukon and its tributaries form the same branching patterns as the blood vessels in my body. I consist of 60 percent water—the river is in me. Travelling down the river, I was in its element, all my fancy gear notwithstanding. The rain ran down my neck, the wet mud of the riverbank sucked at my feet, and the canoe rocked in the push/pull of the rapids. I found my internal clock abandoned city time and became attuned to the angle of light on the water and to my stomach. Time became quite untethered as I watched the layers of clouds pass over me and make fleeting shadows on the land. The river ran on its own time, entirely oblivious to me.

The pace of hand embroidery is removed from modern life: threading the needle, piercing the cloth, the incremental accumulation of stitches. Five backpacks hang on the studio wall, flaps up. I make drawings of them with various additions, even things protruding from pockets. Weeks pass by as I work on other projects, but still I look at them, thinking. Finally, I opt to line them with sunsets I have admired in different parts of the country. Despite the flare of glorious colour, a sunset precedes a descent into darkness. Oceanus's many daughters, the Oceanids, tend to the Earth and the water. I tend to bits of cloth and thread. Like the sea, I hold still sometimes. But when I work, the needle keeps moving. It keeps my mind moving—sometimes in circles, sometimes in parallel ripples, sometimes in strange undertows. I dream of the river's surface.

ABOVE: Bettina Matzkuhn, *Choke* (third opening), from the series *Gear*, 2022. Repurposed outdoor fabric, hand and machine embroidery, paint. | Photo: Bettina Matzkuhn.

RIGHT: Bettina Matzkuhn, *Choke* (first opening), from the series *Gear*, 2022. Repurposed outdoor fabric, hand and machine embroidery, paint. | Photo: Bettina Matzkuhn.

NEXT PAGE: Bettina Matzkuhn, *Choke* (second opening), from the series *Gear*, 2022. Repurposed outdoor fabric, hand and machine embroidery, paint. | Photo: Bettina Matzkuhn.

A CHICKEN TRIES TO FLY

CIARA FARMER

In the back of the grad school classroom, my throat is tight, my vision swirls, my hands are clammy, and I can't steady my breathing. *Fuck*. I bring my right knitting needle behind my left, loop the yarn around it from the back to the front, pick up the loop on my right needle, and slip the remainder off the left needle, pass the new loop through to form the knot of a knit stitch. And then I do it again. Again. Again. I'm knitting a sweater with a Western-inspired fringe across the bust. I still can't breathe. *Run*, my brain demands. I sprint down the hall in tears, the ball of yarn shoved into the front of my shirt so I can continue to produce frantic stitches.

The decision to go to grad school for urban planning was my own. My family didn't pressure me into it, and formal education is not the standard for my friends. I started undergrad three years "late" after multiple European backpacking and acid trips. A major in anthropology and a minor in creative writing meant I had very few required classes. I took any class that caught my eye: Television Theory, Sociology of Cults, History of Drugs. I pursued education for education's sake. But I feared spending my life anxious about money. Worried about housing. Worried about paying for dental out of pocket, or worse, not being able to get my teeth cleaned at all. So, I applied to complete a master's in urban planning at the University of British Columbia almost solely because I wanted to find a good job after school.

As a kid, I had learned the basics of knitting from my grandma, and a knitting class seemed like a fun way to manage the stress of my last term of undergrad and the wait for grad school admission news. At the end of the term, I had a successful honours thesis and a mustard-yellow circle scarf that I immediately unravelled and knitted into a hat that I'd actually wear. I spent the summer before grad school in an old armchair at the Woodrack Cafe, drinking chai and knitting hats for everyone I knew, with the National's "Not in Kansas" playing on heavy rotation.

I applied to grad school for financial stability. I did not apply to the program because I was deeply passionate about urban planning. It never occurred to me to fear the outcome of spending two years in a master's program.

Prior to applying to grad school, I'd considered myself unencumbered by social norms and pressure, at least when it came to my career and lifestyle. When I did ultimately attend undergrad, I felt freed by the vastness of knowledge available to me. The pressure to be conventionally successful mounted only in my final year. In undergrad, I wrote papers about juggalos, the rise of LSD, and *Buffy the Vampire Slayer*. In grad school, I felt like my classmates bought their personalities from a mail-order catalogue, while I struggled to make my vintage clothes work for professional mixers.

Panic attacks—the hyperventilation, the crying, the flushed skin—used to scare me. Some people rush to the hospital the first time they have one, certain they're dying, but I've had them as long as I can remember. I can't say when they started. Only that I can remember being a very young child standing in the hallway of my childhood home, my knees collapsing under me, my vision fuzzy, unable to bring oxygen into my lungs. What I wish someone had told me about my panic attacks is that they are feeding me information about my surroundings.

Find something you can hear, something you can smell, something you can touch. This is a grounding exercise. It brings you into contact with the present moment during a panic attack and out of your swirling head. Something you can hear? The dull clicking of bamboo knitting needles. Something you can smell? Wool. Something you can touch? The effortless repetition of the knit stitch passing through the needles once, twice, three times.

Chicken Run, a stop-motion animation film released in 2000, follows a cletch of chickens and a geriatric rooster convinced he's the sergeant of a battalion all living on a Yorkshire egg farm. In the opening scene, the chickens attempt to orchestrate a *Great Escape*–like exit from the farm. This, we understand through a montage, is in response to inhumane conditions on the farm, the best of which is that the chickens are forced to produce eggs that will never become babies, the worst of which is punishment of death by axe for any chicken who ceases to lay eggs.

In the film, Babs, one of the modelling-clay chickens, knits. I mean, she (or a human working on set, probably) really knits tiny projects with modified toothpicks made to resemble knitting needles and thready yarn. The movie never tells us why Babs knits. But I know that Babs knits because she is trapped in a situation that she can't remove herself from, and knitting is something she can do to create a sense of agency.

Mr. and Mrs. Tweedy, the detestable couple who profit from the chickens' suffering, intend to turn the chickens into pot pies using a machine. The chickens and their labour are commodities for the Tweedys to profit from, with the ultimate goal being industrialization of the process. The Tweedys are a misdirection, though. The actual antagonist in *Chicken Run* is a Yankee-Doodle dingus of a rooster named Rocky. Rocky is a dreamboat from the "land of the free" who arrives on the farm after he is shot from a cannon, which leads the chickens to believe he can fly. After he trains them (unsuccessfully) to fly, Rocky leaves them trapped on the farm. The Tweedys are repugnant and murderous, but they never claim to be anything else. Rocky is insidious because he is initially incredibly alluring. He's suave, handsome, charismatic. The audience believes in the version of freedom he is offering. It's exhilarating to imagine a chicken could fly to freedom.

Find something you can hear, something you can smell, something you can touch. Something you can hear? The swish of the yarn passing over the knitting needles with ease once, twice, three times. Something you can smell? The earthy cotton of your project tote. Something you can touch? Fuzzy mohair fibres on your fingertips.

Panic attacks are a blessing. They tell me in no uncertain terms that something is deeply amiss. *Run.* I sprint from my grad school classroom and duck into the empty student lounge. *Breathe.* Tears puddle in my eyes. I don't know why I'm panicking exactly; nothing specific is happening. I form another knit stitch. And another. The panic attack is a slap across the face that forces me to consider my feelings, to identify a trigger. This is something I am otherwise quite bad at. Panic attacks happen when my body wants to pick flight or fight, but I'm stuck, trapped. Specifically, when I'm suffocated by the weight of my choice to pursue a degree that means nothing to me because it feels like my only other option is lifelong poverty.

See, the chickens thought the enemy was the Tweedys, and I thought the enemy was the poverty that I assumed I could avoid with a master's degree. Rocky is the false hope of the American dream; he's the diversion that I think is better than being on the bottom rung of capitalist society, and then I turn around and find that he's just capitalism with a pretty face and it's too late to take it all back. The chickens trying to fly? That's my grad school. The work I naively produced for someone else. The work I produced because that was what I was supposed to do to break free. And the work I never wanted to do in the first place.

The chickens are worth more than their capital; they deserve a life where their value lies just in their right to exist. Babs deserves a life where knitting is not an escape (at one point, she literally knits a noose) but part of the abundant life where she spends time on things that really matter to her, where knitting is not her only reason to live. Ultimately, Rocky returns to the farm and helps the chickens escape. He abandons the falsified version of the American dream, because it never really existed. Not in the way it was promised. It was just a way for people to get rich from the misery of others. At the end of the film, we see Babs on a makeshift swing made from a pair of old tighty-whities whose elastic is slack from wear. She knits as another chicken pushes her on the swing. The camera pans, and there are chicks, finally born from the eggs that used to just be food for others. In school, the geriatric rooster is their teacher, and the hens are enjoying the sun.

So, Babs the chicken knits. I knit. Knitting is subversive. Knitting is rebellion. It's rebellion in a society that wants your time, your labour, your output for profit. It is the production of an object that you can buy for less than the cost of the joy of creating that object. It's selfish in the way that we should all be selfish. And when Babs is free, she still knits, because when knitting doesn't need to be subversive anymore, knitting is just joy. And when people suggest

I monetize my hobby, I say no. I refuse to let the pervasive millennial "side hustle" take my hobby. My act of rebellion. I knit for me.

Find something you can hear, something you can smell, something you can touch. Something you can hear? Your own measured breaths matching the pace of each stitch. Something you can smell? The steamy tea you sip in between stitches, once, twice, three times. Something you can touch? The cool metal of small embroidery scissors shaped like a bird.

HUNDREDS OF THINGS A GIRL CAN MAKE

LORRI NEILSEN GLENN

A spool emptied of its thread, nails hammered into its flat end. Old yarn Mrs. Hinchey saved for you from the church basement sale. You are in the corner of the schoolyard in the foothills of northern Alberta, your fingers busy, and before the last bell, you have finished the cord and tied it into a bracelet. You barely know who you are, let alone what you can make with your hands.

When I saw the little bookcase tucked in a corner of a museum shop in Duck Lake, Saskatchewan, my heart lifted. Musty hard-bounds and local community histories, bifold flyers, stapled recipe booklets, and coil-bound family memoirs. One of my Métis great-great-grandmothers is buried in this area; could I find a mention in here of Kitty, or perhaps a cousin?

That summer, when the gathering at Batoche ended, I took to the secondary highways and dust-plumed roads of northern Saskatchewan to track down place names and cemeteries I'd found in the archives. When some of my ancestors left Red River in the late nineteenth century, they'd found land and safety in this part of Saskatchewan. Many of the hamlets listed in historical records have now withered, leaving only a few staunch farmhouses at gravel-road intersections, so when I reached Duck Lake, it was a relief to see a museum filled with local artifacts.

I pored over the books and pamphlets on the shelves. No luck. No Kitty Budd.

But look: a salmon-coloured cloth-bound volume, *Hundreds of Things a Girl Can Make.* The Musson Book Company: Toronto, 1941. The pages were as thick as starched fabric. I was raised in Western Canada in the middle of the last century, but this book was new to me.

Do you want your own smelling salts? A cloth cover for your postcards? Raffia serviette rings? It seems you can stitch, embroider, bead almost anything if you put your mind to it. Countless crafts made of cardboard, paper, and cretonne. This book would have been for the generation between mine and my mother's, but it pulled me back to my own days of paper and paint, scissors, rags and thread. Days of paper dolls and paper fortune tellers, those origami creations with jaws that opened and closed between our fingers like bird beaks: one, two, three, four, lift the numbered flap.

And wait—no mention here of a spool knitter? Whenever my mother emptied a spool of thread, I'd nab it and pound four short nails into its flat wooden top, wrap string around the outside of the nails, then systematically loop each lower string over the upper with a nail or my pencil, wrap around, loop, wrap around, loop, until the coil that grew out the other end of the spool was as long as I was tall. Who taught me? Probably a friend. We made bracelets, necklaces, colourful cords to weave into the spokes of our bikes for the July parade. I didn't know they were called French knitters; I thought they were someone's serendipitous discovery, another example of cobbling together what was available to make something from nothing. My hands can do this. What else can they do?

You open the bedroom door to find the parcel from Winnipeg with Gram's birthday surprise. You've never seen a doll so beautiful. She's cradled in a large silk-lined box, wearing a crocheted skater's dress and hat and a hand-stitched fur-lined cape. All white, like the Olympian Sonja Henie, the star of the movie. You have been learning how to figure skate, and when you're about ten, Gram will teach you how to crochet. You're left-handed, and it will be a long session.

Years into my marriage, not long after Gram died, I found a bag filled with wool, crochet hooks, and basic patterns at a Mennonite thrift store. I learned the patterns for basic squares, made several dishcloths and one or two small throws for the couch, but soon tired of squinting at the tiny print on the glossy pages. It reminded me of the tedium of picking out notes for a new tune on the piano. Since I already had the basic stitches down, the "notes," if you will, I preferred to compose basic designs on my own. I could never take on a complicated pattern like the dress Gram crocheted for my doll that year. Besides, for me, crocheting was as much about spilling off nervous energy, mulling over writing dilemmas and family crises, as it was about creating usable items. When our eldest son entered his skating phase—on a board, that is—I crocheted skullcaps for him and any of his sk8rboy friends who might want one. It turned out many did, and for a time I could crochet one cap in an evening. A lot went into the stitches, a kind of Madame Defarge's register, not of French revolutionaries, but of the anguish and turmoil of life stories in draft form: a rebellious teen and his dance with drugs, a functional-needs child and an ineffectual school system, the petty dramas of an often-toxic academic workplace—slipped, looped, and chained through my fingers and out into the world.

Today, as I stepped out the door to take the dog for a walk by the shore, I grabbed my old wool hat, something I'd crocheted with thick-gauge yarn years ago, extra roomy at the back to hold in my hair, now fully grey. Who knows where the skullcaps ended up?

Where is he? Usually, you are inseparable, but tonight, Gord is late for the gathering by over an hour. You and Joyce arrive at the rink early and join the campus crowd. When he finally arrives, you pick him out from a distance by the animal design on his sweater. "I don't know what happened," he tells you. "I blacked out." His speech is slurred. You sink into the shoulder of his sweater, smell the oil of the wool. This has happened before. Should you be marrying this man, you wonder? Does he drink that heavily?

Back then, everyone had a Cowichan sweater. When you're an adolescent, of course, "everyone" means the people you want to hang around with. Years before Gord, when I was in high school, I was a drama nerd, one of a group of students directed by a legendary fireball of creativity known as Mr. Hinitt. We bused to drama festivals around the province of Saskatchewan, bringing home hardware for our dedicated work on his lavish and meticulously planned Shakespearean productions. We sewed doublets and trunks, capes and flounces. I helped only with cutting and basting, but when we all worked together, the energy was electric. We'd come to school early and stay late. My friends Pat and Mardi, along with Wayne and Carol, all had Cowichan sweaters, each distinguished by its particular pattern. I ached for one, but they were expensive in the stores; it would take years of babysitting to afford one.

At that time on the Prairies, few knew the history of Cowichan sweaters or the many ways opportunists exploited the work of the Coast Salish knitters. I was middle-aged when I learned about my Ininiwak ancestors, people known as the Homeguard Cree, who worked for the Hudson's Bay Company in northern Manitoba in the eighteenth and nineteenth centuries. The HBC has profited for decades from the sale of Coast Salish sweaters. As an adolescent, all I knew was that I wanted one for bonfires in the woods on cool summer nights or for the long walks to school on crisp October mornings. I wanted to be like everyone.

When I came home one afternoon to find a lookalike sweater on my bed, I was elated. Then mortified. It was and it wasn't a Cowichan. The wool didn't have that distinctive lanolin odour; it was processed. The pattern—I can't recall which animal—had a uniformity that spoke of a knock-off. My mother raised four children virtually alone; my father travelled extensively. She worked part-time as a nurse for extra money he rarely allowed her, and I knew then she must have spent weeks after her hospital shifts knitting this sweater. I wore it dutifully, ignoring the pitying smiles my friends gave me. When I moved out of my parents' house, the sweater disappeared.

Years later, about to finish university, Gord and I had already chosen a ring. When I went on a long summer trip to Quebec, we exchanged letters, and I called him long distance every night. For several days my phone calls went unanswered. It was his father I finally reached. "Gord is gone," he said. "Gone?" "Yes, dead." I don't remember much after that. Only the confusion—how could he pour out his heart to me in letters and then put a gun to his head? It was quick: a single shot. Twenty years later, after I tracked down his sister, I learned the autopsy had revealed a large mass in his brain that would have caused blackouts and severe depression.

All night through the mountains in a borrowed convertible, and here you are: it's morning in Gastown. You walk the streets—he, determined to find the friends who promised you a bed somewhere in one of these buildings, you, intoxicated with freedom, the delight of a spontaneity you never knew growing up. From an open window, the sounds of Ginger Baker, maybe? On the street, buskers wearing tie-dye. Macramé and beads hanging over a shop door. Macramé everywhere. Your long denim skirt is wrinkled; your legs were tucked under it during the long trip. Why are you worried about wrinkles? You need a shower. Yesterday, before you left, you'd ripped apart the seams on an old pair of jeans and stitched in long flannel panels from an old plaid shirt to finish the full-length skirt. A maxi. It's 1970. Your bottle-blond hair is so long it reaches your ass; you need no makeup. You've been together a few months; his friends call you his shiksa—forbidden flesh. You are performing flower child, a young teacher unaware of how mainstream she is. Unaware of so much.

At first, it was flower-pot hangers, using three basic knots—four, if I count lark's head knots, what I think of as macramé's version of a blanket stitch. Square stitch, half hitch, and spiral. Hemp. Cotton string. Jute. Sisal. Then a pouch, then a godawful vest for him after the two of us return from Vancouver. A year later, after the tears, after my gut sensed that life as a fever dream in the age of Aquarius would not sustain me, after he walked to the highway and held up his thumb, I found myself provinces away, teaching art to adolescents. I ordered dowels and ropes of various thicknesses, sat in my apartment above Winnipeg streets at night, tying knot after knot after knot. Several mats and wall hangings later, some decorated with clay baubles fired in the school kiln and some the length of a door, I was married to the history teacher, happily setting up house in an old four-bedroom apartment on Wellington Crescent.

The gift is huge, and you hope they didn't spend too much. Your elder son and his new wife wait as your younger son—already thirty, how did that happen?—adds a few logs to the wood stove, your husband of over forty years refills everyone's coffee, and the dogs pace between everyone, hoping for a ball of tissue paper to fetch and rip apart. The Pogues in the background, then Chris Rea. You've all emptied stockings and are into the "main" gifts. When you take off the wrappings, you are careful as always to salvage what paper you can, even knowing your eldest might roll his eyes. You've always been a string and wool and paper saver, a habit you picked up from your mother and her mother, Gram. When the layers of tissue are off, your hands fly to your face, and you burst into tears.

"Here, I want you to have this." On one of my trips to Winnipeg, my aunt Kay emerged from her tiny overstuffed bedroom with a bag filled with fabric. Nearing one hundred, she was trying to give things away. Inside the thin plastic bag was a trove of cotton quilt pieces. "This was Mother's," she said. "She died before she could finish it."

Her mother, my paternal grandma, Eleanore, died shortly after I was married but before I could ask her about our ancestry, in particular her mother and grandmother's. As a young woman, Eleanore had watched a riverboat burn off the wharf at Warren's Landing outside of Norway House in Manitoba, her own mother trapped inside. It was that story and Aunt Kay's prompting that took me to the archives, to northern Manitoba, to cousins' homes and into a 320-year past—years of research and travel and discovery—to complete the pattern of my background.

I knew of my Scottish roots (Gram) and my Irish and French roots, but—as other people have learned—some roots were hidden, often intentionally, like invisible stitches behind a smooth seam. Kay knew, and when she was nearing her hundredth birthday, she asked me to find out what had happened to Catherine Kennedy Couture, her Cree/Métis grandmother, my great-grandmother. What happened in that fire? How was it that Catherine and others died while the family, including Catherine's daughter Eleanore, watched helplessly as the boat burned to the waterline?

Later, Eleanore married and moved south to Saskatchewan, where she planted a huge garden. I remember the tall stakes of sweet peas. A large cellar full of preserved fruit and meat. Quilts in every room. I was too young to appreciate the evidence of all her handiwork around me. I recall visiting Kay there, along with her daughter.

When my husband and I moved to Nova Scotia in my thirties, I took a quilting course and managed to sew a small baby-sized quilt, but I stopped after that. Once, in a tourist shop, I heard a customer complain about the price of locally made quilts, and I blurted, "You know, that works out to be about five cents an hour."

Knowing these hand-stitched creations take countless hours, and knowing my challenges with both patience and instructions, I paused that day when Aunt Kay handed me the bag of quilt squares and asked, "Would you be able to finish this?"

"I'll try," I said. But I knew I couldn't do it justice, and the pieces sat in my closet for a year or two. After our son married J, a talented sewer and designer, I brought out the bag, hesitant to ask. Someday, if she had time, and only if she had time, I wondered, would she perhaps sew these pieces together?

And here it is now, in my hands, backed, stitched. An heirloom, whole and beautiful, a part of the family. Before Kay died at the age of 106 and 8 months, I told her that J had finished the quilt for us and sent her a photo. Kay was a woman proud of her Métis roots. When she gave me the quilt pieces, she gave me remnants of my past, and by urging me to solve the mystery of her grandmother's death, I was able to help us both learn the story we had never known.

Oh! Don't forget the tie-dye T-shirts for your friends, the string art you learned in order to teach your students, the satin-lined cape and black pants hand sewn for your first-born, who had to be the Count from Sesame Street *for Halloween. Or the canvas doormats you hemmed and then painted with brightly coloured fish for the porch in your first house in Nova Scotia; the year money was tight, and you scoured second-hand stores for silk and satin anything to sew patchwork scarves as gifts; the countless dishcloths you knitted and crocheted for charity. Innumerable hand-stitched repairs of denim knees, jacket arms, broken seams.*

So much growth; tears and repairs. So many seams.

And now, years on, you know it's time. Some things you need to let go.

To cast off. Like the dark warm sea and coil of blood and breath that brought you here, faith in their presence at your crib before your tongue knew how to name, clasp of guiding hands, your precious doll, and the gingered breath of your dog. They won't come back. Belief that words will give you what you ask, whispers of your schoolyard mates whose maypole orbits leave you alone in space. Let go of these.

While you're at it, first supple brush of mouth on mouth, hot satin of his belly on your own, all you thought you were until you saw your face, plans to make the perfect family, raise the perfect child. Illusions. Veils. Severed seams. Let them go. Let go of certainty that what you water dig plant feed will take root, what you tie knot stitch fold will cover, secure, protect, repair, endure long and long, years into years ahead. Untie.

Carry threads of light and leave no shadow.

WHAT STORY?

CARRIANNE LEUNG

In early 2020, I was writing a novel that I had started just a couple of months before. As the number of COVID-19 cases rapidly increased and the provincial government mandated the first lockdown, I tried not to panic, believing the official missives that it would be only a few days. Work meetings were cancelled, shops closed, and outside my window, the once-busy street emptied of people and cars.

The ordinariness of tasks that filled my hours fell away. There was nothing to do but wait and try to calm my nerves. I thought this would be a good time to focus on finishing the novel, since we weren't allowed to do anything else. But I was wrong. The pandemic introduced new distractions. Two weeks stretched into months. As time dragged on, there were unsettling realizations. At first, signs that read *We're all in this together!* appeared in the windows of storefronts and residences, but the way the pandemic distributed its harm revealed we were not all affected in the same ways.

The numbers showed fault lines; the most marginalized were the ones most vulnerable to and impacted by COVID. While I sheltered in place, ordering groceries online and getting used to Zoom, those without housing, those who kept the city running by delivering my goods, working in the warehouses, attending to the ill, were most exposed to the virus. The deaths in long-term care facilities brought to light a callous disregard for the elderly and disabled.

Incidences of anti–East Asian hate rose alongside the COVID numbers as President Trump proclaimed it the "Kung Flu virus." Racial violence, especially anti-Black violence, also escalated. The discovery of mass graves at residential schools tragically confirmed what Indigenous communities had been telling us for so long. Folks in my city were further disenfranchised by mass layoffs and evictions. Police violently dismantled encampments, scattering the unhoused further into the margins in the middle of a health crisis. The cruelty, the callousness of systems, structures of colonialism, racism, late capitalism left no room to breathe and a wake of harm. If it wasn't clear before, every day revealed new evidence that our ways of doing things were not sustainable. Along with others, I sank into despair, rage, and grief.

Yet I still did not have words. As a writer, my job is to put language to experience, pluck out patterns of meaning, arrange events and characters into some relatable form, so I tried to keep writing through this time, but the blank page intimidated me, and I kept closing my laptop.

Ironically, the novel I was working on was about catastrophe, a series of events that forced radical change in the lives of my characters. I did not expect the real world to crash into my story. My characters stopped what they were doing and glared at me from the screen.

What the hell, Carrianne? What do you want us to do now? I told them I didn't know. We would just have to wait and see.

COVID-19 is quite a protagonist. Some would call it a master villain. Others would call it just a character living its own logic and destiny. There are many ways to tell that story. For now, we have only the inciting event, the scene that launches a story. At the time of this writing, we are still in the middle of it. We haven't reached consensus yet for where we are in these stories. But these last couple of years have been about bracing for what happens next, and unlike a novel or a film, this middle has been a very long one.

Since I could not write those first months, I did something peculiar. I started stitching and painting. Aside from language, I do not have an artistic bone in my body. For example, I love the idea of myself as a knitter, but I have never finished a project, because my scarves look like capes for my dog. I don't like counting. I am not organized enough to keep track of rows and purls and such. Just before COVID arrived in Canada, I had walked into a craft store and bought a bunch of colourful threads and a few sashiko patterns. It was instinct, as everything I do—falling in love, eating cake, choosing what to wear every day—seems to be instinct. I reach before thinking, and I am so glad that I reached for those threads. I had great plans to learn how to stitch, but I quickly forgot about them and left the supplies buried in a drawer.

Without words, I'm in a fog. Writing blocks have happened to me only a handful of times, and what usually follows is a very sad Carrianne. I am empty, reaching for trashy reality TV to make me feel better about my own life. I burrito myself in a duvet until I find words again. This time, when I couldn't continue with the novel, I reached for the threads, itching for a practice to replace the writing. I began by just playing with the sashiko patterns and found them calming. It was easy. The patterns were printed lines on squares of cotton, and all I had to do was follow with simple stitches. My focus on the up-and-down movements of my fingers holding the needle dimmed the switch on encroaching anxiety. When I looked up from my hoop, hours had gone by. Very much like writing.

A couple of friends that first summer had their book launches cancelled because of lockdown. A book launch is a festive event. It's a birth, a wedding, a party all in one. After years of toiling alone, this is the occasion to celebrate with beloveds. My body, not getting a chance to hug, kiss, and love up on my writer friends, found stitching instead, and I stitched their book covers as gifts. I translated the cover images into key lines or a simple graphic image and used remnants of fabric left over from sewing projects. The final pieces were interpretations of the original work. I stitched the book title and the author's name on each. I think the pieces made my friends happy. It made me happy. And so, I kept doing it.

My daily ritual began each morning with thinking of someone special and designing a custom piece for them. I learned how to transfer my designs onto scraps of fabric by tracing images onto paper with heat-transfer pencils. When I was satisfied with the graphic, I would iron the image onto a piece of cotton and be ready to stitch. By summer, I had embroidered and given away over fifty pieces of art. I made a friend in Saskatoon a stitch of the iconic grain elevators. For another friend, I crafted a piece inspired by the memory of a special walk we took at Lake Louise. I stitched blankets for babies.

I posted some pieces I'd made for myself on social media, only to give them away to friends who expressed their delight. The first cherry blossom piece I did, I gave to a friend who said it reminded her of childhood and watching her aunt embroider. It surprised me how much these gifts meant to others, how evocative a simple thing made of needle and thread could be.

I continued using remnants until I ran out. Then I ordered from my local fabric store. I stocked up on threads and bought sheets of broadcloth. Stitching for friends made me feel I could tighten the bonds between us, allowed me to express my care and gratitude for them in this time of loneliness. Ah. There it is. I was lonely too. My daily practice was an insistence that I was not alone, that beauty still mattered even as all around us, tragedy kept striking. If I had a needle in my hand, I was able to speak.

Some of my work was political. I stitched a police car burning during the Black Lives Matter protests. I created a tableau of Hong Kong activists protesting China's imposition of security laws that curtailed their civil rights. I was making an archive of the days we were living through. I wanted to remember these times, to preserve what I felt. There is something so precious about craft, whether writing words or making stitches; both are slow work, intentional and attentive. Perhaps this mark making is primal to humans, our act against forgetting.

I was suddenly being asked to do commissions, but aside from two pieces that I offered as fundraisers for Land Back legal fees and one for a food-security organization, I vowed to never accept payment for my stitching. This new passion would be guided by creative whim. I wanted something pure in my life, and this practice felt unencumbered by expectation. A gift is a gift is a gift. I delighted in the gifting.

I turned to the small beauty I found on daily walks in my neighbourhood. For long chunks of time, my world was reduced to a few blocks. I walked my dog through the same streetscape, the same but not really the same. The weather, the seasons, my moods changed, and I noticed new things in this small space. I started to see my neighbourhood as lines, curves, colours. I completed a series of embroidered so-called weeds, flowers that defy planned gardens and find homes in cracks in the pavement, parking lots, dump sites. I first photographed them and other little scenes, transitory, too tiny to be noticed otherwise, but the stitchwork guided me to pay closer attention to the details around me. I stitched clouds, rain, even lightning.

Deaths happened near and far. The city felt soaked in suffering. The world kept spinning, and every day, through my laptop, came fresh trauma and new fears. I wanted stillness, and the only movement I could focus on was the flash of needle rising and descending. I began to feel a strange remove from the "outside," my life growing ever smaller, and the threshold between me and everything else became more strongly delineated. I grew more isolated, and the only thing I could do was to keep stitching as if it were everything for the moment. The sound of thread being pulled through fabric became the music of comfort.

One of my favourite stitches is called the rice stitch. This stitch requires small marks on the fabric, arranged as if they have been scattered without a set pattern. It is quite deceptive because it requires intention to pull off its seeming effortlessness. Maybe others have different names for it. To me, it is exactly how rice looks if spilt on the floor, something I remember my grandmother saying was a big no-no. Thunder gods would rebel, she told me, stomp all over the land in rage. This story captured how I felt about the great injustices outside my window. But I wasn't a thunder god. I wished the thunder gods would break apart the sky, rearrange the world and lessen the suffering. I thought of this whenever I made that stitch.

Through YouTube, I learned how to make other stitches. The French knot was hard to master and made me feel all thumbs. I persevered, because clusters of French knots resemble Queen Anne's lace. The lazy daisy stitch allowed me to make varied blades of grass or leaves. Precision was not necessary; the more randomly I poked through the fabric, the more organic and interesting the shapes. Mostly, I used the running stitch and the backstitch. The running stitch felt playful, like skipping feet. The backstitch felt like mourning. The stitch moves forward, only to go backward to return to the previous stitch, like memory when one feels loss. With these two simple techniques, I could draw infinite pictures.

Stitching pulled me back from a pit of despair. Maybe you saw that pit too, ready to swallow us if we were not careful. By keeping the needle moving, I was able to hold on to my friends, remember the good in my life; stitchwork offered another kind of language and mode of storytelling while I waited for the words to come.

I eventually returned to writing the novel. The story came suddenly, in a burst. I dove back into familiar waters—cold and thick against my skin. The story took on the shades of what had been happening in the world, a strange book written in a strange time. When I think of this work, I will always think of the words beside the stitches. I will also remember the silence and stillness.

I hope that you are able to find your language to describe these moments and to hold tight to the things that sustain you. The pandemic is still happening as I write this, the world still erupting, changing, unsettling. I like to think that the world is also being made now, in our living rooms, in isolation, in our imagination, through words, through threads. I may have found stories again to write, but I still turn to the needle. Stitches have become as important as words, both part of the vocabulary I need.

Recently, on my first trip outside of Canada since the pandemic, I met a fellow traveller whose birthday was coming up. I had brought along some sewing supplies and, on a quiet afternoon, I stitched her name on a small square of muslin. Around it, I stitched three waves in various shades of blue and green. We were by the sea when we met, both of us great lovers of water. Above her name, I made loose yellow rice stitches to stand in for stars. When I gave it to her, her eyes lit up. What a gift, I thought. Not for her, but for me.

THE ART OF BEING ALONE

ROB LEACOCK

It's Saturday morning, and I'm in the kitchen making the coffee while Stefanie wrestles Matilda into her basketball uniform in the front room. I'm readying Stefanie's to-go mug before they have to head out. It's the team's last game, way up in Sherwood. From where we are in Little Rock, it's a good forty-five minutes in the car to watch eight-year-old girls run up and down the court for half an hour. "Did you want to take her?" Stefanie had asked me on Friday night, "or do you have a match?" She said it with less mockery than she once did. I took my turn taking Matilda to practice earlier in the week, and I'll have plenty of chauffeur duties with Weston's soccer games in the coming weeks.

I have a match. It's Millwall away. Millwall. The Lions. Their ground is called the Den—or the New Den, since they built the current stadium in the nineties, the first stadium of the "new era" in English football following the Hillsborough disaster in '89, when all those kids from Liverpool were crushed to death. The Den, the Lions. But Millwall are still a bit of the old era, grim and notorious with aggressive fans and hooligan firms, the whole bit. I hate Millwall away.

The season has dropped off for West Brom lately. It's been pretty poor, actually. One thing after another. A win against Peterborough was hardly celebrated. The loss against Preston North End was shocking. The supporters are primed for a revolt. The manager is on the brink of losing his job. The players we've brought in during the January transfer window haven't been the golden-booted miracle workers we hoped and prayed they would be. And today the club travels away to Millwall, and I am filled with dread.

I climb the stairs and shut the bedroom door and arrange myself on the bed. I have the match on the laptop. The streaming service was an indulgence, but I don't follow the club *not* to watch the matches. Only, I can't always watch too closely. I have my knitting. It's not that I can't watch the match. I can; I do. I'm cautious not to become too emotionally invested, or so I tell myself. It's hard to love something, because we don't always want to sort through the whys of it. It's easy when things are up. Love isn't only happiness, as much as we may not want to admit it. Can you love something and not worry over losing it? I've got enough on my mind without needing to let a silly football match ruin my weekend. I don't think about it too much myself. At the very least, the knitting will subdue some of the cursing that inevitably comes with football matches.

It's a hat. It's always mostly hats. I knit other things now and again. I spent most of December and a bit of January on that rainbow scarf for Colin next door. I had to start it over six times and knitted it wider than I would've liked just to get the rainbow to lie the right way. That thin thread on those narrow needles—it took forever to finish, and halfway through, I realized one skein wouldn't do it. I had to track down the woman—the dyer—from the craft show at the church where I bought the yarn. It was her stepdaughter who sold it to me. But I tracked her stepmother down and sent her a picture of the yarn, and she told me she thought she could match it. And she

Rob Leacock, hats supporting the West Bromwich Albion FC, 2015–21. | Photo: Rob Leacock.

did. I didn't quite finish it in time for Christmas, but Colin loved it, so I did too. I knitted a sweater once just to see if I could, and I could. I gave it to my friend Amelia.

It's been a solid decade of hats. I've lost count, and I'm not sure I could estimate. A hundred maybe. Or two hundred. It started a few years before the football fanaticism, once I mastered the circular needles and figured out how to purl so the edge wouldn't curl. Two years of trial and error before I made one that fit and could be worn in public without embarrassment. It was like learning to play by ear; I never have followed a pattern. For a while, it didn't occur to me that there were patterns out there. Figuring out the right number of stitches to fit a head, trying out increases and decreases, working out the arithmetic, learning to manage double-pointed needles, going through countless misshapen head coverings until I mastered a proper hat. Now I knit more hats than I have heads.

My wife receives several a year; my children too. Stefanie had me do flamingo hats for the girls that one Halloween, and they turned out pretty great. I made a dinosaur hat for Matilda's school project. An Arsenal hat for Weston. A few for Becca she refuses to wear. My mother, my sisters, my nieces and nephews, Britton and Amelia's daughters. Father Richard in DC gets one every year at Christmas. Made a Sheffield United one for my buddy Mason. Julie at school—two, because of her chemo treatments. Never mind the backlog of people I've quietly promised. I owe Zach a red-and-white one, for Arsenal. Bishop Loya in Minnesota—he loves Chelsea, but I won't knit His Grace a blue one. Some people, I can't remember if I've knit them one or not. I should probably have kept a list. Too late to start one now.

And for myself? For myself, I always do a green-and-white beret every basketball season, for the school where I work, so my students can always find me in the stands. A beret: an inch of seventy-two stitches, K1P1 and then increase to 120 and six more inches, then decrease by four, round and round, switching to the double-pointed needles at sixty stitches, decreasing until I'm done. They don't all need pompoms, but some are better with one. A beret is my preferred hat. I knit a few every year. Am I really the type of person who can get away with wearing a beret? Not really. But if you can knit a beret with your own goddamned hands, you can get away with it.

I learned how to knit at an actual church knitting group from a congress of old ladies. I was a young minister, and I mistakenly wandered into the wrong room to find the prayer-shawl knitters. I say mistakenly, but I was curious. This gang of women straight out of central casting with their oversized bags and their coded lingo all staring at me over their glasses. They sat me down and tutored me through the basics. Weeks and weeks of back-and-forth for a ragged scarf that I never wore (we lived in Texas then), visiting the masters to show them my progress.

I kept at it long after I'd moved on from that parish. Hours and hours on my own in my living room, poke, loop, pull, slide. My left index finger would get dull and numb from pushing the needle tip. Trips to the craft store for yarn and extra needles so I could have more projects going at once. A solitary knitter, maybe even a secret one. I didn't know many other knitters.

I'd been knitting for years before I learned that I knit English style (like my football). I never knew there was a different style to knit in until a Continental tried to convert me, but why change? I'd spent so long knitting and purling this way, throwing the yarn, pushing the needles with my finger and thumbs. A distinct rhythm and metre, like a drummer mixing bass and snare and high hat. Or maybe more like a blacksmith, hammer, iron, anvil.

I'm in the bedroom upstairs with my laptop, needles, yarn, our cat, and the football match. The match is not going well. The club, the players, the manager can't seem to get it together. Can't get the formula right. It seems like we have all the right pieces, but we just can't put them together in the right way. Haven't found the magic. The season started well, but the club seems to be slowly coming apart. So, I am knitting this hat, a K2P2, with the remnants of old mismatched skeins from previous projects.

I am alone. I can be alone. I do this all the time, the knitting or the football or both or whatever alone. I never think about it. It's in me naturally. I learned how to do it from a master: my father with his pristine needlepoint. Pillows and bell pulls and Christmas stockings and church kneelers. Flowers and birds and ponds full of koi. Thousands of hours spanning decades in his chair, stitching. His little skeins neatly rolled in a Ziploc bag and those gold scissors my aunt gave him for Christmas one year, snipping the tiny loose ends into the mug he'd taken his coffee in the week before. The Weather Channel on mute so he could listen to his opera or his baroque chamber music or mariachi. Alone.

He wasn't like the silly dads on TV. Never a ball or a fishing rod or model airplane with us. Never the camping trips or football tailgates, like some of my friends and their dads. He told me plenty, but not through any heart-to-heart. He was the one you went to for math, even though my sisters and I didn't want to. He was the one from whom there was a reckoning over a poor report card. He also scooped the ice cream and would hand out the cash Mother gave him for his lunch at the university if you needed to buy something. I spent hours and hours with him, quietly watching and learning, cultivating how to be alone. Watching him with his patterns and needle and yarn. It gave him a peace that few things did. It was when he was most himself. My father did not have a diverse repertoire for expressing himself, but needlepoint was like medicine to him. Nothing could bother him. If he didn't like a row or a whole section—if he didn't like the way the yarn was laid—he'd rip it out without so much as a wrinkled brow. Alone and untroubled.

It's amazing how easily you can practise the art of being alone, if you want to. Not lonely or isolated, but content. Sure, I could root for the Cowboys or the Longhorns or the Razorbacks or whatever other team wherever we've lived, but then I'd have to be with people.

I'd have to work on fitting in. I follow an English football club four thousand plus miles away that nobody's heard of. I have the shirt to prove it. Okay, several shirts. When you root for an obscure English football club, people think you're daft, and they leave you alone. Oh, you're into soccer—which team? West Bromwich Albion. Blank stare, change of subject. It took Stefanie and my family a few seasons to finally be able to tolerate this life choice.

At the high school where I am the chaplain, I work in the Upper School Commons amid the din of student leisure before lunch. "Are you knitting?" a curious student will ask. They always stand a good distance away, carefully peering on tiptoes but not getting too close. Perhaps they find the needles menacing. They're not quite sure what they're seeing. Have they ever even seen someone knit before? "Yes," I say, "I'm knitting a hat." They nod. "Cool," they say, and they leave me alone.

At my son's weekly soccer practice, I never bother to venture over to the dads' circle. It has something to do with my experiences in middle school, I think. I keep to myself, a grown man huddled in a camping chair wearing a headlamp on a November evening, knitting. And they leave me alone.

My father's last few years were hard. A degenerative neurological condition robbed the man of many things, especially his ability to needlepoint. He was not himself; he was alone but in a different way, slowly drifting from who he was as the progressive supranuclear palsy unfolded within him. That final Christmas stocking for his youngest grandchild lay unfinished in a bin. He had tried a few times from the hospital bed, but his eyes and his hands couldn't manage. He wasn't satisfied with the work. At his insistence, my mother had given it to me to do. What did I know about needlepoint? "You knit," my father told me during a visit to the nursing home. "They're the same concept." He would ask me how the stocking was going when we'd visit for Thanksgiving or in the summer. I'd hem and haw and equivocate. I'd lie. I couldn't bring myself to do it. Stefanie ended up watching some YouTube videos and taking on the project. A beautiful stocking with a choir of angels and Becca's name across the top. She spared me the agony. She does a lot of needlepoint now.

Grieving is the deep practice of being alone. I spent four years readying myself for the moment when my father's condition would worsen, as the doctors predicted it would. Every goodbye in the nursing home was the last. He and I were under no illusions. He had asked for a DNR, and I was there when Mother did the paperwork. I rehearsed my father's dying until I felt I'd got the hang of it. Only I never quite did. I never felt so alone as I did when my father died. Grief is trying not to fall apart, trying not to unravel yourself. My father died, and I grieved. And I knitted. Trying to keep it together—or trying to outpace the sometimes constant unravelling. I still grieve; I still knit. You should have heard those church ladies fawn over my father's church kneelers.

When my club wins, there's no one at hand to celebrate with, and no one to commiserate with (or complain to) when the club is on the brink of fading into mediocrity, as they are today. I am alone, practising the stoic arts. The missed goals cannot be scored, no matter how hard I wish them to be. Letting the past be the past. Non-judgment. Contemplating mortality. Cursing the poor defense. Praying. Hoping. Knitting. Trying not to think about prepping for school chapel or the unfinished sermon I'll have to preach at the church down in Pine Bluff that still hasn't found itself a full-time minister. The cat is untroubled by anything. She won't even bother with the yarn the way most cats do. I am alone with my football, my miserable club that I love, a hat made with clashing leftover yarn that's getting tackier with each round of stitches, a hat for myself this time. Knitting. Trying to hold everything together. I am alone, and I am content.

ON EMPIRE & YELLOW & HOME

LJ AHENDA

1998

I was eighteen months old. My parents brought my siblings and me to Kenya to visit my father's side of the family. We stayed for a month. I've been told one highlight so many times it feels like I remember it. It's vivid, this memory of grabbing a kanga in my stubborn fists. In my mother's arms as she walked through the market, I reached out with my newly discovered reflexes and caught hold of the prettiest thing I saw. I refused to let go, prompting my mother to buy it from the vendor. I've always believed that moment to be formative, as though it threaded itself across my synapses, tailored my composition.

This kanga is the reason I love yellow. Its shade is rich, darker than a sunflower, warmer than the sun. It's the softest garment I'll ever own. It has an intricate border I'm tempted to describe as paisley, although it weaves its own shape. The swirls and circles swoop into each other in black and red. Inside, a repeating

pattern of black and red dots in diagonal lines, above them a repeating pattern of large leaves. Just above the border, a Kiswahili proverb. I don't know what it means.

"Nostalgia is a lie," I remind myself. I learned this when I read a poem by Dionne Brand in a book from the library that I kept forgetting to return. I checked it out when I was trying to finish my thesis, but even the word *thesis* made me want to throw up. I'd hoped this book would give me direction. What I learned was a lesson about empire. Its grip. Its consequences. How its priorities had wormed into my brain, started to chew.

The Kenya my father left is not the Kenya that exists now. I'd passively believed that I'd stop feeling so split down the middle if I could only go back to what my father left and sew it back together. But of course, despite my denial, events occurred. Time carried on, mocking my intentions. The world as I imagine it in the 1980s is not the world that exists now. Keeping my head pointed into history, I was missing the present. Its empire. Its consequences.

2022

My existence has always felt flimsy. I could invent a parable on how it's not in my blood to stay in one place. I could talk about the history—the travel, southward down the river, that my father's ancestors followed until they found places to stay, then the conflicts—and there I go talking about it.

The truth is that I avoid making homes of places. I get antsy when I stay in the same city for too long, or when I'm around the same people year after year. Consistency makes me nervous. When the connection is loose, the loss doesn't bleed so much.

The poem says, "Even our nostalgia was a lie, skittish as the truth these bundle of years."

LJ Ahenda as a baby with her kanga, at her grandmother's house in Kenya, 1998. | Photo: LaDona Ahenda.

In my mind, for years, my kanga was lovingly designed and handcrafted by a woman who lived on the land where my father grew up. I pictured the cotton, the dye, the selection of proverbs from which she chose the perfect one, the hands that stitched the edges, the basket she used to carry it to market, and finally the sale, to a woman whose baby daughter grabbed it and wouldn't let go. I imagined that woman was fond of me.

I tried to learn the history of the kanga. There are several theories about its genesis. One suggests that Portuguese traders carried bandanas to East Africa, where people would sew six together to form one large textile. Another theory purports that the unbleached cotton came from the United States or India, then was dyed by local merchants. All that's clear is that as women wore them and used them and as they grew popular in the twentieth century, textile mills were established in Kenya. Kangas have been mass-produced since the sixties or seventies. Of course. Nostalgia is a lie.

2021

I started to care for my hair properly in the second year of the pandemic. I'd been wanting to repair my hair for a while, but I didn't know where to start. Years prior, I'd straightened it every day. There was a man who liked me better that way, and I'd hoped that I could turn his disdain into love if I responded to his every suggestion with perfect delivery. The damage climbed from my split ends all the way up to the roots, and even though I'd gotten myself far away from this man and his influence, my hair didn't let me forget. I was beginning to worry that my hair and I were beyond saving.

During those pandemic years, I dated somebody who thought I had great hair. Never mind that it barely curled anymore, or that what masqueraded as volume was mostly frizz.

In the last few months of the relationship, when the only thing keeping me there was the crushing fear of being alone, I started to wear my hair in different protective hairstyles. I wanted to hide the damage. I followed instructional videos of very stylish girls braiding cornrows into their hair. I bought a few silk head wraps and learned different methods of styling them. I ordered blue-purple ombré hair extensions and gave myself braids.

All that time, my yellow kanga sat folded at the back of my underwear drawer. I looked at it every day, but I never pulled it out.

2022

I called my sister in Calgary. She was out with her friends, so she could only talk for a minute. I asked how she felt about her kangas. "They're bright; they're flowy, fun colours, you know," she said, and I just knew her face was lit up with the sun. "Like, when you put one on, you know you're gonna be comfy." I wished I were more like her.

She's right. They're flowy. You feel pretty when you drape one over your shoulders. I have another one that's bright pink and orange. It's a garment, not a metaphor.

1993

My parents were married on August 25, 1990, in a small church in Calgary. Even after the wedding, they were undecided on where to settle down and raise a family. My mother's family, Mennonites from the Canadian Prairies, were close by. My father's family, Luo from the Kenyan countryside, were across the world. It wasn't until my brother's first trip to Kenya in '93—a baby so tiny, so vulnerable, so full of potential—that my parents decided to make Canada their permanent home.

I've always understood this as a mutual decision. They both agreed to stay in Canada for the kids' sake. But I've never asked my father what he felt, or whether he had heard that adage about never going home again. If he'd felt a severing. What it did to him.

"Our nostalgia," the poem says, "was a lie, and the passage on that six-hour flight to ourselves is wide and like another world."

2018

My parents went back to Kenya for a visit during the summer when I was twenty-one. My siblings and I stayed behind this time—we were grown, and we had our own lives, jobs, and relationships.

That summer, the internet had a lot to say about unlearning the Eurocentric standards of the beauty industry, so I pulled my kanga out of its drawer. I taught myself several new methods of styling it. I wrapped my hair in it; I wore it as a scarf, a skirt; I even tried to use it as a belt once. I took a girl on a park date and used it as a picnic blanket. I cried when we ended our summer fling, and once I was back in my car, I hugged the kanga to my chest.

My mom showed me the scrapbook she made of their birding safari. She told me all about how friendly and helpful their guide was. He pointed out so many birds that she never would have seen on her own. She made him promise to protect her from the snakes and laughed, but he followed through. She couldn't remember his name.

She said that it was a shock to see how different things were from their past Kenya trips. Many fishers were out of work, as invasive species overtook the waters. The lakes themselves had risen to drown several establishments they'd frequented over the last thirty years. "Not to mention," my mother said, "a lot of the colonial structures are gone, which, for me, was a big part of the charm."

I didn't feel like I could ask my father about being Black—he and I didn't talk like that—so I turned to books instead. I read whatever I could find about African history, poetry, news. Anything to hold on to. I didn't retain much information. I kept the kanga close.

2021

When I ended the pandemic relationship, I called my sister-in-law. I took videos of myself sobbing along to a Spotify playlist called "saddest taylor swift songs that make me want to go to a farm and cry." I cut the braids out of my hair.

I passed that summer in a haze. Each day spilled into the next. I pulled out my kanga and put it up on my bedroom wall, stared at it until I could let the yellow in. I took it with me when I drove along the Sunshine Coast with my grandparents. The heat dome over the coast at the time was unprecedented. At high tide, a slew of boiled purple sea stars splashed around my feet. Low tide uncovered millions of cooked mussels still clinging to the shoreline. This was the first time I'd seen such death. I used my kanga to keep the vulturous sun off my shoulders. Continued to cry about my own problems.

2007

When I was ten, my family went back to Kenya for the month of July. We spent some time on the family's land, some time in the capital, and—my favourite—some time on the coast.

We walked on the beach every day. The season's wind cooled the air against the equator's sun. At the market, kangas billowed in the wind. The bright fabrics painted the sky, the sand, the water. In my memory, all I could see was delight.

I bought my pink kanga with the spending money that my parents gave me. I wore it like a dress over my bathing suit and felt like the prettiest girl on the whole beach. I wore it to dinner. I wore it the next day when we went out in a glass-bottomed boat. We saw fish in every imaginable colour, and I was one of them. I could indulge in this feeling called belonging, though I didn't have a vocabulary for it at the time. I just knew that my lungs felt expansive.

On our final evening in Mombasa, my siblings made me jump in the ocean with them one last time. The water was warm. The sun, gentle, was setting over the horizon. We splashed each other. We sang all the songs we'd made up on the trip. We argued, we laughed, we danced. We said goodbye to the landscape, to the land itself, hoping we'd be back one day, hoping that on our return, we could feel, once again and just enough, something resembling home. "Anyway," the poem says, "it's fiction what I remember."

2022

The poem says, "I have tried to write this thing calmly, even as its lines burn to a close."

I have tried to write this thing calmly. I have felt defensive, inadequate, fraudulent, afraid. I have made maps of my skin, etched my lines according to the wishes of some foreign, imposing king from some century or another. I have clung to that map, even as its lines have burned to a close.

I can't return to something that was never mine, and I can't become somebody I'm not. I have tried to decide who is responsible and be angry with them, from the parents who made a complicated choice for their babies to the men who made brutal choices for reasons of power. That hasn't gotten me very far.

The poem says, "I have come to know something simple. Each sentence realized or dreamed jumps like a pulse with history and takes a side."

I have made metaphors of garments. I have wrapped my hair, my shoulders, my heart in a metaphor and expected it to rescue me. Each sentence twists and pulls me between an empire's stomach and claws. Its poisoned blood and its still-expanding heart.

I have asked and failed to answer the question of selfhood. I was born where I was born. I have lived the way I lived. Loved the way I loved. So be it.

Still, I have come to know something simple. I have come to know how selfhood adheres to the ribs. How its patterns remain intricate; how it billows in the wind; how it brightens the water, the sand, the sky.

I have fallen in love again. I have neglected, then rescued my hair again. Again, I have suffered a winter and welcomed a summer, expecting the sun or some garment to solve my sadnesses. I have tried to tell myself the truth but come out with more questions.

Yellow remains my favourite colour. Hope, my favourite outcome. Love, my favourite home. The poem says, "What I say in any language ... is plenty and pitiless and loves."

WHAT IS THE BODY BUT A MATRIX OF THREADS?

LIA PAS

When I became chronically ill, I began embroidering scientific diagrams. Soon the practice of stitching became something deeper, something that soothed and filled me. I spent hours with needle percussed through taut linen, pulled sighs of cotton thread, colours against colours, stitches, textures. I was overwhelmed with neurological symptoms of pain and tingling but, through meditating on them, began to see these sensations as stitches on cloth. I traced body parts on linen and began to stitch what I was feeling in the moment. How simple vessels lumened through the body. How delicate a lacework. A threading. A circuitry. The craft held more meaning as I stitched my ill state—my ill self—making my invisible symptoms visible. The act of embroidery calmed my nervous system and offered exquisite attention to my symptoms, making them less distressing and more something to explore. How do

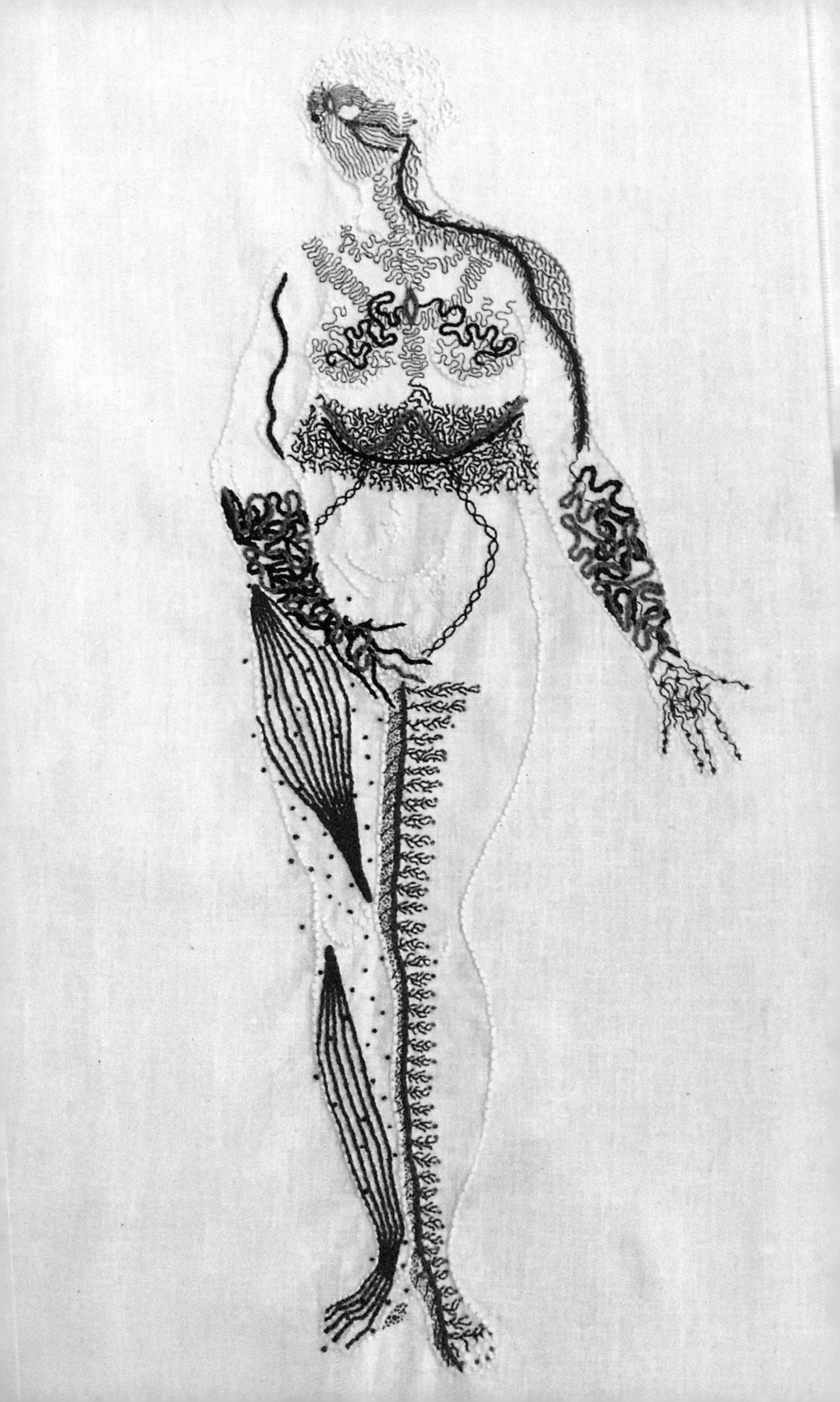

we know what our heart needs to break open within? Veins thread throughout bodies. We are honeycombed in bones. We are filagreed. My creative practice became a curative one.

My interest in SciArt—the blending of science with art—started young. My mother is a scientist, and my siblings and I grew up surrounded by physiology textbooks and scientific papers. I often spent time in my mother's lab and watched her prepare slides and dissect rats. At home she taught me how to sew doll clothes, and I helped her sew my ballet costumes. My ballet obsession turned to modern dance in high school, and I was a "dancing musician" with York University's Dance Ensemble during my music degree. I continued to engage my interest in anatomy and somatics through yoga and other movement classes while working with many dancers during my twenty-five years as a composer/performer. I undertook yoga-teacher training so I could teach as a way to have a stable income while making performance work, and it was through yoga that I returned to science. The teacher training contained both anatomy and kinesiology aspects, and we visited a gross anatomy lab to gain a broader understanding of the body. I continued making performance work and sewing my own costumes, while the science of anatomy kept creeping into my text, image, and movement work.

For so long, the intellect has been considered superior to physical experience because of Descartes's mind-body split. But it is difficult to ignore the physical in a body that is so demanding—in a body that bleeds monthly, in an ill body. Attention given to the body is attention not given to the intellect. And though I believe mind and body are not separate, it is challenging to overcome years of living in that paradigm. The body—not just the brain—contains the mind. The nervous system of the gut is just as important for our cognitive and sensory faculties as the brain. The nerves of the heart send more messages to the brain than the brain sends back down to the heart.

We are threads and nets. We are reds and blues and jewels. We are flowing rivers within fibres within fires within. See these marks

Lia Pas, *Body Map*, 2016. Cotton-thread embroidery on linen cloth. | Photo: Lia Pas.

on our skin—fine and lined engravings—each its own story, its own tributary. See these veins—the intricacies of them placed so carefully. We are embroidered quilts, felted beings armatured in bone. The body demands attention and urges us to act and react in certain ways to all stimuli, including that of the intellect. And if we don't listen to the body's more subtle signals, it makes them louder, so we have no choice but to finally listen.

My first major illness happened in my thirties, during my master's degree in devised theatre at Dartington College in the UK. I was creating work around anatomy for my solo show, *splanchnologies*, using old anatomical texts and engravings—primarily Vesalius's *Fabrica* and *Gray's Anatomy*—to explore the intricacies of the body from both a scientific and an embodied perspective. I became ill with a campylobacter infection that resulted in ulcerative colitis, but I somehow managed to complete my show and dissertation. Though my performance work had been created before I became ill, I found myself using my rehearsals to connect with my physically ill state. The oddly poetic descriptions in Henry Gray's writing allowed my poetic sensibilities to connect with my somatic ones, offering me the terminology as well as the descriptive sense to see inside myself. By the time my family and I returned to Canada, I was extremely ill and underweight and ended up hospitalized with severe anemia from the colitis.

It took two years to rebuild my strength. I continued to work with old anatomical texts and images. With each page of description, I engaged with my own physiology. With each illustration, I visualized my own organs, my own somatics. Though I didn't feel able to perform live at first, I was able to create my videopoem, *susurrations*—a love poem to the heart. I started the piece by writing about how intensely aware I needed to be of my heart lest I overexert my anemic system into a heart attack. I thought I had been aware of the somatics of my body before, but the practice of listening in so profoundly and compassionately informed both my movement and meditation practices, and my creative work was drawn even further into the sciences of anatomy and physiology as a result. There is a refined type of life here. I know how it leaves me breathless. It knows how resilience is built in rest. It knows how each step requires time in repose.

Almost a decade later, I became severely ill again, this time with something much more debilitating and mysterious. I caught an unknown virus and was overwhelmed by tingling all over my body and severe fatigue. I went through Guillain-Barré syndrome and numerous other tests, but no one could find anything measurably wrong with me. I shaved my head because I was too fatigued to wash myself with any regularity, and on my worst days, chewing and swallowing were utterly exhausting.

The only aspect of my daily practices I was able to maintain in the haze between medical appointments and fatigue was meditation. Being so ill, there was a shift in the sensation of time, in what takes place between breaths, in what takes place in each step forward, in each word on the page. Even an experienced meditator like myself can only meditate for so long, especially when the act of meditation sparks ideas for creative work.

I was eventually diagnosed with the neuroimmune condition myalgic encephalomyelitis / chronic fatigue syndrome (ME/CFS), and though there are few treatment options, pacing one's activities is the best way to deal with the overwhelming fatigue. Knowing that exertion beyond my very limited capacity would result in post-exertional malaise (PEM)—tingling, aching, and even more fatigue—I knew I needed to find a medium that would allow me to work while reclined, one that was slow enough not only to support my neurological needs but perhaps even to calm them. And so I returned to needlework.

I am not a flowery person, so traditional embroidery designs held little appeal. I started instead with some text/image pieces I had created based on scientific diagrams, teaching myself stitches as I went.

NEXT PAGE: Lia Pas, *Bleeding Vessel*, 2022. Cotton-thread embroidery and glass beads on linen/rayon cloth. | Photo: Lia Pas.

There were times in the day when even stitching was too much for me, and so I meditated or rested in other ways, then picked up my hoop and thread once I felt able to stitch again. Embroidery became an extension of my meditation practice, absorbed as I was in the slow act of stitching. Both practices developed over time, and I found my neurological symptoms easier to deal with if I focused in on them, shifting my perception from pain, tingling, or burning into discrete parts. What sensations made up the pain? What textures were the various types of tingling? Where did the perceived temperature of the sensations shift? What was this piercing but a way to be in attention? To be in that golden space of now that breathes and expands until we are everything—microcosm and macrocosm—wound about in threads, connections, and shifting nets, woven pieces, and glorious knots. We are all of a tapestry, knowing this small needle as now, as being, as the call to presence.

One day, my embroidery and my meditations coalesced when I saw my neurological symptoms as lines of thread in various colours and stitches. I traced parts of my body on linen and stitched what I felt and saw in my mind's eye in the moment. Through the practice of exquisite attention, my invisible symptoms became visible, each stitch a way inside. These practices further cultivated my relationship to my body, to anatomy, to physiology. I drew my hands in threads, threads through my hands. How we are webbed like a spider's gossamer, venations like leaves, like cloth embroidered. Each stitch a moment. Each stitch a bright singing through warp and weft that was once plants, flowers, or spun cocoons.

My body's knowledge was not lost, only transmuted. I started to hold the ringing again, if not the singing. My hands could dance, slow like a tree's growth. I found presence in each stitch, in each fibre knit together through needles. My body's knowledge was held differently now—deeper and slower, more oceanic and just as wide. It sang within, quietly. It danced there, slowly.

As this symptomatology series grew, I became more involved with the chronic-illness community on social media. I thought these pieces were intensely personal self-portraits of my own neurology, but many people said they illustrated their neurological symptoms as well.

SciArt at its core is about science communication. And though medical and anatomical illustration are fields with a long history, there is often a literalism in them that does little to evoke the human experience—especially the experience of living in a chronically ill body. Neurology is still a young science, and ME/CFS a poorly understood and stigmatized disease. By making these invisible symptoms visible, I am able to communicate sensations that are difficult to explain in words, especially when paired with cognitive symptoms like brain fog. I stitch threads that are nerves, threads that are sensation, threads that are beneath our skin, between bones, reddened, whitened, blued. These illustrations give voice to others when language fails them. Many people have told me they've brought my images to their doctors to show their own symptoms.

I would not have been able to go so deeply, thoroughly, and exquisitely into my symptoms through another visual medium. The slowness of embroidery allowed me to pay attention to what I felt in the moment and translate it freehand into thread. Now I created parts of bodies that voiced with threads—wide and open with colour and shape. The voice of needle and thread a percussion and sigh: high overtones, layers of thread wrought, dancing organs and their sensate forms, lithe and stretching into space, bones decorative and graceful. I wove presence through them. To knot, to create tension that sings. To breathe with each stitch.

inhale . placing needle
exhale . pull thread through

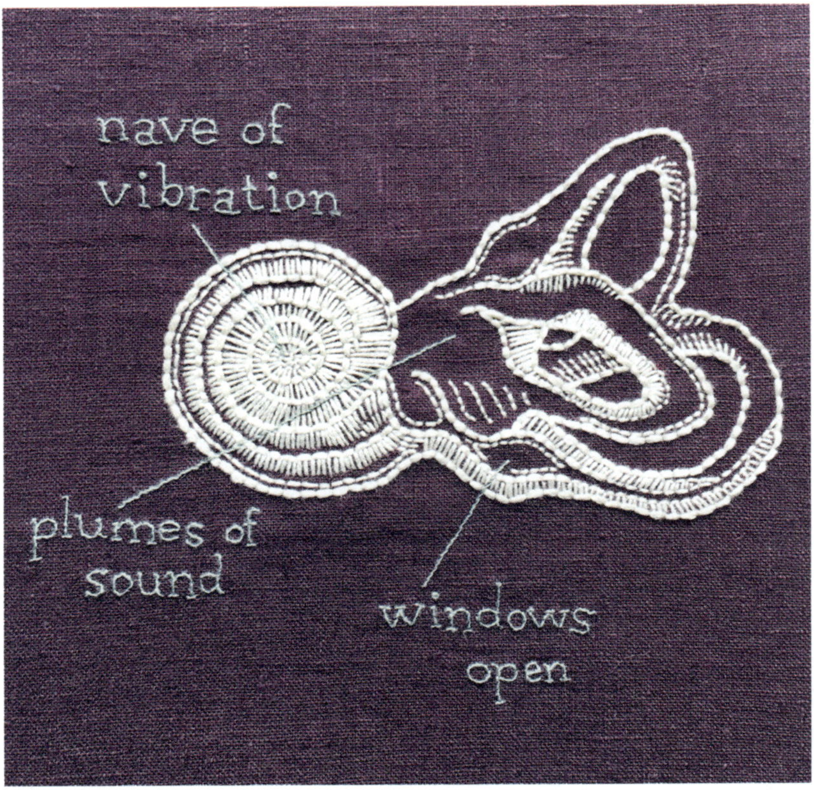

Lia Pas, *Nave of Vibration*, 2017. Cotton-thread embroidery on linen cloth. | Photo: Lia Pas.

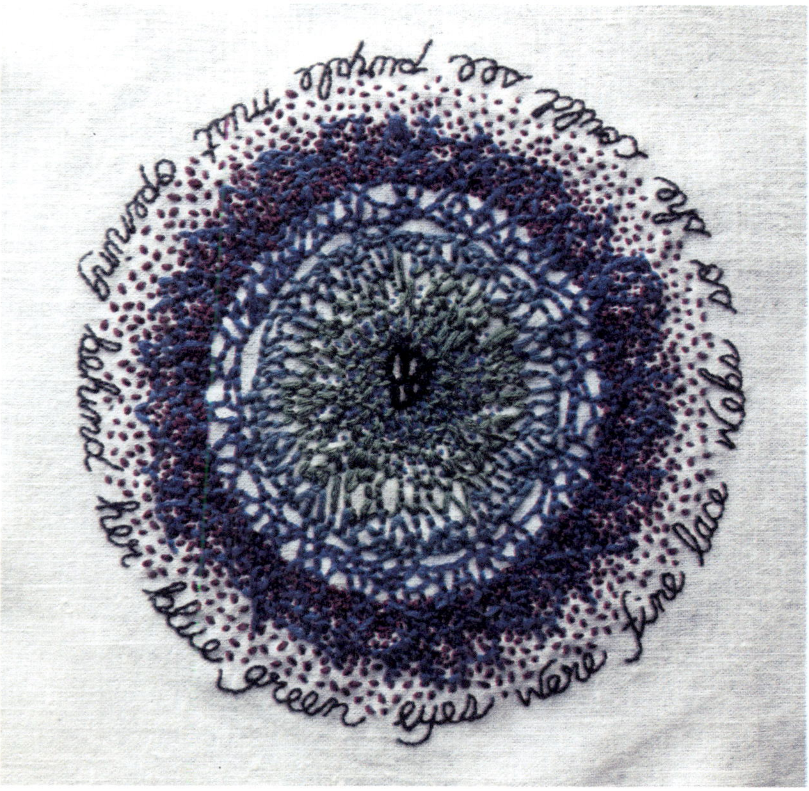

Lia Pas, *Eye Poem*, 2016. Cotton-thread embroidery on linen cloth. | Photo: Lia Pas.

To colour, stitch by stitch, thread by thread. The slowest sort of art. So delicate, so pristine.

The act of sewing echoes the interwoven nature of our anatomy. For what is the body but a matrix of threads? Each vein, each neuron, so thread-like. Each lymph node a French knot. Each organ decorated with fine vesicles—curlicues of life. This reimagining of the body in thread removes the "gross" aspect of gross anatomy, brings attention to our own shapes echoed in nature: an inner ear a tiny shell; the fimbriae of the Fallopian tubes, anemones; the bronchi of the lungs branching like trees. The disturbing made textural and sublime.

The body is a temporal creature, and illness forces us to witness this. The time and care that embroidery takes mirrors the time and care a chronically ill body like mine needs. I must move slowly so as not to aggravate my symptoms—urgency is no longer an option. Attention paid to the body in such an intimate way takes slowness and time, just as each thread must be pulled through carefully, delicately, so it does not end up in a snarl behind the cloth. This is like the slowest singing. Each stitch a note . a note . a note. Rhythms that dance through arms and hands. Rhythms that sing the body. This slowness and care taken—in body, in stitch—is an act of rebellion in a culture that demands speed and moreness in all things. Time stretches—a silk thread. Stitch it here, woven into linen. A shining mark, a stitch, a time taken, a hand. Fingers on needle guiding the exquisite pull through. This hooped cloth a drum. This quick breath a knot. How much of your lungs filigreed with veins. How bountiful the air—each breath sounding reeds and song through honeycomb flesh, each muscle vibrant, quivering. Time stretches—a silken breath. Inhale here—woven into leaves, a calming breeze, tracery. A breath, a time taken, a shadow. Ribs open wide, a shadow guiding the exquisite pull through.

Not always, but often, an ill body is a woman's body. Often, but not always, stitching, a woman's work. Pairing stitching about an ill

Lia Pas, *Paresthesia (face)*, 2016. Cotton-thread embroidery on linen cloth. | Photo: Lia Pas.

body with the often-misogynistic nature of the medical field means bringing awareness to it twofold. Embroidery allows me to flourish in the liminal spaces of medical waiting rooms and, more often than not, begins a conversation. When medical professionals realize I am an anatomical artist, communication becomes easier. Suddenly, we have a linguistic and visual connection, which means I am listened to more readily.

With each layer of my chronic illnesses, I create more pieces. I sketch organs and systems and bring the drawings to my appointments even before I begin stitching. This gives the doctor something to point at, to ease their explanations. When I am able to describe my symptoms and systems in detail, it allows doctors to assess what's going on more quickly, more thoroughly. And when I ask questions about my imaging in order to create a symptomatology piece, that allows me to somatically immerse myself in my meditations, visualizing more readily what is happening in my body, how that might translate into stitch, and how to release the tension that all symptoms bring.

The practice of stitching is an embodied practice. As my pile of completed pieces grows in layers of cotton, linen, and silk, I understand more about what it means to live an embodied life, what it means to live in an ill body, what it means when I am looking for answers and treatments. What it means to create while waiting—each stitch filling time, filling breath, filling understanding. A thousand stitches it took to put myself back together with exquisite attention. Perhaps that was all I needed—to pull thread through skin like a drum, to wait for the rustling, and to watch how I made my time deep and sweet.

ONE BEAD AT A TIME

SANDRA LAMOUCHE

They say it takes five years to learn the hoop dance, ten years to be competent, and twenty years to master it. I started hoop dancing in 2005, in the middle of studying for my degree in Native American Studies. I met my hoop-dance teacher, Jerry First Charger from the Blood Reserve, through a poster calling for Indigenous dancers. I was excited for the opportunity. I had been dancing since childhood. My mother put me in lessons to correct my pigeon-toed stance. I always joke that this was my first experience with the healing power of dance. I stopped in high school. I loved dance, but I was often the only Indigenous person in all of my classes. My family was also from a lower economic status. Even while having solos and taking classes up to five days a week, I felt I didn't belong.

I brought my sisters with me to be part of the lessons. Although I had learned other powwow dances in my youth, I found the hoop dance mesmerizing, particularly the way the hoops were manipulated and how the body almost magically transformed to different shapes;

in a few manoeuvres, one could transform from an eagle into a globe using the hoops. The dance's teachings of unity, leadership, and care for the environment spoke to my passion and experiences in life. I was learning the history of First Nations and colonization in a truthful and honest way for the first time in my life. Jerry First Charger taught the history, protocols, and meanings behind the hoop dance.

At home, our culture, beadwork, and stories were important for teaching my siblings and me about our values, respecting nature, and respecting each other. We learned to conserve power and heat, to recycle, and when we fished, ate wild meat, and picked berries, we connected deeper with the land. My dad used to take us "rock hunting" to look for special rocks, which I now do with my children. They leave stones on the kitchen counter; on the coffee table; or in coat, pants, or backpack pockets. Sometimes they bring me heart-shaped or shiny rocks and crystals as a gift.

After practising for a few months, we were ready for our first performance. We used a dance space on campus at the University of Lethbridge to share the work, *The Manitous*, meaning "the spirits," derived from the Anishnaabe story of the hoop dance. I had volunteered to do extra practice to learn more hoop dancing beyond the basic five hoops that the others were learning, and I became the main hoop dancer. Family members, Native Studies professors, and students were the audience, a small but still intimidating crowd for my first performance. We five dancers wore black leggings and black T-shirts, and I wore my hair in braids. My hoops were plain white, and my mom had made some simple moccasins for me to wear. I was nervous. I felt my heart beating and felt that everyone was looking at me. I worried about what others might think and about making a mistake. I did make a few mistakes, but afterward my friends and family were supportive. I felt proud and fell in love with the dance. Now, hooked by the meanings, symbols, and the spirit of the hoop dance, I had found my why for dancing.

I continued to dance and learned to do beadwork so I could wear beadwork to represent myself, my family, and my culture in a good way. The first beadwork I made was two small butterflies. My intention was for them to be identical, but in the end, one came out short and wide and the other one tall and thin. My mom joked that the fat one was me as a baby and the skinny one was me now. The following year, my mom surprised me on my birthday with beaded leggings and a belt she had made. I continued to do beadwork and made myself earrings, a headband, and a beaded floral hairpiece. Before that point, I did not have a clear image for what type of beadwork I wanted to do. My mom had always done florals. Florals are a traditional Cree style. The styles and symbols used in beadwork can tell a lot about a person, from their nation to more personal stories about their individual family. I chose to do light-pink flowers on my hair ties, earrings, and headband to symbolize the wild rose, the flower of Alberta.

My mom has sewn and beaded since she learned as a young girl. She held on to this because it was one of the memories she had of her mother. I learned about this connection only when I also started doing beadwork. My kokum (grandmother) Sarah Cardinal's death has been an unsolved murder since the 1960s. My mother was only a child when her mother went missing, her body found later. One of the only things my mother remembers about her mother is that she was known for creating beautiful beadwork. My mother continues to do beadwork as a way to carry on her legacy and to stay connected with her mother. Now my sisters and I and many of my extended family keep connected to my kokum Sarah, even though many of us never got to meet her.

Since university I have written and raised awareness about Missing and Murdered Indigenous Women using dance and creativity. Women are often seen as culture carriers; they tell us who we are. They carry the stories, traditions, and ways of life. They are the ones who traditionally were at home to teach. Beadwork is one way

Sandra Lamouche wearing a hoop-dance dress, hoops, and her handmade floral beadwork, 2015. | Photo: Sandra Lamouche.

to learn, carry, and share these teachings. Different symbols, shapes, colours, styles, methods, and materials make it a rich medium for teaching culture and identity. From the preparation of the beadwork to the finished product and how that final piece of artwork moves and is worn into the world, we use beadwork to carry culture and identity.

The more I danced and created, the more I learned about myself, my identity, culture, history, and language. As I got better at sewing and was exposed to more dance, I was able to create increasingly complex and nuanced designs. When my father-in-law gifted me the Blackfoot name Itamspiakii, which translates to "happy dancing woman" and comes from the deer family, I incorporated it into my designs. Over time I have come to understand this name as a guide in life—a reminder to remain positive and happy; encouragement to continue dancing with the strength of a woman, a life giver, and with the gracefulness of the deer. The hoop dance was part of the reason I was given this name and, in turn, it contributed to the designs on my beadwork and outfits as I continued to create. In a way, we create our identity through our actions and through our art.

The inspiration for my recent beadwork came in the form of an image. My husband and I were moving from Peterborough, Ontario, where we each earned our master's, back home to Alberta. We travelled through the US instead of driving the isolated highways of northern Ontario. We made it to Saskatchewan one evening, and as we crossed the border back into Canada, I was in awe of the big, open skies of the Prairies, how the bright colours of the sunset changed to the clear night sky. An image flashed in my mind of an eagle soaring, with the background divided in half by its wings. On the bottom was an orange circle representing the sunset, and the top half of the circle was the moon. I knew this was going to be part of my next design. I held on to this image for years, and it wasn't until almost a decade later that I created it.

When I started to plan the beadwork, I expanded on this image with half a night sky in blue and the other half red, for the sunset.

To me, this was also a representation of balance in the hoop dance. The dance represents the beauty of creation, but as a dancer transforms from one shape to another, they go through a struggle with the hoops. The hoops collapse in and out of themselves, and the dancer juggles and manoeuvres them to create the next image. People see beauty and creation in the hoop dance, but they often do not see that the dance is also about the challenges and struggles in life. The hoop dance is a message of balance and facing our challenges, being responsible so that our struggles can help us grow. Night and day. Light and dark. Beauty and struggle.

The contrast of night and day reminded me of the stars in the sky and the northern lights. My mosom (grandfather) used to call them Cipayak E-nimihitowin, spirits dancing in the sky; they may appear when an Elder has passed on to the spirit world. They are respected and looked upon with awe, but they also symbolize death in this world, sometimes serving as a bad omen. They are a reminder of our ancestors who have gone on. I love the idea of being able to continue dancing, even in the spirit world. Although I have a lot of dancing and creating left to do on earth still, it is a comfort to know that my spirit can continue to dance in the next life. When I spoke to a Cree Knowledge Holder to seek guidance on using the northern lights in my beadwork, she suggested making them a small part because of stories in which the northern lights can sometimes represent death and be seen as a negative sign. I chose to use the colours of the northern lights as a border and as a small strand on my beadwork.

Another symbol I used is a Blackfoot design that represents thunder. My husband and I are involved with ceremonies related to the thunderbird. Its sacred story can be seen as very powerful, particularly the idea of a thunderstorm. We need rain to help things grow, but just like a thunderstorm, if it is too powerful, it can cause damage, flooding, and lightning. I asked a Blackfoot Elder about the image; she had used it on one of her dresses, but she also suggested

Sandra Lamouche, beaded choker, earrings, floral hair ties, moccasins, and leggings featuring wild-rose and deer designs, 2015. | Photo: Sandra Lamouche.

making it small, so as not to be too overpowering. I used the image on the bottom part of my beadwork, underneath the sun and eagle.

This new beadwork was started after my older beadwork began to wear. The original full set had taken five years to complete. I completed in three years the new set with the symbols of balance between the sun and moon, beauty and struggle, and the powerful symbols of the northern lights and thunder adding complexity. This seemed more authentic to me and a step away from toxic positivity, perfectionism, and the romanticization that I have had to deal with in my life as an Indigenous woman, mother, wife, and as an educator, dancer, and artist.

Looking back, I now see how I had been hiding parts of myself, and this was even evident in my beadwork. My wild-rose beadwork focused solely on the flower and its beauty. The thorns were hidden—they were the intergenerational trauma, the struggles I went through, the mistakes I made, and the challenging parts of my identity. I now know that by hiding the thorns, my struggles or imperfections, I am only hurting myself. Exposing and embracing myself as a whole person, including both strengths and struggles, is true self-love and self-expression. Allowing only others to see only the beauty means that they can never see the whole me. If people only love me for the flowers and beauty without the thorns, then they are not truly loving me for who I am. Sometimes these thorns are a protection; they are necessary, they make me strong, and that is beautiful. Over the years and one bead at a time, I have been able to shape my identity, creating myself through my beadwork and outfits.

I recently have been using this beadwork under black light when possible. The bright neon colours of the northern lights glow brightly. The beadwork has taken on a new life, with an emphasis on light in the darkness. I have been focusing on the healing aspect of dance and using dance, beadwork, and sewing as a tool for healing. I have been challenging myself to use dance and art in new ways. This has led to more writing and publishing. More art exhibits.

Sandra Lamouche, beaded leggings featuring northern lights, eagle and sun, and moon; moccasins with colours of the northern lights, 2019. | Photo: Sandra Lamouche.

More contemporary Indigenous dance and choreography. The new challenges we are faced with call for new ways to heal and create. This year I finished an orange jingle dress for a healing dance said to have begun during the Spanish flu pandemic in the early 1900s. Orange is for the children who survived residential schools, including my grandparents, and those who did not. I am also making a red jingle dress to honour Missing and Murdered Indigenous Women. We can use creativity to create our own story, identity, and life. We can also use it to stitch together healing in the midst of challenge. Both are forms of healing. Whether or not we are in the face of great adversity, we can stitch our own self-determination, one bead at a time. The hoop dance itself represents beauty and challenge. The more we go through the hoops and challenges, the more we grow. The more we stitch, the better our designs become. More sturdy, more intricate, more balanced and beautiful.

Sandra Lamouche, earrings, hair ties, and choker, 2019. | Photo: Sandra Lamouche.

MIGRATION THREADS

MACAYLA YAN

I hand-embroider two hoops joined by a thread. On the left side, I stitch a representation of the coastlines surrounding my 爺爺 ye ye's (paternal grandfather) one-road village in 台山 Toisan (Hoisan) county with a mark to indicate the village's location. Instead of using fabric, I embroider on plant-patterned lace that I received from my 婆婆 po po (maternal grandmother) when she downsized her belongings a few summers ago, after my 公公 gong gong (maternal grandfather) passed away.

In the right hoop, on the same lace, I embroider a representation of Lək̓ʷəŋən (Lekwungen, currently imposed with the names Songhees and Esquimalt First Nations) Territory with a mark showing my grandparents' house in North Park, a historically industrial and recently gentrifying neighbourhood. The thread that connects the two pieces begins at my 爺爺 ye ye's village and ends at the North Park house. As part of the diaspora, I find the internet a tentative source of translation. The representations I create are based on screenshots from Google Maps, exacerbating the disparity between the images and the actual land and true forms of each coastline, especially as the land's ancestors knew them. My 姑婆 gu po (paternal great-aunt) said the ocean used to meet the 台山 Toisan village now and again, the tide reaching in to flood the street, but now a mud spa hinders the scope of its rhythmic movement. I can't help but wonder where else these two coastlines were fabricated, altered to meet Western and Chinese imperial desires. These representations also remind me of the subjective complexities of land, particularly when its people are forcibly displaced. In migration, we of the diaspora might (temporarily) forget. I trust the land remembers us, though.

I twist the end of a three-stranded black-cotton thread between my thumb and index finger before inserting it through the eye of a needle. While double-knotting one tail of the embroidery floss, I realize the gaps throughout the lace pose a challenge I've never faced. I must gingerly manoeuvre across the lapses in material, hopping between and around the thin strands of lace. Although I am unable to depict the finer contours of coastlines with precision, I attempt fidelity in shape, not unlike the process of navigating narratives of land and migration. Something is always lost when a jagged line is flattened. As I trace the maps with ink on paper, then thread on lace—each iteration of the image a bit off from the last—my mind meanders between the (story) threads.

My grandparents were born in their respective villages under Chinese imperialism, my parents were born in British-ruled Hong Kong, and I was born in settler-colonial Victoria, British Columbia. How far back must my family reach to locate robust and free community self-determination? I do know my family has become quite adept at filling the in-between space, complying outwardly while inwardly fostering individual and collective cultural survival, blending in without forgetting who we come from. Growing up, my 爸爸 ba ba (father), Russell Yan, frequently emphasized, "We are 台山 Toisan people." The specificity was important to him. In an undergraduate racial history course, I read a journal article that described our community's scant historical allegiance to the Chinese empire, our choosing to identify as 台山 Toisan people. My 爸爸 ba ba didn't factually know this, but I suspect he did in a rooted sense. I saw it in the way he stopped to enthusiastically say hi to people in Chinatown and in Cantonese restaurants. He carried himself with a confident integrity, grounded in his ancestry.

I had little sense of what exactly it meant to be a 台山 Toisan person, beyond the yearly 台山 Toisan banquet gatherings, when my 爺爺 ye ye and his friends wore matching 台山 Toisan Benevolent Association blazers, and the Lazy Susans overflowed with savoury dishes. However, in a white-dominant city, we were different. I silently observed the subtle and blatant ways we were treated as foreign and exotic. Strangers expected me to be pleased if they greeted me in Mandarin or Japanese. White girls told me how lucky I was to be Asian because "white boys love Asians." White men boasted to me about their Asian wives. Hairdressers marvelled at my hair and still spent three hours struggling to cut it. And, of course, I was asked where I was *really* from—when meeting someone new, when waiting for the bus, when serving a customer at my minimum-wage job. I thought maintaining a mental catalogue would help me anticipate the next encounter and feel a sense of control. I remember so viscerally the feelings of discomfort and irritation during two boisterous 台山 Toisan dinners when two different white men recorded us. The first man took a video from the front of the restaurant, the other shot photos of the second-floor restaurant from a fire escape across the street. I was jolted by these violations. The first time, I tried to hide myself from the camera. The second time, exhausted, I gave a bitter look.

We spoke Cantonese, ate fish soup and steamed eggs, prioritized familial and community relationships, and honoured our ancestors. My 爺爺 ye ye and 姑婆 gu po spoke of a distant village with no running water on a land I could not connect to, and despite the reminders that I am a 台山 Toisan person, the concept of being from a homeland remained abstract. I was terrified to reach across the chasm to Asia. My formal and informal Canadian training through school, media, and everyday interactions taught me to distance myself from Cantonese food, language, and people in order to receive an alluring and evasive sense of belonging as a Canadian citizen. I actively rejected my "Asianness" and felt a strange sense of satisfaction at age fourteen when a mixed-race Asian classmate told me I seemed more second- or third-generation Canadian than first.

I was seventeen years old when I stumbled upon a description of white privilege in a blog post, and fragments of my life suddenly clicked together. No wonder I spent so much of my life yearning to look, sound, and simply be white. My skin, nose, hair, and family name would never be white enough to conform. Even my liberal white high school classmate once expressed relief that she wasn't given her mother's maiden name, Lee. When I inquired if that was because it is a common Asian surname, she admitted, "Yeah, you get it, I want to go into STEM; I don't want to just be another Lee on a list." I felt my body freeze at her honesty. I wanted to believe in the illusion of multiculturalism; I oriented my personality around this desire. I convinced myself to love hockey and laugh along with anti-Asian jokes to prove I was integrated into Canadian society, a "good" Asian, rather than an unassimilable one. However, the fantasy of inclusion was so fragile and conditional that it evaporated when observed head-on. I felt angry about the energy I spent contorting myself, seeking that acceptance.

I was twenty years old when I first reached out to my ancestors without a nudge from my family. That afternoon, an Indigenous friend asked me about my family's spiritual traditions. Shy to disclose to someone outside my family that we practised ancestor veneration, I was surprised to be met with excitement. Their eyes brightened, and they passionately affirmed the power in ancestral relationships, which their family also honoured. Their reaction shifted something in me. We shared our awe in silence, and I felt a new appreciation when I recalled laying out food with my grandparents and kneeling at the altar as they told our ancestors how I was working diligently in school and growing bigger. I didn't tell my friend this, but I was proud of my ancestry for the first time. Later, at night, I knelt again and offered a humble orange, and my ancestors told me they loved me. I felt blanketed by their warmth, and tears collected in my eyes. In the space that opened up with my ancestors' extension of solace, I felt the depth of grief for what had been lost across the Pacific Ocean, over two generations.

Snaking the cotton thread in and out of the lace, I grieve again, weighted by the knowledge that my 爺爺 ye ye and 姑婆 gu po will never get to rest in the 甄 Yan cemetery nestled within the village's rice fields. I take a deep breath, knowing they are with our ancestors anyway.

Nayyirah Waheed wrote a poem about how immigrants, upon landing, encounter nothing that wants them.[1] For years, I resonated with these words, but as I form the 台山 Toisan coast with a whirl of needle and thread, I realize that for my family, this is only half true. Sometimes the racism was obvious. My 爸爸 ba ba recounted walking home from school in groups of no fewer than six to minimize the probability of being physically and verbally attacked. I didn't have five friends or know how to dodge the mock accents and slurs hurled in hallways and through virtual space, so I pretended they didn't bother me. Within weeks of securing my first job after my undergraduate degree, I refused unsafe work and firmly maintained the boundary for my own well-being. My team's supervisor complained about me to another white colleague whose desk bordered mine. She kept her back to me but was less than an arm's reach away. At twenty-three, I didn't know how to approach the situation, so I pretended I couldn't hear.

1 Nayyirah Waheed, *salt* (Scotts Valley: CreateSpace, 2013), 5.

Despite these experiences, my family was greeted by something that wanted us. British colonists exploited the labour of my people to build railroads for Western expansion, and because of this, 台山 Toisan people have lived and created community on Lək̓ʷəŋən Lands since the mid-nineteenth century. Migrating needle and thread across the lace, I craft the 台山 Toisan coastline. How many villages in this lush area surrounded by ocean and mountains experienced a mass exodus when people perilously went searching for economic stability? People who hoped to provide for their families.

Until the mid-twentieth century, the rough, rural 台山 Toisan dialect, barely intelligible to standard Cantonese speakers, was the primary language of Chinatowns across North America. The 台山 Toisan banquet dinners were, in part, a celebration of the resilience and resolve of our lineage, a tough braided heritage that refused to forget: "We are 台山 Toisan people." I was so lucky to grow up with frequent visits to Chinatown with my family, grocery shopping for lo bak and gai lan, eating dim sum, and spending the afternoon in Wah Lai Yuen with my grandparents and their friends. During these afternoon visits, I always got a red bean bun, my sister chose a pineapple bun, and my 嫲嫲 ma ma's (paternal grandma) favourite was the coconut bun, because she loved whipped cream.

Throughout my childhood, my 爺爺 ye ye would sit me down during WWE commercial breaks, give me a loonie, and tell me I must study hard to get anywhere in this society. My family stressed the value of education, an education that permitted you to slip by enough to make money without making waves. They had no option but to heed the same education system that had once barred Chinese students from attending. Within a hundred years of the Victoria School District Board officially segregating Chinese children from public schools, I became the first person in my family lineage to complete graduate school.

My departure from academia was a honeyed escape, the kind that allowed my muscles to relax, sweetened by the freedom of choice.

In a working-class immigrant family, choice is a luxury. My 爸爸 ba ba was a server, butcher, lawn mower, warehouse worker, delivery driver, and custodian, many of these concurrently, his pride never too big to provide for his family. A job is a job—you don't have to like it. But I genuinely enjoy the work I do as a counselling practitioner, and I did get to choose it. To this day, I am still amazed by this privilege. When my 爺爺 ye ye urged me to be studious and get a good job, I don't think he envisioned a career in mental health.

I loop the thread to tie the final knot on the hoop that holds my 爺爺 ye ye's childhood village. Were his wishes for my generation constructed by fear? His sister, my 姑婆 gu po, fled 台山 Toisan alone to escape the Communist Party, leaving behind the family village, a first husband who wanted to stay, and seven younger siblings. My 爺爺 ye ye followed her not long after. Without an education in the big city, he found a job in a shoe factory, met my 嫲嫲 ma ma, and they had three children while unhoused. How vividly did he feel the delicate nature of stability?

My family mostly accepted the narratives Canada told us about multicultural tolerance and benevolent colonization. Buying into the belief that Canada was a just mosaic of cultures helped when striving for the Canadian dream. However, my family also rejected notions of white superiority and Canada as a utopia. They told me: save money, respect authority, look after family and community—this country will not protect us. Many of these lessons were because we were afforded less margin for error, were more easily outcast and scapegoated in occupational situations. When I was a child, and still now, my parents and grandparents warned me that if I didn't quietly concede, I would end up desolate. Nevertheless, they also instilled in me the necessity of reciprocity and care. Regardless of how we were treated, we could always choose to take care of each other. My grandparents and their friends regularly fussed over giving each other food. They demonstrated what an honour it is to nourish another. I feel at peace as I tie off and snip the thread—the first hoop complete.

Continuing with the same thread still in the needle, I secure another double knot and commence stitching the coastline of Lək̓ʷəŋən Homelands onto the second hoop. This land received us in our need for refuge. My 姑婆 gu po was brought here by her second husband, a lonely man two decades her senior who migrated during the head-tax era. She worked with textiles, making her living as a seamstress in Chinatown. My 姑婆 gu po never had children of her own, but she saved enough money to eventually sponsor my 爺爺 ye ye and his immediate family. The first time my father had running water and a roof over his head was on this land, and now he "owns" a parcel of it.

Forming the hand-embroidered representation of ancient land, I recognize that Victoria is relatively new. The suite I rent is in a three-and-a-half-storey building at the top of a hill, once a cohesive dwelling but now divided into ten separate units. It was completed in 1904, the year after the Chinese head tax was increased to five hundred dollars per person to thwart Chinese immigration. What would the original owners of this building think of a queer Asian person residing here? What does it mean for me to occupy this land now?

My home is a short distance from the North Park house where my grandparents and 姑婆 gu po lived and where I spent time after school and in the summer. Behind the house, my 嫲嫲 ma ma grew long green pole beans in short, neat rows perpendicular to the clothesline. I felt such glee tiptoeing between the giant stalks and peeking under leaves whenever she let me assist with harvesting. One side of the garden held a short greenhouse made out of an old wooden frame and hazy plastic sheeting. In it, my 嫲嫲 ma ma cultivated winter melon for soups. Perhaps the greenhouse was a portal, the humid air and smell of burgeoning melons transporting her back to a tropical home. How this land receives our diasporic daydreams.

What does it mean to be displaced from your own home only to find economic stability and housing security while partaking in a system that displaces others from their homelands? My family has lived here for fifty-five years, and I love this land. I love the gusts of ocean air and the diversity of tree shapes and the rocky outcrops and the tiny flowers and the hummingbirds who stop by if you have something sweet to share. I can only imagine the immensity of love the Lək̓ʷəŋən Peoples have for the Land.

Along with the established Cantonese community, my family joined the Canadian settler colonial project. A consequence of their pursuit of survival, my family entered an oppressive system that sought to legitimize and entrench the dispossession of Indigenous Homelands. Although we are not viewed as the ideal settler family, we are still settlers, and we carry responsibility as such. And so, we live in an in-between space where we are welcome in the sense that our existence on these lands aids in the occupation of Indigenous Territory, especially if we remain unassuming, unquestioning model minorities. Slowly guiding the needle between the fibres of lace, I can only attempt to appreciate the enormity of grief and pain wrought by settler-colonial domination.

Halfway through stitching the piece, honouring each bumpy inlet, I realize the area I am covering does not include the Songhees and Esquimalt First Nations Reserves. That speaks to how far away they were removed to build a settler paradise. Does my art also disappear Lək̓ʷəŋən Peoples from their Land? Although my intention was to highlight that this is all Lək̓ʷəŋən Territory, this is a reminder to be an active and mindful participant in the larger movement—in the slow, arduous work of systemic transformation.

At least monthly, someone, usually a friend or client, asks me, heavy with unease, how I maintain hope despite the destruction and despair that envelops us. How could I not when transformation occurs every day? Buds become blooms, and humans alchemize art. Life-affirming reminders surround us. I experience it in my role as a counsellor as well. At one job, I work with immigrants and refugees, holding space for complicated feelings about migration and cross-ocean families split by ambitious visions and thorny decisions.

NEXT PAGE: Macayla Yan, *Threads of Memory*, 2021. Hand embroidery on lace. | Photo: Macayla Yan.

How could I not nurture hope when every week I bear witness to the intense emotional process of tears, sighs, and energetic movement as people alter their relationships with themselves, their families, and their ancestors?

What a juxtaposition and false dichotomy between my art and counselling practices. In my art, I am a storyteller. In my work, I am a story listener. Through both, I am changed.

As I steer the needle through the lace, a stretch of the Lək̓ʷəŋən coastline is a smooth curve constructed for settler pleasure. Less than a half-hour walk from my home, this is one of my favourite places to visit the ocean. This beach has observed me laughing, crying, and slowly slipping into love. One year on my birthday, the wind was ferocious, the waves giving me a big, cold hello when I got too close.

In a previous job, I created and facilitated an accessible Indigenous Studies curriculum for adults with developmental disabilities. On an outing, we visited the lower causeway of the Inner Harbour to learn from one of the spindle-whorl Signs of Lək̓ʷəŋən designed and carved by master carver Butch Dick and his son, Clarence Dick Jr. That entire area had been a muddy flatland where Lək̓ʷəŋən People dug for clams and other food. It was filled in, without Lək̓ʷəŋən permission, to construct the Empress Hotel, which is why the building was sinking. Confused, one person inquired, "Wait, if the Lək̓ʷəŋən People didn't agree, why don't we give the land back?" I dream of settlers working together against the power structures and systems that prop up settler colonialism in service of Indigenous sovereignty and leadership.

I add the final piece to the work: a burgundy thread connecting 台山 Toisan to Lək̓ʷəŋən Homelands. This is the first time I've embroidered a piece that transcends the borders of a hoop. I am grounded by the memories of prayers, burnings, and food offerings that directly connect the North Park house to the village. During significant times of the lunar year, my grandparents would set up a mah-jong table in the living room against the fireplace, with framed photos and a small porcelain smiling Budai perched along the mantel. Cloaked with modest cloth, the table abounded with carefully selected fruit and home-cooked foods in special dishware. In the centre of the kitchen, we burned hand-folded incense paper for our ancestors in a tall, square metal bin. My 嫲嫲 ma ma emphasized how we must care for our ancestors just as they take care of us. Once, when I mentioned that I engage in practices to honour my ancestors, someone asked if I'd learned this from a book. I was fortunate to have my grandparents and 姑婆 gu po to introduce me to our ancestors.

Truthfully, I haven't laid out any food for my ancestors in several months, though each stitch is a prayer: In. For the people. Out. For the land. In. For the waters. Out. For the ancestors.

Years ago at an event, Lək̓ʷəŋən Elder Joan Morris spoke about Chinatown as a refuge, just across the Gorge waters from the old Songhees Reserve. She described how Cantonese people would hide Indigenous children in their homes and businesses so they could evade being taken away to residential school. She recalled playing pool and eating Cantonese food with friends and family. She told the room Lək̓ʷəŋən and Cantonese people banded together so that white people would not mess with us. Settler and Indigenous accomplices in solidarity against white supremacy, they weren't afraid to get physical.

I long for those historical relationships of committed care and communal support. I feel at a loss as to how to rebuild those connections, especially as someone not fluent in Cantonese and who is known in Chinatown only as "Russell's daughter."

I examine the two hoops, feeling the tension of how they are tethered together. What does this mean for me? I believe in the necessity of Indigenous sovereignty and collective liberation, but what does that mean in practice, especially when I am so indebted to the Lək̓ʷəŋən Land and Nation? As I sit with this question, I appreciate the ways my family taught me to live in the in-between space while remaining grounded in our ancestry. Even more so, I am deeply grateful for the communities and ecosystems that I learn, heal, resist, imagine, build, and love alongside.

TURNING THE HEEL

KEVIN SHAW

1.

My mom knits socks on double-pointed needles, looping a very thin piece of yarn between four very thin lengths of steel. What begins as a fuzzy, barely there halo grows, round by round, into a tube variously decorated with patterns of repeating diamonds or lacy garlands. Occasionally, she sets the work in her lap and makes notes on a scrap of paper or the back of a used envelope. The list of numbers appears random but tells her enough to keep the design intact and the length and width of the socks precisely fitted to whomever she's giving them.

A knitter friend once told me that making someone a pair of socks is one of the most intimate gifts, as it brings comfort to less-appealing body parts. While I'm not religious, my friend's observation made me think of Jesus washing the feet of his disciples: "If I then, your Lord and Master, have washed your feet; ye also ought to wash one another's feet." Commemorated in the Christian calendar on Maundy Thursday, washing the feet represents Jesus's instruction to love with humility.

"I know you don't believe, but I'm praying for you anyway," Mom often tells me.

She spends hours upon hours working on these socks that are barely glimpsed by anyone but the owner in their short transit between a dark drawer and a sweaty boot. Against the heel, where the wool meets heat and moisture, the sock's fibres begin to felt, which strengthens the fabric while sacrificing the decorative stitches. Over time, the sock's beauty becomes abraded by the force of its own purpose. Perhaps, for my mom, knitting these socks represents the steady refusal of futility.

2.

Several years ago, my mom's brain began to drop her body like a stitch. She would be crossing a street or about to step off a bus and momentarily black out, then collapse. After several months, a physician finally ordered an MRI. The image revealed a colloid cyst that had been growing within a ventricle of her brain since birth. "Benign," the surgeon pronounced, until the cyst began to block the flow of cerebrospinal fluid and increased pressure on her brain, leading to headaches, failures of memory, and loss of consciousness.

My grandmother theorized that the cyst was the remainder of a twin lost in utero that had somehow been absorbed into my mother's fetal body. Aside from the fact that my aunts are twins, I'm unsure of the origins of my grandmother's theory, but it's now a chapter in the story of my mom's brain surgery, a macabre, counterfactual element that provides a narrative for an exceedingly rare failure of the body otherwise lacking a cause.

3.

When does matter become material? When the sheep feed in West Yorkshire? When the shepherd shears the wool, or when the wool is spun? Is colour a kind of form, so that when the wool is dyed this patina green (or is it moss, malachite, sea?), the yarn is already more of what it's becoming than what it's been?

In his book *Fewer, Better Things,* the craft scholar and theorist Glenn Adamson considers such questions and follows Aristotle into a hypothetical forest: does the tree felled to make a table already have a form, or does its form only begin to take shape when the sawyer picks up his saw, or the carpenter applies her hammer and nails? Adamson writes, "'Matter' only becomes a specific 'material' when someone sees its potential and puts it into action—thereby finding a way to put an intention into the world." It's the will to furnish one thing from another thing that makes all the difference.

Still, I'm taken with the idea that the objects we touch and hold in daily life—particularly handcrafted objects—carry various legacies, physical and emotional. My sock contains an archive of my mother's love, as well as all the labour that made the yarn from the wool of a sheep that, at this moment, chews the grass in some pasture across the ocean.

Words, similarly, unspool their long etymologies. It seems too perfect when I discover the origin of the word *matter* in the Latin word *mater,* which means "source, origin," or, of course, "mother."

4.

After the emergency brain surgery, a nurse ushered me inside the ICU, where my mom still slept under anaesthesia. Observing her shaved head attached to countless wires, I imagined she looked as if Dr. Frankenstein had made a wife for his creature after all.

My siblings had chosen to wait at home while I stayed at the hospital. We were all in our twenties by then, and I thought they were being childish, absconding from reality and responsibility, but perhaps they had intuited what I only discovered in the ICU: there's something monstrous in the fallibility of a parent. I was already familiar with my parents' failures by then, no better or worse than my own eventual missteps: bad relationships, poor job choices, the wrong word uttered at the wrong time. That surgery was the first time I witnessed a substantial failure of my mother's body, the mater's matter. The line of stitches across the top of her scalp marked the thin, porous boundary between life and death. While the surgeon and nurses had assured me that she would be fine, it was too easy in that moment to imagine she'd been lost irrevocably to the other side of the line.

5.

For the first hour or so in the recovery room, her eyes closed, Mom knitted without yarn or needles. I watched her fingers repeat the familiar dance, pulling at threads that didn't exist, creating small loops of air. She was usually so intentional with her patterns and measurements—each pair for a specific person—I wondered whose feet they were supposed to fit.

Perhaps when makers get to work in liminal states—dreams, anaesthesia, coma—they're crafting at the level of ideal forms. In daily life and in our usual waking state, any creative person must face the gap between the envisioned end of their labour and the actual object that results. Often, the limit of our ability is a horizon, and the ideal endlessly recedes. Where else but in dreams could we be certain of making exactly what the mind intends?

A neuroscientist would likely inform me that Mom's knitting was really just some misfired electron in her recently mined brain, but I want to believe that the pair of invisible socks she knitted in recovery is among her finest work. I imagine them on permanent loan to the museum of objects made in the minds of unconscious craftspeople.

6.

Red notices from the hydro company began to appear in my mom's mailbox. She'd been several months past due on the utility payments even before the emergency brain surgery kept her out of work. Dodging collectors wasn't new for me and my siblings. We knew to let the blocked numbers on the phone go to voicemail. We never went hungry, but there had been many weeks when we'd wait eagerly for some cheque to clear—my dad's child support, or the meagre pay from one of my mom's jobs—in order to restock the fridge and cupboards with food beyond the basics. We knew financial precarity; we tiptoed along its edges as if afraid the bill collectors could hear us trespassing in our own rented house. But a hand-delivered notice—on red cardstock, no less? That was a new threat.

I was a university student dealing with my own financial struggles and had already moved out to live with my boyfriend, but the cliché "you can't go home again" doesn't apply when you grow up adjacent to poverty. The problems at home remained my problems, as if I had one finger tied to a dwindling ball of yarn in my mom's basket of wool.

I remember making frantic phone calls, asking for help, assuming the power was to be shut off at any moment while my mom was in the hospital, but I forget who paid the bill in the end—a loan from my dad or one of my aunts? The details of those days have dimmed, but the anxiety and shame remain electric. This memory is like a closed-off room lit by a naked, flickering bulb.

7.

When Mom awoke in her recovery room, she spoke to me as if I were my father, as if they were still married. I sat in a chair in the opposite corner of the room, and we observed each other from across two decades. The present came back to her in pain: pressure, migraines. Later, she told me that she'd dreamt the surgeons were knitting her nerves through the hole they had made in her head. She fell asleep again. Before I returned to the waiting room, I watched her eyes roaming beneath their lids, like swells pushing against the surfaces of two small lakes.

When she was a child, my mom's arm got caught between the rollers of a wringer washer while she was helping my grandmother with the laundry. Rather than hitting the mechanism that would simply release the rollers, my panicked grandmother cranked my mother's arm out in the opposite direction. Now, Mom's stories often move in the same way, somewhat illogical, rolling backward and forward in time.

Her memory has never fully recovered. The lapses are sometimes barely perceptible, but still present. She tends to tell stories in spirals, relaying the insignificant details—the colour of a bowl, the name of a pet bird—while often forgetting the crux of an event. It seems a cruel irony that the cyst she's carried her whole life, like a pebble caught in the undercurrent of her brain's fluid, makes the recent past more difficult to access.

8.

When we were growing up, Mom told us how Grandma sewed some of her clothes when she was a kid and how it was a marker of economy rather than fashion, or the kind of thing a bourgeois parent committed to organic living might do today. Aside from some Halloween costumes, Mom didn't make our clothes. The socks came later, and they're highly prized—while Mom was embarrassed as a kid by her handmade fashions, I proudly wear my socks like objects of hipster currency.

"You should sell these," I say, showing her online listings where socks like hers, hand-knitted in intricate patterns with gorgeous, rich wools, fetch a high price. She could use the money. Some months, she's just scraping by on disability insurance, but she resists any of my attempts to help her capitalize on her talent and market these socks for the masses of urbanites seeking artisanal knitwear. She's afraid she'll lose the pleasure of making them for friends and family. Besides, there are some months when she can't make anything at all.

I know several people whose parents gifted them every financial advantage, from university tuition to the down payment on a home. While I'm angry that we've maintained a system where the transfer of generational wealth continues to deepen and reify social inequality, I'm also aware that the same inequality has fuelled craft innovation in so many cultures for centuries, often through labour performed by women. Necessity is the mother of invention, as they say, but it might also be the mother of memory, as handmade objects transmit the past's struggles to the present. Hand-knitted socks made specifically for my feet carry the values—spun together as so many threads—instilled in me by my mom: a reverence for history and the visual arts, an appreciation for the well-made object, and the truth, inherent in any handmade garment, that mastery of a skill takes both time and discipline.

9.

As I revise these paragraphs, looping them like yarn between the needles, I'm reminded of my mother, eyes shut, knitting without notions in her hospital bed. The word *text* descends from a Latin verb meaning "to weave," and I often wish I could craft sentences from a language I could hold in my hands, as if I could write an essay or a poem as beautiful and useful as my mother's socks.

As with writing, ending a sock may be the most challenging part of its making. To move from the ankle to the foot, Mom slips several stitches from the needles and picks them up later, a manoeuvre that narrows and reorients the fabric. I imagine these slipped stitches reflect how her mind remembers now, in threads that come and go and leave small eyelets in the fabric of her memory. The expression knitters use for the task, "turning the heel," sounds like a backward gesture, something connected to the past, even as the fabric keeps growing toward the toe, where the loose ends will be woven back into the sock. There's no closure to the story of Mom's recovery. The migraines and lapses of memory will recur through the years, the same way she knits a sock in a circle. Her loose ends will always remain too easy to pull.

SEAMS: PIECEWORK IN TWENTY UNEVEN STITCHES

THERESA KISHKAN

seam (noun), from Proto-Indo-European root *syu-*, meaning "to bind, sew"

I know it has all been confusing, or at least it was to me, but it's the same confusion as when I am confident that every person who has ever lived knows exactly what I mean when I describe feeling like a snake on the path in the dappled sunshine that turns out, on close inspection, only to be a snake's discarded skin.

—ANNE BOYER, *THE UNDYING: PAIN, VULNERABILITY, MORTALITY, MEDICINE, ART, TIME, DREAMS, DATA, EXHAUSTION, CANCER, AND CARE*

Theresa Kishkan, detail of quilt, 2023. Stitched spirals like elegant snails or meandering tendrils. | Photo: Theresa Kishkan.

1.

By the big window, curtains drawn against the delicate maples where finches gathered during daylight as the pretty leaves fell, I sit with the two quilts I've brought with me for the duration: a patchwork of six-inch squares arranged in a grid, a Christmas gift for a young woman who is married to one of my sons; and a village of four log-cabin squares gathered around wide green trails for a dear friend on another continent. Tonight I thread three needles at a time with lengths of strong cotton, and I push them in and out, drawing the layers of pieced work, soft batting, and plain backing together. The stitches make their own new pathways on the surface, tiny marks like the trail a finch leaves in the damp earth beneath the trees. I saw these marks when I left to walk to the hospital twice earlier today. I saw the footprints of the finches and the samaras the finches have plucked seeds from, and both of them led me away from the building toward you. It's a map a child might have drawn, the short clipped marks of the finches' feet, the arrows of samara. This way? Or that?

A little over a kilometre away, you are drugged in your high bed in the recovery ward. Earlier, your surgeon called to say the surgery had gone smoothly, as expected, and that you were cheerful in the recovery room. Visit him in about an hour, he advised. So I did. "Are you in pain?" I asked. "Not too bad." You were groggy. You had two new hips. Everyone was masked because of the pandemic—I wore a three-layered cotton mask I'd fashioned from leftover quilt fabric and fusible interlining. No one here will know what I look like, after. A nurse checked your pulse, your blood pressure, the dressings on each flank, where your surgeon removed the hips you were born with, replacing them with prosthetic joints of metal and ceramic. Your left foot was moving, the toes a little swollen but animated. Your right foot slept. No one was yet concerned, though you kept saying, "I don't know why I can't feel it." I wished you sweet dreams and walked back in the dusk to this place where I am staying. My phone was alert with messages. Our children, a few good friends. I called our children and then sat at my computer to compose a letter to send to the friends who I knew were waiting for news.

The fire at the centre of each log cabin burns with hope.

2.

I wash grapes, pour another glass of the lovely French Chablis I brought from home, and sit in a big chair with my quilting basket beside me. Thread needles. Run my thumbs over the spirals I've sewn so far into the green trails on the log-cabin quilt. Think. Think. I close my eyes. Where am I going, my thumb carefully describing the journey inward to where the spiral begins, a knot behind it on the back of the quilt. Where am I going, easing the needle in and out, in and out, a track to a place as yet unknown. What am I going to do.

The last time we were in Paris, maybe eight years ago, we went to the Musée des Arts et Métiers to look at its collection of scientific and technological objects, including Foucault's pendulum, timepieces and navigational devices, binoculars from 1681, early planes, calculators, even a maquette for the Statue of Liberty. We spent ages by a case of artificial hips, an exhibit detailing their development, from an early model of ivory invented by one Themistocles Gluck in 1891, to the more contemporary versions made of metals and ceramics. "Imagine having one of those in your body!" Who said it? I remember we touched our own hips tenderly and went on to the next exhibit room.

I read far into the small hours because sleeping interferes with the state of alertness I need during this period. I'm alone because we were advised to treat you as immunocompromised and to limit interactions with others to keep you safe. I arrange the unfinished log-cabin quilt, its trails leading to the unknown, over the foot of the bed. Will my phone ring? Better not sleep, because what if I don't hear the phone? When it does ring early in the morning, I almost don't realize it's the phone. My ringtone is "Brown Eyed Girl" (I don't know how to change it), and for a few minutes, I think it's the radio or someone singing nearby. Then I jump out of the bed. "Hello, hello?" It's you, the day after your surgery. By now you have lost the euphoria of coming out of anaesthesia with the new hips you have been waiting so long for, more than two years. Closer to three. So long that the single bad hip became both hips. Now you are concerned about your right foot. Your surgeon just told you that the sciatic nerve was compressed during surgery, and your foot is paralyzed.

Preparing for this sojourn near the hospital, looking at maps to determine where I'd be in relation to everything else, I wondered what it would be like to have so much time alone here at UBC while you recover. We were both students on this campus in the last century, you earlier than me, in the 1960s. I did most of an MFA here after Forrest's birth in the early 1980s, driving across town from North Vancouver for seminars and rushing home to nurse my baby. I didn't ever learn to find my way around the campus. I always felt hurried. Harried. We were building a house, we were learning to print on the big old Chandler & Price platen press we'd recently acquired, and I wasn't writing much. Eventually I realized that it wasn't a good use of my time to race across the Lions Gate Bridge two or three times a week in order to complete a degree, particularly not when I knew by the second spring that I was going to have another baby. What I remember is that I always parked in the lot at the Museum of Anthropology because I could put money in the meter and get two hours of parking, which was just about enough if I raced back to the car as soon as my seminar ended. I knew the quickest way there and back. I bought a ticket online to the museum for later this morning. Almost nothing else seems the same. It's like a city here, with residences everywhere, building projects happening on every corner, though not many people on the sidewalks, because of course classes are online right now. Empty buses passed me as I walked back from the hospital yesterday.

When I got back, I looked out the window of the suite where I am staying and tried to figure out which direction I was facing. Those house finches were still in the maples, many of them, and I wished I had my trusty *An Exaltation of Larks* at hand to determine what the collective noun for finches might be. I've just looked online, and there are three: a charm, a trembling, a trimming. I'll keep these in mind to tell you, because they are also words for a man who is waking this morning with new hips and a paralyzed foot.

This morning it's still too dark for finches. I look out the window, hazy with rain, and there's someone walking on the dark trail with a flashlight. I recognize her tentative step. It might be me, nearly forty years ago or later today, trying to find my way.

> I am out with lanterns, looking for myself.
>
> —EMILY DICKINSON, LETTER TO MRS. J.G. HOLLAND, JANUARY 20, 1856

3.

Your bright room, with its view of tall pines and a ginkgo, the North Shore mountains tipped with snow as its horizon, is grey when I arrive to visit. By now you've had physiotherapy, two capable men taking you through an exercise routine and helping you to the bathroom with a walker, and they've managed to fit your numb foot into your shoe with a splint designed to cradle your heel. You felt pressure as they pushed but nothing else.

It's hard to know quite what to expect. Doctors keep coming in, looking at their clipboards, checking the honeycomb dressings over your incisions, then leaving. When we ask about the damaged nerve, the potential for healing, they are noncommittal. We ourselves don't know what to commit to, what to attach our hope to.

4.

Reading is best at bedtime, to settle into a novel about Topeka, Kansas, and quilting is good by the window in the late afternoons and early evenings, after my second visit of each day, when the weight of what's to come in the next few months is heavy, not just in a metaphorical way but in my limbs, my thinking. I anticipate that you will make a very good recovery from your bilateral hip replacement surgery. It's the unexpected thing that presents uncertainty. Will you regain the use of your right foot, or will you have to learn a whole new way of moving in the world, compensating at every step for the loss of feeling, the damage to your nerve. Whatever happens, we will do our best. When it's light out, the trees brilliant gold and deep orange, the house finches busy at the work of opening maple seeds, I am ready for anything. But when the weight settles, I pick up my quilt and stitch freehand spirals into the sashing between the log-cabin blocks. The process of moving out from the centre and then letting the thread find its way out into the open space is calming, in the way I suspect meditation might be. My meditations are of the practical sort, though; they always have been. Kneading dough, weeding, watering tomatoes and easing their unruly stems around strings to lead them upward. So, I'll stitch and hope that the threads will take me—*us*—in the direction we need to go now. Sure-footed or not.

5.

> To take a set of objects and actions from one system and reclassify these as elements in another system is like fortune-telling. To a fortune teller, birds flying north spell out tomorrow's happiness and tea leaves tell a story about two lovers and the third who will ruin them.
>
> —ANNE BOYER, *THE UNDYING*

I can't sleep. I read for most of the night, Anne Boyer's *The Undying*,[1] possibly not a good choice given its subject—the author's experience of a breast-cancer diagnosis and her treatment in a market-driven capitalist health-care system—but so compelling and well written that I forget for a moment a foot isn't waking up as it should, forget the difficult journey home we will face in a few days, and read until the room begins to lighten through the curtains at dawn. I push the curtains aside and watch for the finches. "What news do you bring?" I ask them through glass.

I bought the book today at the university bookstore when I went to find you a little gift to commemorate our forty-first wedding anniversary tomorrow. On my way to the bookshelves, I pass through an area with small whimsical objects, and I buy our grandchildren tiny terrariums with sundews so that they can learn about meat-eating plants. I buy them houses for mason bees. And I find a volume of poetry by Liu Tsung-Yuan, translated by Red Pine. The store is almost empty, and I read, leaning against a heavy shelf. I pay for the books and read all the way back to my rooms.

Yesterday, at the Museum of Anthropology, I also bought Christmas gifts. I suspect this is a year when I won't have the time I usually do to make interesting food to put into packages for friends and family, so I looked for beautiful objects: earrings for the young women, an African basket, a bentwood box, books. When I arrived for the afternoon visit, I told you about the shopping, but you were far away. In pain, in shock. I sat in the chair by your bed, and we held hands. "We can do this," I told you. "You'll see."

1 Anne Boyer, *The Undying: Pain, Vulnerability, Mortality, Medicine, Art, Time, Dreams, Data, Exhaustion, Cancer, and Care* (New York: Farrar, Strauss and Giroux, 2021).

6.

The bruising is phenomenal. Your flanks, both of them, are deep blue and purple, streaked with red; they're swollen, the swelling extending down your legs to your feet.

The trees are turning, the birds so lively in their branches, and even the rain against the window reminds me of time spinning from my spools of thread, drops finding a trail over the silver glass. Time easing its way through three layers of cotton, guided by a needle so sharp it draws blood.

To take a set of objects and actions from one system and reclassify these as elements in another system is like fortune-telling.

7.

Forty-one years ago, you and I were married one late morning in a room overlooking the sea in Sidney, on Saanich Peninsula. Who knew what the years would bring?

They brought everything. A house we built ourselves, three children, books we wrote and books we read, together and apart, a garden, friendships, some travel, lots of happiness, and also some sorrow. In sickness and in health, the old wedding vows asked you to promise, and although they weren't part of our ceremony, it's been true. There's been far more health than sickness, thank goodness, but you don't get to choose.

This morning I wake alone in my bed while you recover in the hospital. That's the easy part, though having watched you take a few tentative steps on a walker, assisted by a physiotherapist, I know it's not easy. The more difficult path ahead will be one you'll have to walk with a newly paralyzed foot. We are hopeful that the nerve will regenerate. The process takes two years, and it's not inevitable that it will be complete and successful. But we will continue to hope.

Yesterday was warm, like summer, and in the night, I kept waking to hear wind and rain against my window. We've celebrated our anniversary in many different places—Cox Bay, near Tofino; Vienna; Paris; a motel in Merritt—but mostly at home, where we make a special meal and open a bottle of spectacular wine. This is the first time I'll walk to a hospital with pastries and a book of Chinese poetry to wish my beloved you another year of happiness. A few more days in the surgical ward, then the physiotherapist will help you into our car, and we'll drive home for the next chapter of this story.

8.

How long will a path of thread last, how long will the layers hold together, the strong cottons, the batting, the pieced backs? Under the honeycomb dressing, your skin is held together with surgical staples, though once a needle would have seamed your leg together, tied fine threads to guide your skin to healing. The bird tracks are washed away by the third morning.

9.

People we know who've had hip surgery suggested surgeons, gave advice on a comfortable return from hospital, given that our home is a long drive and ferry trip away. The health authority's osteoarthritis team consulted with you by phone instead of in person, because of COVID-19. We borrowed or bought the necessary equipment. We felt we were prepared.

> We are never our spirits' containers. No person's body is marked with a measuring line.
>
> —ANNE BOYER, *THE UNDYING*

On your flanks, the mark of the pen used to determine the site of incision. Your feet are pink with disinfectant.

10.

> The boundaries of our bodies break. Everything we were supposed to keep inside of us now seems to fall out.
>
> —ANNE BOYER, *THE UNDYING*

When I arrived in your room this afternoon, hoping to be present when the physiotherapist took you to climb stairs and then descend to the little rhyme we used this morning on the pretend stairs, up and over a little bridge, in the big room at the end of the hall, you weren't there. Your day nurse said you were on a different floor for an echocardiogram, required because of some irregularities in your heartbeat.

There's uncertainty about what to do for your heart. It's fluttering. It's done this before. You want to sleep but you have trouble staying asleep for very long.

Everything is documented. Your atrium chambers, your potassium, magnesium, and sodium levels. You keep throwing up. No one is sure when you'll be discharged because of the low levels of important elements. There's a balance you need to achieve. Your digestion is a mess. When you feel steady enough to stand for ten minutes, I take you into the bathroom and fill the sink with warm water. I wash you all over like something fragile. The deep-rose and purple bruises darken your flanks and your thighs. As the water sluices down your shoulders and back, your buttocks, you groan a little, saying, "That feels so nice." "Lift your arms." I wash with a soft cloth and then dry you with the small towel the nurse has given me. A clean hospital gown, a faded cotton bathrobe I asked the nurse to find, having seen several patients walking slowly in the corridor in identical robes and deduced they were hospital issue. Some lotion for your feet. "Do you feel a little better?" Tears come to your eyes. Everything is so close to the surface—pain, swelling, muscle spasms, tears. Sometimes when I walk back to where I am staying, I cry. So few cars, almost no people, though I find a golden-crowned kinglet on the sidewalk in front of a row of residences. I hold the tiny bird in my hand and realize it's dead. I place it on some yews just in case it's only stunned by impact on the tall window facing the street, but the next day it's still there, a sleeping king. I cry, for the bird, for you in your room looking north, for the empty rooms I'll return to, and I cry as I drink my glass of wine and stitch long diagonals across the squares of the quilt I am making for Cristen. Around the border, a running nerve, the peroneal nerve, often yellow in illustrations, though these stitches are white, regenerating itself tiny section by section, each the length of an eyelash, all the way down your leg to your sleeping foot. When I sew, I can make progress. As though my stitches might shadow the nerve and its uncertain renewal.

11.

Back at my rooms, I try not to think too much about how we will get home and how I will manage, and of course I can't think of anything else.

We thought we were well equipped, but now I am thinking of our quirky house and your damaged nerve and wondering how we will manage. I keep buying bottles of wine, and I drink glasses of it by the big window, sewing my way into the night, then reading my way through it. Spirals on the green trails, needle gliding in and out, travels into the cancer ward with Anne Boyer, listening, listening to branches brushing the window in the wind.

12.

My thinking is a tangled nest of threads in the big basket I keep my quilts in. How is it that things have become so knotted and entwined? The fine white strands of love, the coarse red yarn I use for darning, fearfully plucking until it frays, because how will I know if what I am doing is enough, if it will serve us? There are the blues—indigo, peacock, an ultramarine; they fill me with hope. Tease them out, wind them onto old wine corks to keep them ready until I need to ease them through the needle's unblinking eye, following their trail.

13.

We were advised to spend at least one night, if not two, near the hospital after discharge in case of emergency. I clean the bathroom in the suite of rooms, I smooth the sheets, arrange a waterproof pad on your side of the bed. You will want more than dry-roasted peanuts, grapes, and yogurt to eat, so I make sure there's a simple supper.

I bring you back to the rooms I have been sewing in, and you go to bed, the unfinished village of log cabins over your legs, the light of their square red fires warm on the frozen foot. I follow not long after. In the night, you wake and tell me you've been making a poem in the dark. "Do you want me to write it down?" "Yes." So, on the page where I've been keeping notes about meds and pee volume, there's a poem to mark everything that's happened. I see this as light in the trees, a charm for the future.

Be still, old heart.
It's only the excitement
of going home.

14.

All the things I thought might go wrong on our journey home by ferry didn't go wrong. I drove; you slept in the seat next to me. It took us most of the day to return. Into the house, where I made a good fire and brought in the chair with the special foam cushion, and we sat there, grateful to be home. I'd bought food we could have by the fire, and just as I was about to put it out, our neighbour phoned to say she was going to leave something on our deck. The something was a carton of her delicious squash-and-apple soup, a pan of warm cheese biscuits, and a jar of the most beautiful dahlias. There are angels among us, even in this frightening world.

I slept on the other couch so I could be near if you needed me in the night. Hear you if you were sleepless, in pain, troubled. (*Only the excitement of going home.*) But you got up on your own, and I heard you go down to the bathroom, slowly navigating the hall with your walker, and when we woke again, it was 6:30 a.m. I'd dreamed that I'd taken Anne Carson to Egmont to show her around, and we watched two grizzly bears on the opposite side of the inlet entering the water to swim across to where we were standing. To my surprise, Anne didn't recite Sappho.

In the night, while I waited for you to return to your bed, I watched the moon through the big window at the end of the room. A waxing gibbous moon moving toward its blue-moon state next Saturday. After you returned, the sky was pricked with stars, and over you, a quilt I made thirty years ago, Ohio stars pieced of soft blue cottons. Maybe Anne was too busy watching the grizzlies swimming toward us to remember Sappho's Fragment 34, but I'm sure this was the poem she'd have remembered if she'd been in our house last night:

stars around the beautiful moon
hide back their luminous form
whenever all full she shines
on the earth[2]

15.

I have almost finished the patchwork, its bright squares reminding me of France as I sew. My seams are not as tidy as I'd hope, but I'm distracted. And I can't bear to work yet on the forest trails between the four log cabins with their Dupioni fires at each centre. My needle wants a clear route, diagonals across the squares, not the wandering possibilities of the green paths, where I could sew spirals like elegant snails or meandering tendrils. I made the cabins thinking of a village, but we are alone in our house. I keep those needles threaded and waiting, hopeful that the time will come when I'll want to sew freehand again, to find where I'm going by following the needle's eye, anchored by the small knot, part of a cluster of houses. Right now, no.

16.

Your heart won't settle. We go back and forth to the hospital in Sechelt as one thing happens, then another, and then they admit you for a few days. One incision opens and becomes infected. I am taught to clean it, swabbing the edges where you were opened, your hips removed, new ones inserted. There isn't much time to sew, but sometimes I sit with a quilt in my hands. I trace the line of stitching from one square to the next, a field, a trail, thinking my way forward, because I have never needed a guide as much as I do now, sharp needle pulling red thread, blue, creamy white, the knowledge of the knot that anchors the stitching in place.

2 Sappho, *If Not, Winter: Fragments of Sappho*, translated by Anne Carson (New York: Alfred A. Knopf, 2002).

17.

At home we begin to sleep in our bed again, our white-linen curtains left open to the night, the bedspread with a starry quilt. You come up at bedtime, a crutch under your right armpit, left hand on the railing, and I sing the rhyme, *"A B C, able foot, bad foot, crutch; C B A, crutch, bad foot, able foot," following you in case you tumble.*

18.

Mornings are best. I get up at seven, head downstairs, followed by the cat. I feed him, make the fire, put the kettle on, and prepare a breakfast tray for you. Maybe a poached egg on whole-grain toast, with jam or marmalade in a tiny egg cup. Yogurt with a few almonds and some raspberries, a clump of grapes. Decaffeinated coffee, because of your medications, those in a little bowl taken from the basket I keep on the worktop, with each day's dosage written on a file card so I don't have to think about it—just shake a blue tablet, a white one, a miniscule yellow one, and gather them together. Upstairs, I unfold the wooden tray that was your Sheffield grandparents' and put the tin tray with its cheerful flowers on the wooden one. Leave you to your breakfast.

Downstairs, I drink my coffee and read the morning's email in front of the fire. This could be any fall morning, the warmth filling the kitchen, the smell of strong coffee welcome. It could be.

When you are ready to come downstairs, we reverse the chant: "*C B A, crutch, bad foot, able foot.*" But I don't like calling it your bad foot, so we change it to "sad foot." It is. It gets cold. You do the exercises and try to lift your toes. They are inert as stones.

19.

Up and down the stairs. Soon you are doing this more than once a day. You leave the crutch by the coat rack and use your cane, your right foot moving into air without feeling but purposeful nevertheless. Outside, you sweep the patio, begin to rake windfall debris from the grass. Friends come and talk from a distance, bringing soup, flowers, a bag of pine mushrooms, a dish of baked halibut.

There is time again for the other things I love. I begin to sew the paths on the log-cabin quilt, the spirals and tendrils and threads leading into the strong seams that hold the sashing to the blocks. Sometimes I bury my stitches in the very seam itself and tie a knot to hold them. It looks like they disappear into nowhere, but I know the work involved, what I can do, what I can't. What a seam can repair and what it can't.

20.

In the old stories, the journey is perilous, through wild terrain, the warrior cloaked in fine silk embroidered with silver thread. In our version, we wore surgical masks in the hospital where you were taken away to be opened and given new hips, and when you woke, you had no feeling in your right foot. For a week, you got out of your bed in a high ward, and you learned how to move in a new way, helped by men who were strong and kind and who taught you to adjust for your injury, who taught you to use the stairs, to lie on your bed and coax your legs to work again.

Sometimes you cried, because it hurt and because you were disoriented and you knew you'd lost something. I cried too, for those reasons, and others. At night you were alone. At night I was alone, stitching, or reading about a woman who entered hell and returned, parts of her body missing. When we came home to the house we built four decades ago, we were not the same. Our house was filled

with strange equipment we'd borrowed or bought. "Diagnosis," said Anne Boyer in *The Undying*, "takes information from our bodies and rearranges what came from inside of us into a system imposed from far away." But I remember, after your heart had stopped fluttering like a frightened bird in your chest and after the foxglove had become habit and after your doctor told you to consider yourself no longer at risk, just take your medications, and after we'd learned a new pattern for our days and nights, we held hands in our bed, the stars as bright as they'd always been, Christmas coming, owls in the darkness, and it was each other we loved, the beauty of our fire in the mornings, poetry some afternoons, as you read me Louise Glück or I read you Eavan Boland:

> Only when it's laid
> right across the floor,
> sphere on square
> and seam on seam,
> in a good light—
> a night-sky spread—
> will it start to hit me.
>
> These are not bits.
> They are pieces.
>
> And the pieces fit.[3]

This was the season we left home and returned changed. What changes? The heart is a finch in its nest, a kinglet fluttering against glass. The passage of my needles through the layers of cotton, stitching seams to hold them together, to hold us together in our tattered bodies, new seams on your legs. It seems these might hold, though

3 Eavan Boland, "Patchwork," from *Outside History: Selected Poems, 1980–1990* (New York: W. W. Norton & Company, 2001).

Theresa Kishkan, detail of quilt, 2023. Freehand spirals in the sashing between log-cabin blocks. | Photo: Theresa Kishkan.

sometimes we are heavy and sad. I fold the patchwork quilt into a box to send to Cristen. The cabins will take longer, their paths elaborate, leading somewhere still unknown until I mail them to Europe to cover a bed I haven't even seen. The logs I bring from the woodshed gladly burn the whole night through, keeping us warm while we dream.

ACKNOWLEDGMENTS

First and foremost, we owe a huge debt of gratitude to our wonderful contributors. Thank you for trusting us with your stories; without you, this book wouldn't exist. We'd also like to acknowledge and thank all the writers who submitted work for consideration—every piece we read was deeply affecting, and we only wish we had had several anthologies to fill.

Thank you, Sam Haywood, for believing in this project when it was just an idea and for championing it with such enthusiasm. And thank you to our amazing team at Arsenal Pulp Press—Brian Lam, Robert Ballantyne, Catharine Chen, Jazmin Welch, Cynara Geissler, Erin Chan, and Jesmine Cham—your thoughtfulness and care through every step of the editing and publishing process have made this book so much more than we imagined it could be.

We're extremely grateful to the Vancouver Art Gallery, in particular Stephanie Rebick, Danielle Currie, and Ian Lefebvre, for allowing us to excerpt text and images originally published in *Jan Wade: Soul Power* (Vancouver Art Gallery and Information Office, 2022).

Big thank you to the second half of our hive mind—Jennica Harper and Laisha Rosnau—for cheerleading and advice whenever we needed it. And thank you to the UBC School of Creative Writing and the University of Victoria Department of Writing for their ongoing support.

Nancy would like to send a special thank you to Nancy Chen and Monica and Dave Ilett for their constant love and kindness. And, of course, immeasurable gratitude and love to John and Rudy the corgi, her two favourite stitches.

Marita is deeply grateful for the love, patience, and support of Kevin, Atticus, Avner, and Harriet—how lucky she is to have the absolute best family. She would like to thank Gwen Dachsel for continuing to be an inspiration, as well as the Logans and the Slades for all their support during the creation of this book and beyond.

CONTRIBUTOR BIOS

LJ AHENDA works at House of Anansi Press. She holds an MFA from the University of Guelph.

JENNY BARTOY is a French American writer and freelance editor based in the Pacific Northwest. Her work has been published in *Room*, *Permafrost Magazine*, *Literary Mama*, and *WhipUp*, as well as in sewing publications. She is managing editor for *Literary Mama* and formerly edited *Quiltfolk* magazine. She holds a master's degree in sociocultural anthropology from Columbia University.
WEB jennybartoy.com
INSTAGRAM @jbartoywriter
TWITTER @jbartoy

JUSTINA CHONG is a Hong Kong Chinese Canadian writer living in Shanghai. In previous lives, she managed projects for a software company, edited copy for an art museum, wrote scripts for children's television, and once had a job inserting contact lenses into people's eyes on a movie set. She has an identical twin and another sister.
WEB justinachong.com
TWITTER @justinaforever
RAVELRY @justinaforever

LAURA COK knits, cross-stitches, sews (badly), needlepoints, and embroiders in Guelph, Ontario, when not working at her day job in corporate communications. Her debut poetry collection, *Doubter's Hymnal* (Mansfield Press, 2019), was shortlisted for the Gerald Lampert Memorial Award.
WEB lauracok.com

CIARA FARMER is a non-fiction writer. Policy Analyst by day and Story Slam participant by night, she writes at the intersection of oft-lowbrow pop culture and the sometimes too personal. She lives in Edmonton, Alberta, with her cat, Pippi, and her extensive collection of mushroom homewares.

ANNE FLEMING is the author of five books of fiction and poetry, including *Gay Dwarves of America* (Pedlar Press, 2012), *poemw* (Pedlar Press, 2016), and *The Goat* (Groundwood Books, 2019), a novel for children. The sixth, a novel, will be out in 2024 with Knopf Canada. She teaches Creative Writing at UBC's Okanagan Campus.

DR. TIKENYA FOSTER-SINGLETARY teaches literature and writing at Clark Atlanta University, with research interests in African American literature, American literature, and television and popular culture. She is a frequent presenter at the College Language Association and the Popular Culture Association of the South conferences. Her work has been published in *MAWA Review*, *Obsidian: Literature in the African Diaspora*, and *Southern Quarterly*. Co-editor of *Pearl Cleage and Free Womanhood*, she is a 2019 Georgia Governor's Teaching Fellow.

DANIELLE GELLER's first book is *Dog Flowers* (One World/Random House, 2021). Her work has appeared in *Guernica*, *The New Yorker*, and *Brevity*. She teaches at the University of Victoria and for the low residency MFA program at the Institute of American Indian Arts. She is a citizen of the Navajo Nation.

LORRI NEILSEN GLENN's *Following the River: Traces of Red River Women* (Wolsak and Wynn, 2017) is a hybrid work about her Métis grandmothers. Former Halifax Poet Laureate, Lorri teaches in the University of King's College MFA program. She has published fourteen books and has won awards for her writing, teaching, and research. She is Professor Emerita at Mount Saint Vincent University.

JENNY JUDGE is a craft-based installation artist whose work incorporates materials such as glass, ceramics, and fibre. She holds an MFA from the University of Minnesota in sculpture and was first introduced to fabric arts in a residency at the Banff School of Fine Art in 1984.

THERESA KISHKAN lives on the Sechelt Peninsula with her husband, John Pass, in a house they built and where they raised their three children. She has published sixteen books, most recently *Blue Portugal and Other Essays* (University of Alberta Press, 2022).
WEB theresakishkan.com

SANDRA LAMOUCHE is a nehiyaw iskwew from the Bigstone Cree Nation. She is a champion hoop dancer and an award-winning Indigenous educator, two-time TEDx speaker, writer, and artist. She holds an MA in Indigenous studies from Trent University, where she studied Indigenous dance and well-being.

ROB LEACOCK is an Episcopal priest, school chaplain, religion teacher, and middle school soccer coach in Arkansas, where he lives with his wife, three children, and a cat. He's been a knitter for the past fifteen years. An avid soccer fan, Rob is a supporter of the West Bromwich Albion Football Club.
INSTAGRAM: @robertleacock

CARRIANNE LEUNG is a fiction writer and educator. Her debut novel, *The Wondrous Woo* (Inanna Publications, 2013), was shortlisted for the 2014 Toronto Book Awards. Her collection of linked stories, *That Time I Loved You* (HarperCollins, 2018), was named one of the Best Books of 2018 by CBC, shortlisted for the 2019 Toronto Book Awards, longlisted for Canada Reads 2019, and awarded the Danuta Gleed Literary Award in 2019. She is currently working on a new novel titled *The After*.

DR. DANIELLE LUSSIER, Red River Métis and citizen of the Manitoba Métis Federation, is mum to a trio of tiny Métis. As a beadworker and textile artist with a PhD in law, she is keenly interested in the relationship between law and beads and the use of beadwork practice as a pedagogical tool to (re)build community, facilitate learning, and mobilize knowledge. She encourages you to #ReadTheBeads and practice #LawWithHeart.
WEB daniellelussier.ca
TWITTER @daniellelussier

BETTINA MATZKUHN explores stories about ecology and landscape through a focus on embroidery. She holds a BFA in visual arts and an MA in liberal studies from Simon Fraser University. Her work is held in public and private collections. She exhibits internationally, writes on the arts, lectures, teaches, and volunteers. She lives in Vancouver, BC.
WEB bettinamatzkuhn.ca

SADIQA DE MEIJER's writing has won the CBC Poetry Prize, the Governor General's Literary Award, and other honours. In 2020, she and artist Amy Rubin formed the textile arts duo the Woolgatherers. Sadiqa is currently working on new collections of poetry and essays.

LIA PAS is a Saskatoon-based multidisciplinary artist who works in image, text, and sound, exploring body and states of being. She focused on performance-based work until 2015, when she became disabled with a chronic illness. Since then her work has focused on text and fibre arts. Her symptomatology and anatomy embroideries have been featured in numerous online publications and can be seen on her website and social media.
WEB liapas.com
TWITTER @lia_pas
INSTAGRAM @lia_pas

ANDREA REXILIUS is the author of *Sister Urn* (Sidebrow, 2019), *New Organism: Essais* (Letter Machine, 2014), *Half of What They Carried Flew Away* (Letter Machine, 2012), and *To Be Human Is to Be a Conversation* (Rescue Press, 2011). She is the program director for Regis University's Mile-High MFA in Creative Writing.

RENÉE SAROJINI SAKLIKAR is the author of five books, including the award-winning *Children of Air India* (blewointment, 2013) and *Listening to the Bees* (Nightwood Editions, 2018). Her essays and short fiction have appeared in many literary magazines and anthologies, including *Exile Editions, Chatelaine, The Capilano Review,* and *Pulp Literature.* The latest volume of her epic fantasy in verse, *Bramah's Quest,* is forthcoming with Nightwood Editions in 2023. She was Poet Laureate for the City of Surrey, 2015–2018.

KEVIN SHAW lives in Ottawa. He's the author of a poetry collection, *Smaller Hours* (icehouse, 2017), and his essays have been published in *The New Quarterly, Event, Literary Review of Canada,* and the *Best Canadian Essays 2018* anthology and broadcast on CBC Radio.
INSTAGRAM @thiskevinshaw

Hard to believe, but **ELIANE LESLAU SILVERMAN** took early retirement as head of women's studies at the University of Calgary, then promptly moved to Salt Spring Island, BC, where she discovered quilting and open-water swimming. Her many passions in life are her daughters, her grandchildren, books, gardening, women's reproductive well-being, choir, friends, cooking, and food.

JESS TAYLOR is a Tkaronto (Toronto) writer and poet. Recently, her second short story collection, *Just Pervs* (Book*hug Press, 2019), was a finalist for the 2020 Lambda Literary Award for Bisexual Fiction. Her story "Two Sex Addicts Fall in Love" was longlisted for the Journey Prize, and "Paul," the title story from her first collection, *Pauls* (Book*hug Press, 2015), received the 2013 Gold Fiction National Magazine Award. Her debut novel will be released in 2024.

DR. KELLY S. THOMPSON is an award-winning author and holds an MFA and a PhD in creative writing. Kelly has published widely, with essays appearing in *Chatelaine, Maclean's,* the *Globe and Mail,* and many literary magazines and anthologies. Her military memoir, *Girls Need Not Apply* (McClelland & Stewart, 2019), was an instant national bestseller, and her second memoir, *Still, I Cannot Save You* (McClelland & Stewart), was released in January 2023.

For over thirty years, **JAN WADE** has been creating mixed-media paintings, textiles, and sculptural objects, drawing upon her lived experience as an African Canadian person and her mixed cultural heritage. *Jan Wade: Soul Power* (Vancouver Art Gallery and Information Office, 2022) brings together Jan's diverse body of work, alongside new pieces made specifically for a retrospective at the Vancouver Art Gallery.

KATHLEEN WINTER's books include *Annabel* (House of Anansi Press, 2010) and *Boundless* (House of Anansi Press, 2014). Her new novel, *Undersong* (Knopf Canada, 2021), is inspired by Dorothy Wordsworth's unpublished diaries. Winter was born in the United Kingdom and lives in Quebec's Eastern Townships.

MACAYLA YAN is a Cantonese and Toisan settler residing on the homelands of the Lək̓ʷəŋən Nation. As such, Macayla is deeply grateful to the stewards of this land. Macayla is also a counsellor, emerging textile artist, community organizer, workshop facilitator, and eldest cousin. Everything Macayla does is grounded in belief in the necessity and power of individual, collective, and ancestral healing and liberation.
WEB macayla.info
INSTAGRAM @mac.ay.la